[英]休·鲍登 著　程璐 译

牛津通识读本·

亚历山大大帝
Alexander the Great

A Very Short Introduction

译林出版社

图书在版编目（CIP）数据

亚历山大大帝 /（英）休·鲍登（Hugh Bowden）著；程璐译. —南京：译林出版社，2022.7
（牛津通识读本）
书名原文：Alexander the Great: A Very Short Introduction
ISBN 978-7-5447-9143-4

Ⅰ.①亚…　Ⅱ.①休…　②程…　Ⅲ.①亚历山大大帝（前356-前323）-传记　Ⅳ.①K835.407=2

中国版本图书馆 CIP 数据核字（2022）第 063014 号

Alexander the Great: A Very Short Introduction, First Edition by Hugh Bowden
Copyright © Hugh Bowden 2014
Alexander the Great was originally published in English in 2014. This licensed edition is published by arrangement with Oxford University Press. Yilin Press, Ltd is solely responsible for this bilingual edition from the original work and Oxford University Press shall have no liability for any errors, omissions or inaccuracies or ambiguities in such bilingual edition or for any losses caused by reliance thereon.
Chinese and English edition copyright © 2022 by Yilin Press, Ltd
All rights reserved.

著作权合同登记号　图字：10-2018-429 号

亚历山大大帝　[英国] 休·鲍登 / 著　程璐 / 译

责任编辑	王　蕾
装帧设计	景秋萍
校　　对	王　敏
责任印制	董　虎

原文出版	Oxford University Press, 2014
出版发行	译林出版社
地　　址	南京市湖南路 1 号 A 楼
邮　　箱	yilin@yilin.com
网　　址	www.yilin.com
市场热线	025-86633278
排　　版	南京展望文化发展有限公司
印　　刷	江苏扬中印刷有限公司
开　　本	890 毫米 × 1260 毫米　1/32
印　　张	8.375
插　　页	4
版　　次	2022 年 7 月第 1 版
印　　次	2022 年 7 月第 1 次印刷
书　　号	ISBN 978-7-5447-9143-4
定　　价	39.00 元

版权所有·侵权必究

译林版图书若有印装错误可向出版社调换　质量热线：025-83658316

序 言

陈 恒

有"说不尽的莎士比亚",就有"说不尽的亚历山大",他们都是人类文化史上的伟大奇迹。亚历山大对我们来说永远是个陌生的熟人:历史中的亚历山大、传奇中的亚历山大、学术中的亚历山大,乃至媒体中的亚历山大,我们从中可以看出亚历山大在激发人类想象力方面所起的巨大推动作用,在人类文明史上所具有的特殊地位,在塑造世界格局中所占据的奇特位置。

历史学家工作的基础是史实与材料,有一分材料说一分话,但我们研究亚历山大的文献非常有限,主要依据是所谓的"亚历山大史家",这构成亚历山大历史知识的来源。这些历史学家笔下的文献出自不同的目的,因此在19世纪上半叶德国古典学界出现了一种"史源研究"(Quellenforschung)的潮流。根据"史源研究"的方法,古典研究者们分解出古代晚期学者们所编写的汇编作品中的不同来源,并建立这些史料来源之间的关系,从而追溯古代世界哲学、历史、宗教、法律、雕塑等领域相关记载的最早起源。学者们认为,通过这种方法可以更准确地评估这些记载的可靠性，从而提出更合理的判断。这种研究方法有助于我们认识真正的亚历山大。但只依据古典作家保存下来的有限又可疑的文献来构建真实的亚历山大，是远远不够的。好在当代学术已经在考古、铭文、纸草、钱币、天文记录、图像等领域取得不俗的业绩，我们可以利用这些成果来不断完善、丰富亚历山大的真实形象。

通过铭文，我们知道亚历山大所承诺的"为希腊人争取自由"只不过是一句空洞的口号；钱币告诉我们，亚历山大大帝的耳朵周围有的公羊角是埃及神阿蒙的象征。公元前331年春天，亚历山大造访了绿洲中的阿蒙神庙，并开始声称自己是阿蒙的儿子，这是亚历山大与同伴生怨的主要原因；通过巴比伦天文志，我们知道了高加米拉战役的确切日期；在公元前100年左右的一幅"亚历山大大帝镶嵌画"中，我们了解到罗马时代庞贝城的贵族希望通过这幅画，使自己与亚历山大大帝作为勇士之王的形象产生某种联系，希望来访者在主人身上发现亚历山大美德的折射。19世纪末和20世纪初挖掘出的大量纸草文献，大大完善了这一时期的年代和政治史。

透过这些支离破碎的证据，我们得以还原历史上较为真实的亚历山大。但亚历山大形象的构成是多元的，传奇就是一个主要的因素。两千多年来，除耶稣外，没有哪个历史人物能像亚历山大大帝一样如此持久地成为人们关注的对象：他是一位王子，具备天生的优势；他是一位勇士，是后人模仿的对象；他是一位将军，打开了古代世界的大门；他是一位先知，寻求不朽的秘密；他是一位哲人，与印度圣人讨论生命的目的……起源于公元前3世纪埃及的《亚历山大传奇》（我们能读到的最早版本是公元3世纪的）是描写亚历山大生平的虚构文学，几乎被翻译为中世纪欧洲和中东的每一种语言，在古代和中世纪广泛流传，并不断被美化，虚构的元素变得越来越夸张。

如果说亚历山大开创了希腊化时代，那么德罗伊森（Johann Gustav Droysen，1808—1884）便开创了希腊化时代研究。他于1833年出版了博大精深的《亚历山大大帝史》（1836、1843年又出版了另外两卷）。1877年再版时该书被命名为《希腊主义史》。"亚历山大的名字标志着世界上一个时代的结束，另一个时代的开始"，这是修订的总基调，当时德罗伊森已经70岁了，正处于他的权力和声誉的顶峰，再版是对他的作品在德国统一时所取得声望的一种敬意。他对马其顿的腓力和亚历山大研究的设想并不打算作为当前的政治宣言，但人们热切地认为它预示着在普鲁士君主制领导下的德意志各邦可以取得什么成就。一个以开明的文化和政治原则为基础的专制政权首先征服了世界，然后实现了文明，这个过程可能会在现代重复。在这种情况下，人们很容易接受亚历山大作为一个新时代开创者的形象。尽管德罗伊森的说法遭受过某些非议，但还是几乎获得了普遍的接受。亚历山大自觉或不自觉地创造了一个以希腊文化和绝对君主制为基础的新世界，这个世界一直持续到罗马作为世界强国的统治地位，德罗伊森将这个过程称为"希腊化"。这种说法并不新鲜，因为这个词在亚历山大之后一直在流行，是地中海东部非希腊人所说和所写的希腊语的标签，但德罗伊森把一个单纯的语言学概念扩展为对整个时代本质的概括。① 20世纪上半叶的历史学家大多

---

① Glenn R. Bugh, ed., *The Cambridge Companion to the Hellenistic World*, Cambridge University Press, 2006, p.9.

追随德罗伊森的观念研究亚历山大,比如英国塔恩(W. W. Tarn, 1869—1957)的《亚历山大》把亚历山大作为普世兄弟情谊观念的传播者,这些说教自然帮助了那个时代的帝国主义者、侵略者和政客。后来反战思想的盛行则使德罗伊森、塔恩等人的观念显得过时了。生于犹太家庭的巴迪安(Ernst Badian, 1925—2011)目睹了其父在1938年"水晶之夜"被纳粹虐待的场景,后来波普尔(Karl Popper, 1902—1994)帮助他们一家逃离维也纳,来到新西兰。巴迪安成为第二次世界大战后西方学术界重要的古典史家,他的著作终结了对亚历山大的美化与幻想,让人们相信亚历山大大帝是极端暴力的、野蛮的、偏执的。

上述几点是休·鲍登撰写《亚历山大大帝》一书的依据、主线和底蕴,是作者的努力方向,并且在简短的篇幅内基本做到了。作者叙事能力高超,主线明晰,重点突出;材料梳理能做到点面结合,张弛有度,但又不失深度;利用当代研究成果拨去历史重重迷雾,来尽量展示亚历山大真实的一面。但全书对亚历山大东征时的东西方文化交流着墨不多,只是在亚历山大图书馆建设时稍有提及,而对亚历山大与亚里士多德的关系也未设专章介绍,似有遗珠之恨。不过作者在有限的篇幅内,尽力展现有趣的事例和数据,又不时给出一些耐人寻味的叙述和判断。如,罗马将军大西庇阿说:"城市、国家和帝国覆灭的必然性:这样的命运降临在曾经幸运的特洛伊城,亚述人、米底人和波斯人也曾遭遇这样的命运,他们的帝国曾经是最伟大的,最近马其顿的辉煌帝国也是如此。"借西塞罗之口说亚历山大:"他的气质和自制力都是最好的,但即使是亚里士多德的学生,一旦被称为国王,也会变得傲慢、残忍和放纵。"这一切都在激活读者的想象力,让人掩卷长思:事实并不为自己说话,历史学家为它们说话,并在一定程度上通过它们说他们想说的话。作为纯粹历史人物的亚历山大与作为文化偶像乃至意识形态意义的亚历山大,其价值并非一致,作为后者的亚历山大来自历史又超越历史,其意义远远超出了他所建立的短命帝国。

亚历山大的重要性与其说是通过他的历史丰功和战略伟绩来衡量的,不如说是通过这种英雄人物的权力象征和绝对君主的权力模式来衡量的。亚历山大的事迹早已超越叙事本身,超越时空的限制,超越历史的真实性,是军事活动的动力源,是政治权力的象征,是一切要成为强者的那些人的精神支柱。可比肩亚历山大的拿破仑牢记神父雷纳尔(Abbé Raynal, 1713—1796)的话:"因为埃及跨两大洋,位于东西交界处,所以亚历山大认为,世界帝国之都应该建在这里,这样,埃及将作为世界经贸的中心。由此可以看出,如果要统一亚、非、欧,那么埃及将是其中的关键。"拿破仑认为埃及是至关重要之地,他去埃及是追寻亚历山大大帝的足迹,创造辉煌的历史!在雕刻自己作为世界统治者的形象时,他以不久前在庞贝古城的灰烬下发现的一幅壁画为蓝本,在这幅画中,亚历山大被描绘为具有宙斯的姿势和属性。因此,1806年,新皇帝让安格尔(Jean Ingres, 1780—1861)以古代亚历山大·宙斯的姿势为他画像……历史没有国界,历史总在重复上演,但并不是重复自身,历史同认识一样,永远不会在一种完美的理想状态中完结。

献给伊莎贝尔和克莱尔

致 谢

多年来，我一直在伦敦国王学院古典文学系教授有关亚历山大大帝的课程，写这本书的灵感便来源于此。我从学生们身上学到了很多，也希望他们会欣赏我的成果。这门课程通常是与林赛·艾伦博士共同授课的，她让我意识到近东材料的重要性。我特别感谢她，同时也感谢所有国王学院的同事。我也从同事那里学到了很多东西，我曾在世界各地的会议和讲座上与他们讨论过亚历山大，包括苏洛恰纳·阿西尔瓦萨姆、伊丽莎白·拜纳姆、菲利普·博斯曼、布莱恩·博斯沃思、彼得·格林、瓦尔德马尔·赫克尔、蒂姆·豪、罗宾·莱恩·福克斯、萨宾娜·米勒、丹尼尔·奥格登、弗朗西斯·鲍纳尔、约瑟夫·罗伊斯曼、安德鲁·斯图尔特、理查德·斯通曼、帕特·惠特利、约瑟夫·维舍夫和伊恩·沃辛顿。大部分的写作是我在担任辛辛那提大学古典文学系玛戈·蒂图斯研究员时完成的，我很感激那里的教职工们，他们慷慨大方，热情好客。感谢牛津大学出版社所有参与本书制作的人，包括卡罗尔·卡耐基、凯·克莱门特、凯莉·希克曼、安德里亚·基冈、艾玛·马、乔伊·梅勒和苏布拉马尼亚姆·文加塔克里希南。最后，一如既往，我要感谢我的家人，谢谢我的妻子吉尔和我的女儿们，她们给予了我无尽的支持，这本书要献给她们。

目 录

亚历山大生平大事年表　1

亚历山大征战路线图　5

引　言　1

第一章　辉煌前奏　10

第二章　王子：马其顿宫廷里的亚历山大　24

第三章　勇士：亚历山大的军队　33

第四章　指挥官：亚历山大和希腊人　44

第五章　法老：亚历山大和埃及　56

第六章　世界之王：亚历山大和波斯　68

第七章　旅行者：亚历山大的阿富汗和巴基斯坦之行　79

第八章　终有一死：亚历山大在巴比伦　92

第九章　亚历山大死后　98

索　引　108

英文原文　121

亚历山大生平大事年表

关于日期的说明

现存的关于亚历山大的古代文献并未完全给出精确的时间顺序信息。巴比伦天文志中提到的事件日期可以精确确定，但是对于希腊作者提到的事件，即使他们给出确切日期，我们也只能提供近似对应的时间，因为希腊和马其顿的历法不是以365天为一年的，常常与太阳历不一致。因此，这里的大多数日期是按季节给出的，但即使是这些日期也必须被视为近似值。

公元前356	夏	亚历山大出生
338	夏	喀罗尼亚战役
337	春	科林斯同盟成立
336	春	马其顿军队在帕曼纽的带领下进入亚洲
336		腓力二世被暗杀；亚历山大即位
335	春	亚历山大进军色雷斯和伊利里亚

	秋	洗劫底比斯
334	春	亚历山大横渡赫勒斯滂海峡进入亚洲
		亚历山大在特洛伊
		格拉尼库斯河战役
	夏	亚历山大解放希腊城邦
	秋	亚历山大在卡里亚
	冬	亚历山大在利西亚
333	春	亚历山大在戈尔迪乌姆
	夏	亚历山大在奇里乞亚
	秋	伊苏斯战役
	冬	围攻提尔开始
332	夏	围攻提尔结束
	秋	围攻加沙
	冬	亚历山大进入埃及
331	春	亚历山大拜访锡瓦的阿蒙神庙
		亚历山大从埃及行进到提尔，又向幼发拉底河进军
	10月1日	高加米拉战役
	10月20日	亚历山大进入巴比伦
	冬	亚历山大进入苏萨
330	春	亚历山大进入波斯波利斯
		亚历山大焚烧了波斯波利斯宫殿
	夏	大流士三世之死；贝苏斯宣布自己为国王（称阿尔塔薛西斯五世）
	秋	审判和处决菲罗塔斯，处决帕曼纽

329	春	亚历山大进入巴克特里亚和索格狄亚那
		贝苏斯被俘
	秋	亚历山大渡过雅克萨提斯河
328	秋	杀害克雷图斯
327	春	亚历山大占领了索格狄亚那岩山
		亚历山大与罗克珊娜结婚
		"侍从的阴谋"；逮捕卡利斯提尼斯
	夏	亚历山大进入兴都库什山脉
326	春	亚历山大占领奥尔努斯岩山
		亚历山大渡过印度河
		亚历山大在海达斯佩斯河打败波鲁斯
	夏	亚历山大抵达比阿斯河,随后返回印度河
	冬	亚历山大在与马利作战时受伤
325	夏	亚历山大抵达印度河三角洲
	秋	亚历山大行军穿过格德罗西亚
	冬	亚历山大回到帕萨尔加德和波斯波利斯
324	春	亚历山大到达苏萨,为印度战役获胜而奖励士兵
		亚历山大与斯妲特拉和帕里萨斯结婚,这是一场集体婚礼的一部分
		亚历山大惩罚在他不在时滥用职权的总督
	夏	亚历山大重组军队
		亚历山大下令希腊流亡者返回他们的城市

	秋	赫费斯提翁死亡
	冬	亚历山大征战科萨亚人
323	春	亚历山大进入巴比伦
	6月11日	亚历山大死亡

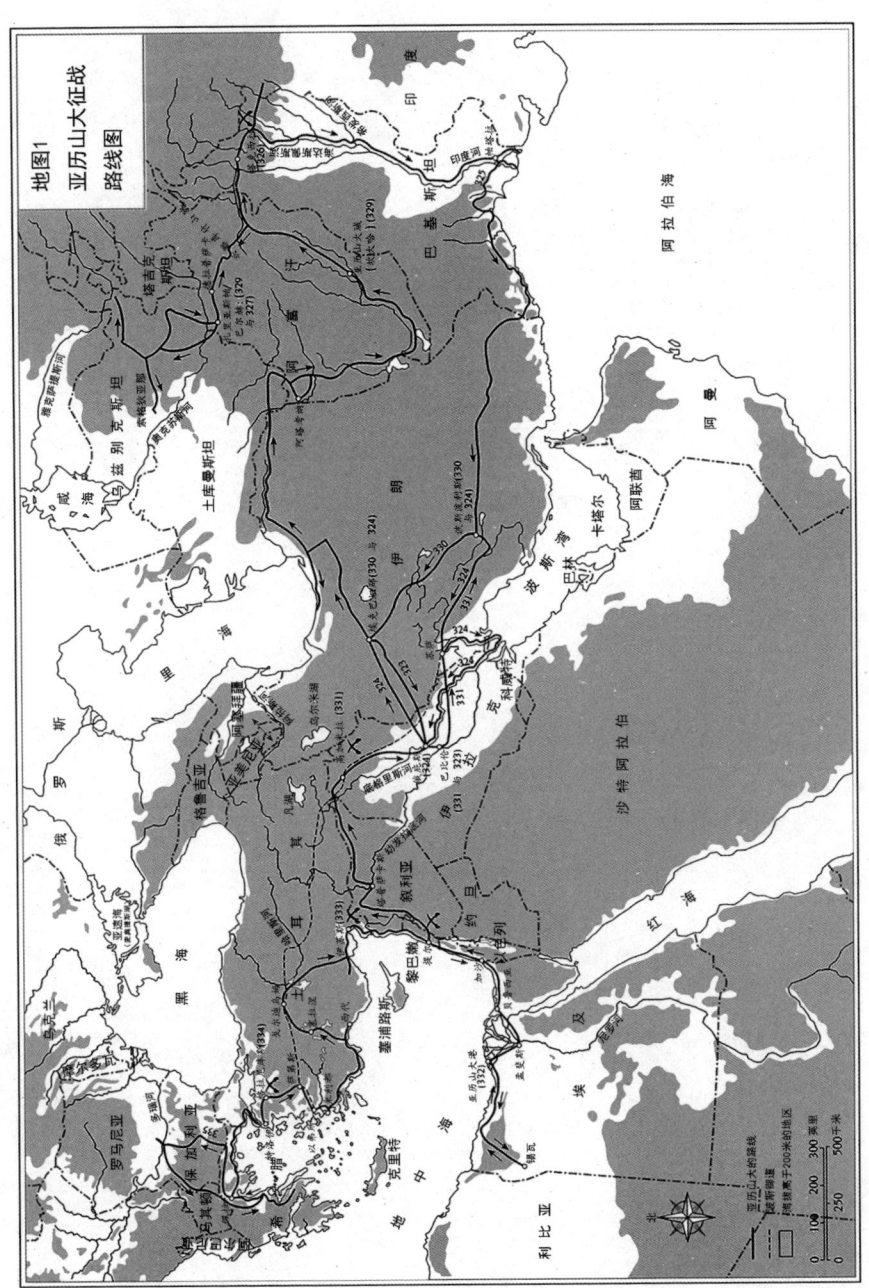

引　言

　　意大利国家考古博物馆位于意大利那不勒斯市，在博物馆的两层楼之间，有一幅描绘一场战役的大型镶嵌画（图1）。尽管画的左边部分已经严重受损，但仍能轻易辨认出亚历山大大帝的身影，他未戴头盔，骑在马上，定睛看着大流士三世，大流士三世则站在战车里，高于大批的战马和人群，惊慌失措地看着并指向亚历山大。就在大流士身后，他的战车御者正鞭打着马队，以带他远离这迫在眉睫的危险：亚历山大刚刚用长矛刺穿了挡在他与大流士之间的最后一个波斯骑士。画的后面是一条天际线，上面布满了马其顿人的长矛，而画的前景则到处都是遗弃的武器和倒下的波斯人。马其顿人的胜利不可避免。这幅镶嵌画长近6米，高3米多，是公元前100年前不久，为庞贝古城的"农牧神之家"的主人创作的。农牧神之家是庞贝城最大的私人住宅之一，可能是由一位意大利贵族建造而成，这幅镶嵌画在住宅中具有突出地位，覆盖在接待室的地板上，每一位重要的访客都会在这里看到它。主人显然认为，通过这幅画，他与亚历山大英

1

图 1 亚历山大大帝镶嵌画：这幅画反映了意大利人对亚历山大大帝的看法，以早期希腊绘画为基础，描绘了亚历山大大帝在伊苏斯战役（也可能是高加米拉战役）中的胜利场景

勇的勇士之王的形象便产生了某种联系，从中受益匪浅。

亚历山大大帝生于公元前356年，自公元前336年到公元前323年去世，是马其顿国王。其间，他率领一支军队，进入阿契美尼德波斯帝国领土，并控制了包括现在的希腊、保加利亚部分地区、土耳其、叙利亚、黎巴嫩、以色列、巴勒斯坦、约旦、埃及、利比亚部分地区、伊拉克、伊朗、阿富汗、乌兹别克斯坦和塔吉克斯坦部分地区以及巴基斯坦大部分地区在内的领土。在他死后，人们不断重新讲述他的征战故事，这在古典时期的人物中几乎是独一无二的。从他生前直到今天，在整个欧洲和近东，他一直存在于人们的想象之中。因此，亚历山大成为他去世两个世纪之后的一幅意大利艺术作品的主题也就不足为奇了。而对这幅镶嵌画提出一些问题，将有助于我们思考亚历山大本人，以及我们对他的真正了解到底有多少。事实证明，亚历山大比他看起来还要神秘。

那么，亚历山大镶嵌画是什么？它又代表了什么？人们一致认为，这幅镶嵌画本身创作于公元前120年至前100年间，但许多学者认为，这是一幅更古老的希腊绘画的复制品，这幅希腊绘画可能绘制于公元前4世纪后期，大约在画作描绘的事件发生后不久。有人曾试图将其归于一位有名的画家，有可能是埃雷特里亚的斐洛克塞诺斯，抑或是一位女性画家，亚历山大港的海伦。由于任何一位古代画家都没有确切属于他的作品留存下来，我们无法深入研究作品的归属。关于这幅镶嵌画描绘的是哪一场战争，人们有过争论，因为亚历山大曾两次遇到大流士，分别是在伊苏斯战役（公元前333年）和高加米拉战役（公元前331年）。大多数学者倾向于伊苏斯战役，但并没有得出确定的结论。这幅画是否准确地描绘了这场战争，抑或在很大程度上是艺术想象之作？画中的其他人物呢？那个头戴镶有金色花环的白色头盔，与众不同，立于亚历山大大帝左侧的人是谁？是他的先知，特密苏斯的亚里斯坦德，还是他的保镖之一，后来成为埃及统治者的托勒密？也许正是托勒密委托制作了这幅镶嵌画？有些人理所当然地提出了这样一个问题：把亚历山大镶嵌画简单地看作一幅"罗马的复制品"，源自一幅公元前4世纪创作的希腊绘画，是否合适？我们现在看到的是一件意大利艺术品，应该注意它的创作背景是公元前2世纪后期的庞贝城：这幅画对它的委托者、创作者，甚至对造访农牧神之家时看到它的人们来说，意味着什么？这些问题回答起来并不容易，但至少都是关于我们所拥有的这件艺术作品，而不是那幅想象中的原作的。

当我们研究对亚历山大一生中某一时刻的艺术表现时，这些关注似乎并不重要。但关于亚历山大生平的文字证据，也存在类似的问题。现存的关于亚历山大生平事迹的叙述可以追溯至公元前30年到公元2世纪或3世纪。最早流传下来的记载是西西里的狄奥多罗斯撰写的《历史丛书》40卷，记载了从神话时代开始一直到尤利乌斯·恺撒之死的历史。这部著作的大部分已经遗失，但记载亚历山大事迹的第17卷却大多保存了下来。此外，还有公元1世纪克劳狄乌斯或韦斯巴芗统治时期，罗马人昆图斯·库尔提斯·鲁夫斯写的传记《马其顿国王亚历山大大帝》，公元100年左右由希腊人喀罗内亚的普鲁塔克所写的亚历山大传记，以及由另一个希腊人尼科美底亚的阿里安所写的征战记录，阿里安是哈德良皇帝的朋友，写作于公元2世纪的前三分之一时期。在这之后,另一位罗马作家查士丁创作了《庞培乌斯·特洛格斯〈腓力史〉概要》,也就是狄奥多罗斯同时代作家庞培乌斯·特洛格斯的作品《腓力史》的缩略版本,其中包含了对亚历山大统治时期的描述。这些作家统称为亚历山大史家。显然,他们的叙述直接或间接基于亚历山大死后几十年的记录,有一些是由亚历山大征战的参与者所写的,但尚存文本的作者是否忠实传递了他们所读的内容则无法确定。很明显,这些幸存的有关亚历山大的记录,或多或少对他进行了塑造,以便能够吸引当时的读者,也就是说,这些读者多是由强大的皇帝统治的希腊人和罗马人,亚历山大大帝成了这些皇帝统治的典范。从根本上讲,叙事来源中的亚历山大是一个罗马人眼中的亚历山大。

正如这幅亚历山大镶嵌画一样,有关亚历山大生平的叙述可能保存了许多材料,可以追溯到亚历山大所处的时代,但我们所拥有的这部分是零碎的,而且,这些记录总体上是通过后世之人的作品进行传播的,他们在传播的过程中改变了材料,以适应新技术和口味的变化。对于任何想要讲述亚历山大生平和征战故事的人来说,寻找有效的方法来解读这些叙述,无疑是一个极大的挑战。许多时候,亚历山大史家对于同一组事件提供了相互矛盾的版本——事实上,阿里安指出,有时甚至目击者们的消息来源也不一致。另一方面,当同一个故事出现在几个不同的叙述版本中时,我们无法确定哪个是真的:有些关于亚历山大的故事是在他生前或死后不久虚构出来的,例如,他遇见了神话中的亚马逊女王并与之上床,这些故事很快就成为叙述传统的一部分。关于他的故事盛行一时,没有一个作者能够忽视,即使在早期作家的记述中根本找不到关于他的故事。尽管对亚历山大史家的资料来源进行了数十年的研究（德语称作"Quellenforschung"，即"史源研究"），我们仍然没有可靠的方法来确定他们的记述中有多少是可信的。

但是，通过对亚历山大周围的世界建立更全面的了解，我们可以或多或少在确定事件发生的可能性方面取得一些进展，为此，我们需要研究更多的物证。在大英博物馆古伊朗展厅的一个展柜里，陈列着一小块灰色的陶土残片，宽4到5厘米，高6厘米，上面刻有整齐的楔形文字（图2）。这块残片用阿卡德语所写，是巴比伦天文志的一部分，记录的是国王统治的第十四年第二个月。在残片的底部可以看到这样的文字："第二十九日，国

图2　巴比伦天文志残片，记录了亚历山大统治第十四年第二个月发生的事件，包括国王的去世

王崩；云［……］天空"。日期对应的是公元前323年6月11日，时任国王是亚历山大大帝。这一小块黏土是亚历山大几近同时代的证据，但这与镶嵌画上的亚历山大非常不同。这样的天文志涵盖了公元前652年到公元前60年这一段时期。每晚都有人站在巴比伦王宫的屋顶上，观察天空。天气晴朗的时候，他们会记下行星的位置，以及任何其他不寻常的现象（彗星、日食等等）。这些观察结果将被记录在天文志中，每个月的观察之后，还会有一份关于市场上主要商品价格的报告，以及对发生的重大事件的记录。这些观察的目的是确定诸神对城市，特别是对国王的态度：如果天空中有迹象表明国王面临危险，就可以采取措施保护他。亚历山大第一次进入巴比伦是在公元前331年10月20日，当时几乎已经被认可为巴比伦的新国王。公元前323年春，他回到了这座城市，几个月后就在这里去世了。当他身处巴比伦一带时，整个巴比伦的学者-祭司都在关注他的安康，他的行为被记录在王家纪事和其他文本中。除了罗马的亚历山大，还有巴比伦的亚历山大。

　　在亚历山大死后发行的钱币上，可以看到他更多的形象，这些钱币是由控制他帝国各个部分的人发行的。亚历山大本人根本没有发行印有自己肖像的钱币；相反，他遵循了马其顿人早期的做法，将赫拉克勒斯的头像印在银币上。而他的继任者们开始发行印有他肖像的钱币，这表明，就像后来农牧神之家的主人一样，他们认为与亚历山大的联系对他们有利。但是，这些钱币上的亚历山大头像有着不同寻常的特征。一些钱币肖像显示，亚历山大的耳朵周围有公羊角（图3）。这些角是埃及神阿蒙的象征，亚历山大修复了底比斯城的阿蒙神庙，并于公元前331年

图3　亚历山大的继任者利西马库斯发行的一枚银币,银币上亚历山大的头像上刻着埃及阿蒙神的象征——公羊角

春天造访了利比亚沙漠锡瓦绿洲中的阿蒙神庙。根据亚历山大史家的说法,正是在这次造访之后,亚历山大开始声称自己是阿蒙(或宙斯,阿蒙被认为与宙斯是同一的)的儿子,这些说法是亚历山大的士兵和同伴愤恨他的主要原因;大多数现代学者都接受了这一观点。但这些钱币表明,这些同伴中的一些人实际上却选择去宣传亚历山大和阿蒙神之间的关系。可能他们对亚历山大说法的态度在他死后发生了改变,也可能这些公元前4世纪后期的钱币所讲述的故事比几百年后书写的故事更为真实。

此外,还有其他一些亚历山大的形象可以帮助我们更好地了解他的同时代人或近时代人是如何看待他的。希腊的城邦中竖立着的雕塑上雕刻着他制定的城邦法令。雅典演说家在他们存世的演讲中提到了他的事迹。他的名字和肖像,以法老的风格,雕刻在上埃及神庙的墙壁上,那里还以他的名义进行了修复工作。还有一些同时代文献和文物可以帮助我们更全面地了解他所处的世界,即使其中并没有提到他的名字。

这本"牛津通识读本"中的《亚历山大大帝》不仅没有忽视亚历山大史家所提供的叙述，反而比以往更加重视这些同时代文献，并指出了哪些是我们知道的，哪些又是我们不知道的。虽然本书结构大体上是按时间顺序排列的，但并不打算直接叙述亚历山大的生平和他的征战行动。普鲁塔克的《亚历山大传》是古代文献中记录了亚历山大的童年以及他成为国王后的各种行动的唯一一部，虽然不一定可信，但碰巧的是，全书内容长度与本书相似，适合搭配阅读。本书提供了时间轴，以及显示亚历山大进军路线的地图（地图1），应该足以防止读者在庞大的时间线中迷失方向。第一章"辉煌前奏"将简要介绍阿契美尼德波斯帝国和马其顿王国发生冲突之前的历史，而最后一章将探讨亚历山大死后几千年来，对他的记忆如何一直萦绕在世界上。在中间的章节，我们将在亚历山大自己的世界里考察他：不仅是希腊和马其顿，还包括构成古代近东的整个复杂的网络。

第一章

辉煌前奏

　　狭窄的博斯普鲁斯海峡连接着黑海和马尔马拉海。约公元前513年,波斯国王大流士一世(公元前522—前486在位)修建了一座横跨博斯普鲁斯海峡的大桥,并率领一支军队从亚洲进入欧洲。次年,大流士返回亚洲,留给他的指挥官梅加巴佐斯一项任务,命令他征服爱琴海北岸的领土。当地的统治者把土地和水源赠予波斯人,以示臣服,马其顿人阿敏塔斯就是其中之一。他因此被授予马其顿总督的职位,而马其顿则成为阿契美尼德波斯帝国的一个省。阿敏塔斯将自己的女儿吉盖娅嫁给了一位名叫布巴雷斯的波斯领袖。约公元前495年,阿敏塔斯去世,他的儿子亚历山大一世继承了他的总督位置,亚历山大一世仍是大流士与其子及继任者薛西斯的忠实臣民。就这样,波斯人亲手扶植起了这个当权的家族,而正是这个家族,将在180年后推翻他们的帝国。人们熟知的亚历山大大帝,即亚历山大三世,便是亚历山大一世的六世孙。

波斯阿契美尼德王朝的崛起

居鲁士大帝(约公元前559—前530在位)建立了波斯阿契美尼德王朝,他最初是安善国王,这个头衔代表了他对古埃兰王国的统治,古埃兰国位于今天的伊朗西南部。公元前559年,居鲁士大帝成为波斯人的首领。他掌权后不久,开始向外征战,击败了北方邻国米底(公元前550年),并迅速将势力扩张到整个伊朗高原,向西进入安纳托利亚高原,并在此击败了吕底亚国王克洛伊索斯(公元前546年),将他的帝国扩展到了爱琴海海岸。之后,他将注意力转向了位于美索不达米亚的巴比伦,当时近东最强大的城市。巴比伦人在那波帕拉萨国王(公元前626—前605在位)和尼布甲尼撒国王(公元前604—前562在位)的统治下,推翻了新亚述帝国,结束了新亚述帝国对美索不达米亚及其以西地区(约为今天的伊拉克、叙利亚、黎巴嫩、以色列、巴勒斯坦和约旦等国)长达数个世纪的统治,并建立了自己的帝国。公元前539年,居鲁士大帝在底格里斯河畔的俄庇斯击败了一支巴比伦军队,顺利进入巴比伦,废黜了国王那波尼德斯(公元前556—前539在位),让自己的儿子冈比西斯取代他成为巴比伦国王。居鲁士大帝的征战一直持续到他去世为止,之后,冈比西斯(公元前530—前522在位)进一步扩张了帝国,吞并了塞浦路斯和埃及(公元前525年)。

冈比西斯在从埃及返回的途中逝世,死亡原因不明,他死后,理应由他的兄弟巴迪亚继承王位(公元前522年)。然而,就在此时,发生了一场政变,波斯贵族大流士自立为王,他可能是居鲁士家族的远亲。大流士成功镇压多起叛乱,并在掌权后继续推行其前任的扩张政策。在东部，他将帝国的疆域延伸至今天的巴基斯坦境内的印度河，并在北非扩张领土，吞并了昔兰尼加地区（今利比亚）。他跨越博斯普鲁斯海峡，在黑海沿岸与斯基泰人作战（约公元前513年），尽管结果并不理想，但如我们所见，这场战役使大流士控制了爱琴海北岸和多瑙河之间的土地，包括色雷斯和马其顿。

统治波斯帝国

要统治一个如此庞大而分散的帝国，就需要有效的组织。阿契美尼德王朝体系的核心便是国王本人。波斯王室铭文强调国王的身份和统治权，并强调国王得到了众神之首阿胡拉·马兹达的支持。国王出现在王宫等地的雕塑中，他或是坐在他的宝座上，或是站着。在雕塑中，国王总是比其他人都要高大，他的头顶上方经常雕刻着代表阿胡拉·马兹达的飞盘。阿契美尼德王室的肖像画继承了亚述王室的特征，诸如国王狩猎狮子这样的场景。这些图像被用在印章上，因此传遍了整个帝国。大流士进入欧洲后，他和他的继任者们就开始在吕底亚首都萨迪斯铸造金币，称"大流克"，在爱琴海地区流通。金币上的国王被描绘成一个手持弓和矛的战士。

帝国有许多个首都：居鲁士在米底的埃克巴坦那、巴比伦和他在法尔斯兴建的帕萨尔加德进行统治；大流士在埃兰的苏萨为自己建造了一座宫殿，并在距离帕萨尔加德不远处的波斯波利斯建造了另一座。国王和他的宫廷每一年中都要从一个首都缓慢地迁移到另一个首都，部分是为了应对气候（伊朗高原上的埃克巴坦那在夏季比较凉爽，而巴比伦和苏萨则更适合冬季)。王室的巡行采取的是大队列的形式,国王大部分时间都住在帐篷里,而不是石头或砖块的建筑里,正如他在军事行动时所做的那样。这种游牧风格是独特的波斯风格,与美索不达米亚从前的君主们以城市为中心的风格形成了鲜明的对比。首都的宫殿也是展示王室权力的地方。由大流士一世建造并由他的继承人薛西斯(公元前486—前465在位)扩建的波斯波利斯宫殿遗址是现存最壮观的例子。其"apadana"(觐见大殿)外侧檐壁上的雕刻描绘了国王的臣民从帝国各地为他献上贡品的场面。每一群人的衣服、发型和携带的礼物都不尽相同。宫殿里储存着大量黄金、白银等不易腐烂的物品(根据古代作者的说法,除了黄金白银之外,亚历山大在储藏室里发现了至少价值2500吨白银的贵重金属)。除了接受贡品外,国王还向朝臣和臣民赠送礼物,尽管这种礼尚往来的关系并不公平。例如,国王进餐的同时,他通过"国王的餐桌"制度来监督他的家人、臣仆和侍卫的饮食。

帝国的各省由国王任命的总督管辖,这些人通常是波斯的主要贵族,但正如我们所见,像马其顿的阿敏塔斯这样的地方统治者也可以掌权。他们通过联姻与国王和彼此之间建立联系,尽管有些总督职务会通过家族传承,但与国王的个人纽带仍然很重要。总督要为国王和自己收取税金与贡品,并在国王的军事行动需要时召集军队。这些男人(偶尔也有女人)在自己的首都拥有宫殿和自己的朝廷。有些人在称为"天堂"的大型狩猎公园内建造了避暑宫殿和行宫,他们可以在此模仿国王猎杀狮子和其他动物。修建于哈利卡尔那索斯(今博德鲁姆)的摩索拉斯,即卡里亚总督(公元前377—前353在位)陵墓等遗迹被列入世界七大奇迹，显示了当地统治者作为总督的野心。西方诸侯的朝廷和宫殿经常被帝国边缘以外的领袖们造访，并成为爱琴海地区，尤其是色雷斯和马其顿王室的典范。国王监督总督的活动需要良好的通信交通，而阿契美尼德帝国的道路系统在古代就备受推崇。它使得信使（希罗多德在公元前5世纪的一篇文章中写道："无论是风霜雨雪，烈日炎炎，还是月黑风高，都不能阻止他们以最快的速度完成既定的任务"）和宫廷巡行可以快速行动，并且加快了军队的机动速度——不仅有利于国王的军队，也有利于入侵者的军队。

波斯和希腊人

在大流士的儿子及继任者薛西斯的统治下，阿契美尼德帝国达到了它最大的疆土面积，尽管只持续了短暂的一段时间。公元前480年，薛西斯征服了希腊北部和中部的大部分地区，包括雅典。66年前，居鲁士打败了吕底亚国王克洛伊索斯，并接管了他的王国，其领土包括爱琴海东岸的一些主要希腊定居点，冈比西斯征服塞浦路斯后，更多的希腊城市被纳入帝国。这些城市由个人或小团体管理，这些管理者由总督掌控，并为总督的利益服务。公元前499年，许多管理者起义反抗波斯的统治，并得到了一支舰队的支持，这支舰队由20艘来自雅典的船只和5艘来自优卑亚岛埃雷特里亚的船只组成。公元前494年，起义被镇压，希腊最大的城市之一米利都被洗劫一空，其中位于狄迪马的阿波罗圣地和神庙遭到大规模破坏。

在爱奥尼亚人起义前的几年里，即约公元前511年至公元前506年，雅典经历了一段内乱时期，主要发生在"僭主"希庇亚斯和另外两个人——伊萨戈拉斯和克里斯提尼——之间，后者后来建立了雅典的民主制度。在斗争的过程中，伊萨戈拉斯向斯巴达求援，作为回应，克里斯提尼通过吕底亚总督与波斯人展开了谈判，甚至可能向国王投降。因此，在大流士看来，雅典和爱奥尼亚以及塞浦路斯的城市一样，是一个反叛的主体。公元前492年，波斯将军马多尼乌斯率领一支联合军队和舰队穿越赫勒斯滂海峡，穿过色雷斯和马其顿，打算向南进军埃雷特里亚和雅典，但由于大部分舰队在阿索斯山附近失事，远征被取消。两年后，大流士派遣另一支军队，在达蒂斯的率领下，横渡爱琴海。许多希腊岛屿都向国王投降，埃雷特里亚也被洗劫一空，但军队随后在马拉松战役（公元前490年）中被雅典人击败，这场征战就此结束。

大流士死后，薛西斯继承了他父亲的计划，公元前481年，他率领马多尼乌斯将军沿着先前走过的路线行进。这一次战役取得了成功，薛西斯接受了沿途所有希腊城市的投降，在塞莫皮莱击溃了一支斯巴达人领导的小型军队，并成功洗劫雅典，将战利品带回苏萨。然而，这种成功是短暂的。公元前480年，薛西斯的舰队（其中包括大量的希腊船只）在萨拉米斯被希腊舰队击败，次年他的军队于普拉塔亚战败，并撤回亚洲。

在接下来的几年里，剩下的波斯军队被赶出了北爱琴海，安纳托利亚西部的希腊城市在几十年的时间里从波斯的控制下解放出来，成为雅典领导的联盟成员。然而，没过多久，波斯当局就在爱琴海东岸恢复了统治。希腊城市之间的不信任与日俱增，最终导致在雅典和斯巴达及其各自盟友之间爆发了伯罗奔尼撒战争（公元前431—前404），而这场战争的真正胜利者是阿契美尼德帝国。双方都试图赢得国王阿尔塔薛西斯一世（公元前465—前424在位）和大流士二世（公元前423—前405在位）的支持，正是大流士的小儿子居鲁士对斯巴达人的支持赋予了他们所需的海军力量，迫使雅典人投降。作为回报，斯巴达人同意把亚洲大陆上的希腊城市交给波斯人。

大流士二世死后，斯巴达人和波斯人之间的关系破裂，因为斯巴达军官携一批雇佣兵支持居鲁士，试图从他的哥哥阿尔塔薛西斯二世（公元前405—前359在位）手中夺取王位，但没有成功。雅典作家色诺芬参加了这次战役，在《远征记》一书中进行了描述，这部作品为阿里安的《亚历山大远征记》提供了一个典范。公元前386年，阿尔塔薛西斯最终通过"国王和平协议"解决了爱琴海地区的事务，协议承认了阿契美尼德王朝对亚洲大陆城市的统治，国王威胁说，如果岛屿和欧洲大陆上的希腊人不尊重该协议和彼此的自治权，他将动用军队或金钱进行干预。在随后的几十年里，波斯向希腊的主要政治家提供资金，确保他们所倡导的政策不与国王的利益相冲突，因此，希腊人与阿契美尼德帝国的势力之间几乎没有直接冲突。

公元前4世纪的阿契美尼德帝国

薛西斯的继任者们很少刻立王室碑文，因此我们对帝国其他地方发生的事情的了解比早期要少得多。希腊历史学家尼多斯的克特西亚斯曾在阿尔塔薛西斯二世的朝廷任职一段时间，他写了一部波斯史，目前只能通过其他作者的引用来了解，但这并不能给予我们很多信息。尽管埃及在公元前404年脱离了阿契美尼德王朝的控制，直到公元前343年才被阿尔塔薛西斯三世

（公元前359—前338在位）收复，但阿契美尼德王朝基本保持完整。我们从一些巴比伦文献中了解到帝国最后几年的事件，包括所谓的王朝预言，其中报道了阿契美尼德宫廷的一些阴谋事件。阿尔塔薛西斯三世的死因可能是中毒，也可能是自然死亡，在他死后，宦官巴戈阿斯唆使杀害了阿尔塔薛西斯三世的大部分亲属，并扶植他唯一幸存的儿子阿尔塔薛西斯四世（公元前338—前336在位）上台统治。两年后，巴戈阿斯将其杀害，由于王室家族其他成员已经死亡，巴戈阿斯扶植了一位王室远亲登上王位，即大流士三世（公元前336—前331在位）。大流士曾是一位成功的军事领袖，因此，对巴戈阿斯来说，扶植大流士三世显然是个错误的选择，他很快便被国王下令诛杀。大流士三世就是要直面亚历山大大帝的人。

马其顿王国：最初的150年

与此同时，在马其顿，薛西斯在爱琴海战败之后，阿敏塔斯的儿子亚历山大一世（约公元前495—前454在位）保住了自己的位置，他被称为"爱希腊者"（"希腊人的朋友"），希罗多德的故事显示，亚历山大一世一直在密谋反对波斯人。他的王国危机四伏，有时还要面临来自内部的挑战。马其顿的中心地带是爱琴海西北角的广阔平原，阿利阿克蒙河和阿克西奥斯河流经这里，被称为下马其顿，其首都埃盖位于平原南缘。亚历山大一世向西部和北部的高地（上马其顿）扩张，向东也延伸到斯特里蒙河流域，控制了17000多平方公里的领土（面积比英国历史上的约克郡略大，比美国新泽西州略小）。该地区不仅有大量肥沃的土地用于农业和畜牧业，还拥有森林和金银矿藏。然而，它的四面八方都被潜在的敌人所包围。东边是色雷斯王国,西北和西边是伊利里亚与伊庇鲁斯王国。而在爱琴海沿岸,特别是在哈尔基季基半岛,有一些建立于公元前7世纪和前6世纪的希腊城邦。

马其顿国王有时会有多个妻子,因此往往会有几个同父异母的儿子。这种一夫多妻制的做法使国王可以大量利用联姻来达成外交,这也意味着男性继承人数量充足。另一方面,这意味着马其顿国王的死会不止一次导致一段时期的不稳定,因为他的继承人会为了王位互相争斗。这种情况发生在亚历山大一世死后,他的继任者佩尔狄卡斯二世(公元前454—前413在位)花了几年时间才掌权。在他统治时期,马其顿王国经常受到邻国的威胁,只能采取有限的军事行动(并不总是成功的)和谈判相结合的方式来解决。

他的继任者阿奇劳斯(公元前413—前399在位)加强了马其顿的军事力量,修建了道路和防御工事,可能还引入了新的步兵阵型。他还将首都迁往位于马其顿平原的佩拉,并设立了一个宫廷,吸引了希腊艺术家和作家搬迁至此,其中就包括雅典悲剧家欧里庇得斯。阿奇劳斯死后,他的继任者之间发生了更多的争斗,直到他的堂兄阿敏塔斯三世(公元前393—前369在位)即位。阿敏塔斯三世统治期间,伊利里亚的扩张主义加剧,哈尔基季基半岛的希腊城邦的敌意也与日俱增。这些压力在他死后继续存在,随着马其顿王国开始更直接地参与希腊南部城邦的事务,新的压力也随之增加。阿敏塔斯三世死后,他的儿子亚历山大二世(公元前369—前368在位)征战色萨利,随后被暗杀,其继任者托勒密(公元前368—前365在位)可能是亚历山大二世的弟弟佩尔狄卡斯三世的摄政王,他与希腊城邦底比斯结盟,派遣人质去往底比斯,以示诚意,其中包括后来的腓力二世,亚历山大二世和佩尔狄卡斯三世的另一个兄弟。在佩尔狄卡斯三世(公元前365—前360在位)统治时期,马其顿王国曾一度与雅典结盟,而不是与底比斯结盟,但这种联盟是短暂的,因为佩尔狄卡斯三世本人在对抗入侵的伊利里亚军队的战斗中被杀害,把王位留给了他的兄弟腓力二世(公元前360—前338在位),也就是亚历山大大帝的父亲。

腓力二世

腓力二世用了不到三年的时间,通过外交、军事重组和优秀将才三者的结合,改变了马其顿王国的命运。除了要对付不断挺进的伊利里亚军队外,腓力二世还遭到上马其顿帕埃尼亚起义的威胁,同时可能还面临着三个同父异母兄弟与雅典和色雷斯支持的另外两个觊觎者对王位的挑战。他与雅典人谈判,并贿赂色雷斯人,消除了最后的危险,他还处决了同父异母的兄弟阿奇劳斯。腓力二世还提供金钱,利诱帕埃尼亚人停止起义,并与伊利里亚人谈判,达成了暂时休战协议。这给了他时间改进军队的训练和组织。腓力对马其顿战争方式的创新有多大的贡献,他的前任实现了多大的成就,又有多少有待于他的儿子亚历山大去完成,这都存在一些争论。这是一本关于亚历山大的书,因此回顾亚历山大统治下的军队更有意义,这一部分将在第三章中展开。然而,人们普遍认为,腓力通过招募更多的步兵和骑兵,并进行更正规和更彻底的训练,提高了马其顿武装部队的能力。到公元前358年,他已经能够向伊利里亚人进军,并把他们赶出了上马其顿。

腓力通过一系列的婚姻，与邻国建立了稳定的关系。他共有七个妻子，第一个妻子是菲拉，来自上马其顿以利米欧提斯地区；随后，他娶了伊利里亚王室成员奥妲塔，还有两名来自色萨利希腊城邦主要家族的女性，尼塞波利丝和费里娜；公元前357年，腓力又娶了伊庇鲁特王室成员奥林匹娅斯；在他统治的后期，他娶了色雷斯国王的女儿美妲为妻，最后娶了马其顿世家望族的成员克莉奥帕特拉。腓力的父亲阿敏塔斯三世在两次婚姻中育有六个儿子。相比之下，腓力的妻子们生了好几个女儿，却只给他生了两个儿子：费里娜生下了阿里达乌斯，但因为某种原因，阿里达乌斯被认为不适合继承王位；奥林匹娅斯是亚历山大大帝的母亲。没有儿子的妻子在宫廷里几乎没有影响力，人们对这些女子知之甚少。然而，奥林匹娅斯活过了亚历山大的统治时期，并发挥了相当大的影响力。我们将在下一章进一步了解她。

腓力在此之后的行动清楚表明，他认为侵略是确保马其顿利益的最有效途径，但他同时也采取了其他行动，表明他既可以与希腊人合作，也可以与他们对抗。在公元前357年至公元前354年间，他控制了哈尔基季基以外的所有希腊城邦，从东部的安菲波利斯到南部的彼得那。他还占领了克里尼德斯城邦，并将其改名为腓力皮，这里拥有高产的金银矿藏。公元前356年，他驾驭战车，参加了奥林匹克运动会，并获得了胜利。这不仅仅是一种炫耀行为：在希腊，人们认为奥林匹克运动会的胜利者得到了宙斯的青睐，会受到特别的尊重，因此腓力的胜利使他备受关注。

公元前356年，在希腊中部，福基斯和维奥蒂亚之间爆发了一场战争,战争的部分原因是争夺德尔斐的阿波罗圣地和神庙的控制权。现代学者称之为第三次神圣战争。位于马其顿和福基斯之间的色萨利各城邦也卷入了战争,腓力的妻子费里娜的家乡拉里萨号召他保卫这座城市,以抵抗支持其竞争对手费莱的福基斯人(费莱是腓力的另一位妻子尼塞波利丝的家乡,有可能正是在这些事件之后两人举行了婚礼)。公元前352年,腓力打败了福基斯人,被选为色萨利全境的统帅。渐渐地,他被卷入希腊各大城邦的事务之中。

南侵与东进交替发生。腓力回到马其顿,向色雷斯国王塞索布勒普提斯开战,随后进攻哈尔基季基,并于公元前348年攻占了那里最强大的希腊城邦奥林索斯。随后,公元前346年,他向南进军到福基斯,占领了温泉关隘口(在那里,薛西斯曾打败斯巴达人,控制了希腊中部和北部之间的陆路通道),结束了与维奥蒂亚人长达十年的战争。位于德尔斐的阿波罗神庙以及温泉关周围地区由希腊人委员会监管,该委员会被称为德尔斐近邻同盟(Delphic Amphictyony),主要由来自圣地周围地区的代表组成("amphictyon"的意思是"近邻")。在此之前,人们还不完全清楚谁有资格成为该委员会的成员,但战后,作为和解的一部分,福基斯人被驱逐出委员会,腓力取代了他们的位置。目前还不清楚该委员会的影响力,其主要任务是监督每年两次在温泉关庆祝的皮莱节,以及保护德尔斐的圣地。但与他在奥林匹克运动会上的胜利一样,德尔斐近邻同盟的成员资格使腓力成为许多希腊人眼中值得尊敬的人。之后,他回到色雷斯,于公元前342年吞并了塞索布勒普提斯的王国,并向北进军到多瑙河。

腓力当时的终极目标是什么,现代学者对此有不同的看法,他的同时代人也不清楚。希腊南部较大的城市,包括雅典和斯巴达,对北爱琴海地区的自然资源很感兴趣,有时还与希腊北部城市和色雷斯王国结成联盟:马其顿的发展可能会威胁到他们的利益。雅典人尤其依赖黑海的粮食供应,因此不可能让敌对势力控制博斯普鲁斯海峡或赫勒斯滂海峡。腓力的东进对波斯国王也是一个潜在威胁。公元前340年,腓力包围了马尔马拉海北岸的城市,包括拜占庭。阿尔塔薛西斯三世派遣补给和雇佣军部队支援这些城市。他还像他的前任统治者一样,向雅典和其他地方的政客们捐款,鼓励他们尽可能地反对腓力。另一方面,希腊城邦的领袖们认为腓力能够保护他们免受对手的攻击,并邀请腓力介入色萨利和希腊中部地区。在控制了马其顿周边地区之后,腓力很可能想与其他希腊人保持和平关系。一些雅典政治家和政论作者可能受到了他的恩惠,主张支持腓力进击波斯人;另一些人则持相反的观点,他们同样可能从阿尔塔薛西斯那里获取了金钱。

爱琴海两个角落发生的事件导致腓力和雅典之间发生了最后一次对峙,这次对峙之后,他在希腊的征战圆满结束。公元前340年,雅典人与拜占庭结盟,拜占庭此时正被腓力围困。他随之夺取了雅典的运粮舰队,于是雅典人宣战。同年晚些时候,德尔斐近邻同盟指控德尔斐以西的安飞沙城在阿波罗圣地耕种,并开始对其发动军事行动。第一轮军事行动没有达成和解,腓力被召去处理这个问题。他向安飞沙进军,然后向西威胁雅典。德摩斯梯尼是雅典最能言善辩的演说家,也是接受波斯国王馈赠的人之一,他鼓动雅典人出兵反对腓力,并说服底比斯加入他们。双方于公元前338年8月在喀罗尼亚会战,腓力获胜。随后，他在底比斯驻军，但并没有试图惩罚雅典人。相反，他开始组织他的下一次征战。

公元前337年春，除斯巴达以外的希腊所有城邦代表都聚集在科林斯，宣誓效忠腓力，并建立了一个组织，现代学者称其为科林斯同盟。在会议上，腓力宣布了入侵阿契美尼德帝国的计划，公开宣称其目的是为薛西斯造成的破坏而惩罚波斯人，并再次解放亚洲的希腊城邦。召集战役所需的全部部队需要时间，但在公元前336年3月，一支由1万人组成的马其顿先遣部队，在腓力麾下将军帕曼纽和阿塔罗斯的带领下，从欧洲越过赫勒斯滂海峡进入亚洲。

第二章

王子：马其顿宫廷里的亚历山大

公元前356年7月，亚历山大大帝出生在佩拉的王宫里，当时他的父亲腓力二世正在哈尔基季基半岛与希腊城邦作战。正如人们所预料的那样，对于一个成就如此惊人的人来说，关于他出生之预兆的故事后来广为流传。据说，以弗所的阿耳忒弥斯神庙在亚历山大出生的那天被烧毁，有人认为，与生育有关的阿耳忒弥斯忽视了她的神庙，是因为她当时正在参加马其顿王子的出生仪式。还有人说，在腓力得知亚历山大出生的消息的同一天，还得知他的战车赢得了奥林匹克运动会冠军，他的将军帕曼纽打败了伊利里亚人。基于这种巧合，预言家们预言亚历山大将是"无敌的"或"不可征服的"（希腊语的单词是aniketos）。后来的作家们经常用这个词来形容他。

在亚历山大史家中，只有普鲁塔克记载了他的童年时代。普鲁塔克所说的一些话得到了其他作家的支持，特别是他对亚历山大在哲学家亚里士多德指导下接受教育的描述，但一些更具戏剧性的故事似乎也包括在内，倒不是因为这些信息有多可靠，而是因为它们预示了亚历山大后来的成就。这些故事中还包括亚历山大如何驯服他的马比塞弗勒斯，这匹马几乎难以驯服，亚历山大和他的父亲打赌说他能做到。亚历山大似乎对这匹马有着特殊的感情，据说这匹马在伊朗北部被盗时，他曾悬赏重金要把它找回来。比塞弗勒斯在亚历山大征战旁遮普的过程中死去，亚历山大为纪念它在该地区建立了一座城市，并将其命名为比塞弗勒斯。他驯服比塞弗勒斯的故事是否解释了这种感情，或者这个故事是否受到亚历山大后来行为的启发，这个问题仍然悬而未决。

王室女性

对于亚历山大时代的希腊人和马其顿人，以及亚历山大史家时代的希腊人和罗马人来说，一个有序的社会是由男性做出决定的社会。妇女可以通过向家庭中的男性成员呼吁来保护其子女的利益，特别是儿子的利益，但不能以自己的名义行事。早在荷马的诗歌中，希腊文学就展示了积极的女性形象，这些女性可以影响自己的丈夫，让他们善待陌生人，或尊重神灵，但也提供了消极的危险女性形象，她们挑战事物的正常秩序。在民主政体中，女性的影响力必然有限，但在君主制中，王室女性可以拥有相当大的间接权力，并有望为其子女使用这些权力。马其顿也不例外。

普鲁塔克讲述了许多关于亚历山大的母亲奥林匹娅斯的故事。亚历山大与母亲一直保持着密切的关系。即使在他征战期间，他们也通过书信联系，他还把胜利的战利品寄回给她作礼物。普鲁塔克的故事并不利于奥林匹娅斯：在与亚历山大父亲腓力的关系中，她表现出的是嫉妒和猜疑，同时还有狂野和危险。对此的部分解释是，亚历山大死后，奥林匹娅斯卷入了继承人之间的竞争和冲突，各种各样的人都有理由对她持负面看法。我们很难知道这些描述背后的真相是什么，但通过观察其他王室女性的经历，可以更平衡地了解女性在马其顿宫廷中的地位。我们对亚历山大的祖母欧律狄刻和他的妹妹克莉奥帕特拉的了解，可以帮助我们更多地了解他的母亲。

欧律狄刻

欧律狄刻是阿敏塔斯三世的妻子、腓力二世的母亲，她很可能在亚历山大的童年时期依然在世，她的生涯证明了女性在生活和名誉上能够取得什么成就，以及她们可能必须忍受什么。欧律狄刻要么是伊利里亚人，要么是林卡斯人，阿敏塔斯娶她是为了与潜在的危险邻国保持良好关系。欧律狄刻为他生了三个儿子，这比其他任何事情都更能提高她在马其顿宫廷中的地位。阿敏塔斯死后，欧律狄刻被迫进入外交领域。她的长子亚历山大二世要么此时已经离世，要么正在前线与伊利里亚人作战，而觊觎王位者帕萨尼亚斯正在向马其顿快速挺进。欧律狄刻带着两个年幼的儿子佩尔狄卡斯和腓力去见雅典将军伊菲克拉特斯，他当时正试图控制希腊城市安菲波利斯。伊菲克拉特斯曾被阿敏塔斯收养，所以欧律狄刻可以认他为继子。据雅典演说家埃斯基涅斯的记载，欧律狄刻把她的两个儿子放在伊菲克拉特斯的膝头，请求他像保护兄弟一样保护他们。这一行为对一个女人来说可能不太合适，但对家庭关系的呼吁使人们能够接受这一行为，伊菲克拉特斯把帕萨尼亚斯赶出了马其顿。另一个不太可靠的故事说，欧律狄刻不久之后就嫁给了一个名叫托勒密的男人，托勒密成了佩尔狄卡斯的摄政王，这样她就可以继续保护儿子们的利益了。这个托勒密是谁还不确定，但有人认为，托勒密是欧律狄刻的女婿，曾杀死她的儿子亚历山大二世。如果是这样的话，那么欧律狄刻就是为了保护另外两个儿子而嫁给了杀害她儿子的凶手。查士丁讲述了一个更加骇人听闻的版本：他声称，欧律狄刻为了嫁给托勒密，企图谋杀阿敏塔斯未果，而在阿敏塔斯死后，欧律狄刻先是杀害了亚历山大二世，然后又杀害了佩尔狄卡斯。埃斯基涅斯所叙述的故事令人同情，这个故事讲述于事件发生后不到30年，而查士丁的消息来源庞培乌斯·特罗格斯则是在300多年后写作的，带有罗马人对女性干预政治事务的厌恶，但查士丁的说法一直被接受为事实，直到最近为止。欧律狄刻的形象，在古代和现代学者口中，从一个依靠家族关系来保护儿子的母亲，转变为一个准备杀死自己儿子的野心勃勃的阴谋家，因此，研究她的儿媳，亚历山大大帝的母亲奥林匹娅斯的故事时，我们应该停下来思考一下。

克莉奥帕特拉

亚历山大的妹妹和她的舅舅举行了婚礼，她的舅舅也就是奥林匹娅斯的哥哥，通常被称为伊庇鲁斯的亚历山大，正是在他们的婚礼上，腓力被暗杀了。克莉奥帕特拉和奥林匹娅斯一样，经常收到亚历山大送来的战利品，有一次，她还代表安纳托利亚的一个地方王朝向亚历山大求情，这对于她作为妹妹的身份来说倒不是什么不恰当的行为。伊庇鲁斯的亚历山大在征战意大利时去世，留下了儿子涅俄普托勒摩斯和女儿卡德梅亚，克莉奥帕特拉担任摄政：大约30年后，涅俄普托勒摩斯成为伊庇鲁斯的统治者。亚历山大死后，腓力的女儿克莉奥帕特拉成为将军们争夺权力的潜在力量，他们争相娶她为妻，但公元前308年，克莉奥帕特拉被杀害，情况不明，死时约50岁。她的生活，就像她的祖母一样，尽管赋予了她重要的责任，但归根结底是由她与家庭中男性成员的关系决定的。

奥林匹娅斯

　　奥林匹娅斯的生平与她的婆婆和女儿并没有太大的不同。她是伊庇鲁斯的摩罗西亚的涅俄普托勒摩斯之女，她和腓力的婚姻照例是出于外交原因。作为亚历山大大帝的母亲，她在宫廷中的地位很高，但在亚历山大成为国王之前，很少有关于她的叙述，甚至仅有的叙述也很可能是幻想，而不是事实。亚历山大出生的故事与很多奇迹事件联系在一起，随着时间的推移，甚至连他投生的故事也越传越多。一个可能起源于公元前3世纪的埃及的传说声称，亚历山大是宙斯或埃及阿蒙神的儿子，他化身为蛇来到奥林匹娅斯身边。普鲁塔克记述了这个故事，还给出了一个看似合理的解释。他说，奥林匹娅斯像该地区的大多数女性一样，是俄耳甫斯和酒神仪式的信徒，酒神仪式是对狄俄尼索斯神的狂热崇拜，她还为这些仪式准备了很多大蛇。传说，俄耳甫斯被酒神狄俄尼索斯的信徒或酒神女祭司撕成碎片的故事确实与马其顿的皮埃里亚有关。欧里庇得斯的悲剧《酒神的伴侣》中，底比斯的国王彭透斯在酒神祭司的狂热仪式中被他的母亲和其他女人杀死，这一剧目最早在马其顿的阿奇劳斯宫廷演出。在公元前4世纪的马其顿陵墓中陪葬的一些华丽器皿上也发现了酒神的画像。但是，即使奥林匹娅斯确实参加了酒神仪式（当然这一点并不能确定），即使他们确实接触了蛇（这也不太可能），奥林匹娅斯痴迷蛇的形象也纯粹是虚构的。在我们有明确证据表明女性参与了酒神活动的地方（这一时期的马其顿并不包括在内），女祭司的行为也并没有被视为离经叛道。

腓力死后，奥林匹娅斯作为国王的母亲，继续在马其顿宫廷中扮演着重要角色，而亚历山大则在征战。普鲁塔克和阿里安都提到了亚历山大和奥林匹娅斯之间的通信，尽管他们接触到的文本通常被认为是不真实的。她很可能与亚历山大的摄政王安提帕特关系不佳，因此在公元前330年左右搬回了摩罗西亚。亚历山大死后，奥林匹娅斯的地位取决于亚历山大的幼子亚历山大四世的命运。公元前315年，奥林匹娅斯被安提帕特的儿子卡桑德杀死，当时，她的地位相当于亚历山大四世的随从。奥林匹娅斯和她的婆婆欧律狄刻一样，在现存的叙事中被描绘成了反面人物；但试图推翻这些说法，将奥林匹娅斯塑造成一个强大而独立的女性，也并不一定更接近事实。她的地位，像欧律狄刻一样，取决于她的儿子，后来又取决于她的孙子。如果我们能够了解现存古代叙事的误导性表述背后的真实情况（当然我们无法做到这一点），那么我们很可能会发现，她既不是女英雄，也不是怪物，但是她完成了马其顿社会中一个女性的预期角色，尽职尽责地为她的孩子们工作，不惜一切代价。

王子的生活

在过去的几十年里，在下马其顿王家遗址进行的考古挖掘，比其他任何事物都更能揭示亚历山大成长的世界。自公元前5

世纪末以来，佩拉一直是马其顿的王家中心，尽管亚历山大出生在佩拉，但对靠近现代韦尔吉纳的埃盖宫殿和陵墓的挖掘，扩大了人们对亚历山大时代马其顿公众生活的了解。

埃盖宫殿可能是腓力二世建造的。它矗立在形成埃盖古城卫城的山坡露出的岩层上，俯瞰着下面的城市，有一个面向城市的宏伟入口。宫殿的中心是一块空地，四周围着一条柱廊。在这个开放的庭院里，国王可以向他的朝臣们讲话，在面向柱廊敞开的房间里，他们可以成群进餐，可以容纳多达30人坐在一起。宫殿里还残存着一些镶嵌地板，向人们展示着这座宫殿曾经装饰得多么华丽，但不可避免地，墙壁装饰和建筑内容都没有保存下来。然而，从最著名的考古发现，即马其顿王陵韦尔吉纳-埃盖遗址当中，我们可以猜测出他们的财富和辉煌。这些陵墓（其中一个可能是腓力二世的陵墓）之中有丰富的随葬品，包括用黄金和象牙装饰的家具，以及珠宝和其他金银装饰品。在马其顿的其他地方，人们也挖掘出过奢华的墓穴，里面装满了金、银和青铜器皿。王家陵墓上都绘有神话和宫廷生活的场景，宫殿或许也是以同样的方式装饰的。马其顿艺术的一个主题特别值得注意，那就是王家狩猎。

狩 猎

毫无疑问，狩猎是马其顿精英生活的重要组成部分。作家瑙克拉提斯的阿忒纳乌斯在他关于饮食的文集《欢宴的智者》中，引用了一位公元前3世纪历史学家黑格桑德的话：只有在不使用捕猎网的情况下杀死了一头野猪的马其顿人，才会被允许入席宴饮。针对亚历山大大帝的阴谋之中，有一个就是源于在一次狩猎中，亚历山大的一名侍从杀死了一头野猪，而这头野猪原本是亚历山大想要猎杀的，他因此鞭打了这名侍从。一次成功的野猪狩猎标志着从男孩到男人的转变，所以亚历山大用殴打来羞辱一个刚刚完成转变的年轻人，是一种特别令其蒙耻的行为。狩猎是马其顿艺术的一个常见主题。佩拉的镶嵌画和韦尔吉纳-埃盖王家陵墓中最大的一幅画都描绘了腓力和亚历山大骑马或步行时猎杀狮子的场景。在那个时期的马其顿可以找到山狮，但猎狮不如猎野猪常见。描绘狮子的原因之一很可能是在模仿波斯国王和之前的亚述国王，他们用猎狮以及国王与一只或多只狮子近距离搏斗的场景装饰自己的宫殿。亚历山大穿过阿契美尼德帝国的领土时，造访过总督和以前的国王建立的一些狩猎庄园，并曾在那里狩猎。

　　正如我们所看到的，马其顿君主制的早期历史与波斯国王大流士在北爱琴海地区的征战有关。即使在薛西斯入侵失败后，波斯军队离开了欧洲，小亚细亚的波斯总督的宫廷仍然是西边的色雷斯和马其顿国王的有力典范。一些学者认为，腓力二世在策划对抗波斯帝国的战役时，就已经准备好要效仿这位伟大国王的宫廷规范了。他借鉴了贵族把年幼的儿子送到王宫当侍从的做法，特别是要陪伴国王狩猎；据公元前4世纪的历史学家色诺芬描述，波斯国王也有同样的陪伴方式。亚历山大的成长经历不仅为他统治马其顿做好了充分的准备，也为他应对马其顿东部强大的帝国奠定了良好的基础。

亚历山大大帝即位

　　因与父亲争吵，亚历山大在马其顿宫廷的生活中断，被放逐到伊利里亚。他的父亲不久前娶了他的最后一任妻子克莉奥帕特拉，一个马其顿女人，腓力麾下阿塔罗斯将军的女儿。普鲁塔克记述了这一事件，他暗示，亚历山大作为腓力继承人的地位受到了威胁，尽管这似乎不大可能。没过多久，亚历山大就回到了马其顿，正好赶上参加他的妹妹和她舅舅伊庇鲁斯的亚历山大的婚礼。他们在埃盖举行了盛大的婚礼庆典，邀请了希腊各城市的大使参加。亚历山大的父亲腓力就是在这场婚礼上遇刺的。

　　凶手还没来得及逃跑就被逮捕了。他是腓力的护卫之一，名叫帕萨尼亚斯，他的刺杀可能完全出于私人目的。然而，不可避免地，有许多人认为他参与了一个更大的阴谋。上马其顿林塞斯蒂斯家族的两名主要成员，希罗门尼斯和阿里哈贝厄斯，被指控参与了这场阴谋，并与帕萨尼亚斯一起被处决，而他们的兄弟亚历山大并没有受到牵连。据说亚历山大大帝后来指控波斯国王大流士密谋暗杀腓力：他的死肯定对大流士有利，但似乎没有一位古代作者把大流士和帕萨尼亚斯联系起来。普鲁塔克提出的另一种理论在当时广为流传：奥林匹娅斯是暗杀的幕后黑手；而查士丁则认为亚历山大本人也参与了这场阴谋。然而，很难想象腓力此时的死会给亚历山大带来什么好处。奥林匹娅斯在亚历山大不知情的情况下替他行事，这也不合理。关于腓力的死还有很多不清楚的地方，但亚历山大确实因此继承了他父亲的所有职位，最重要的就是作为马其顿国王，领导了一支希腊远征军，对波斯人在公元前481年至公元前479年造成的破坏展开报复。

第三章

勇士：亚历山大的军队

　　亚历山大大帝在位期间一直开展军事行动。在他率领军队攻打波斯帝国之前，他必须处理马其顿东北部和西部地区的起义，随后，他包围并洗劫了希腊城市底比斯。进入亚洲后，他分别在格拉尼库斯河（公元前334年）、伊苏斯（公元前333年）和高加米拉（公元前331年）与波斯人进行了三次主要的战役，并在海达斯佩斯河（公元前326年）与印度国王波鲁斯展开了一次激战，此外，还有一些较小的交战。亚历山大大帝成功包围了安纳托利亚西海岸和黎凡特的一系列城市。他在阿富汗也面临着长期的叛乱（公元前329—前326）；在沿着印度河流域行进的过程中，他在巴基斯坦遇到了更多麻烦。但最终，他总能取得胜利。我们已经看到，"不败"的称号贴在了他的身上：他当之无愧。

　　关于亚历山大的将才和他的军队，已经有了很多书，并附有他的各种征战计划。然而，这些描述和计划所依据的证据并不易使用，关于亚历山大的成就，有很多仍然是猜测。尽管阿里安本人有过军事指挥的经验,并写过战术方面的著作,但关于亚历山大战役和攻城战的古代记述却很少涉及军事编队与指挥结构的细节,他更感兴趣的反而是阐明战争中不太实在的方面。

武装力量

关于亚历山大军队的一些基本信息可以被认为是可靠的。他率领大约3.2万名步兵和5000名骑兵进入亚洲,开始了他的征战。在那里,他与腓力二世两年前派出的约1万人的部队会合。其中,7000名步兵和600名骑兵来自科林斯同盟的希腊城邦,5000名步兵是希腊雇佣兵,其余的是马其顿人和他们的同盟军。希腊各城邦也向亚历山大的舰队提供了船只,但他要在年底前解散这支舰队。随着战役的进行,由于疾病、死伤和退役等情况,亚历山大在战斗和围城中损失了许多人,但他从马其顿和希腊,以及后来新征服的帝国内部,得到了定期增援。古代记述中关于他的军队规模的数字始终一致、可信,但他所面对的军队规模的数字却并非如此。例如,在高加米拉战役中,他与大流士三世的第二次也是最后一次交锋,波斯军队的步兵人数在20万到100万之间,骑兵人数在4万到20万之间。而现代作者普遍认为,军队总人数低于10万。

亚历山大从他的父亲腓力那里继承了他的军队,许多古代作者都提及了它的基本要素,因此我们能够理解它的大致构成。考古学的证据,特别是墓葬的证据,也有助于我们了解其武器和盔甲。骑兵手持冲锋骑枪(但骑行时没有马镫,这限制了他们冲锋的冲击力);步兵的核心是所谓的马其顿方阵,装备有6米长的长矛(sarissas)。人们普遍认为军队两侧是手持长矛、长剑和圆形大盾牌的人，就像希腊城邦的重装步兵一样。除此之外，还有装备标枪、弓箭或投石器的轻装部队。但如果想要了解更具体的信息，就面临一个问题：古代作家为更具体的军队分类给出了许多名称，但没有解释它们是什么，有时可能用相同的名称来表示不同的军队，或用不同的名称来表示相同的军队。方阵中的士兵被称为pezhetairoi（"伙友步兵"），但也有人提到asthetairoi：我们不确定这个词是什么意思。同样地，重装步兵可能被称为hypaspists（"持盾卫队"），但在战役结束后，则更多地提及argyraspids（"银盾步兵队"），他们可能属于精锐部队。这些不确定性并不会在战争重构中造成重大问题，但它们已经产生了一个小型学术行业，试图弄清楚这些术语所指的内容。

古代军队的组成不只是士兵，古代作者偶尔也会记录军营侍从的存在。每一个骑兵都有一名侍从，虽然据说腓力限制每十个士兵只能有一个侍从，但军官们的侍从数量应该更多。随着战争的进行，士兵们会获得战利品，需要奴隶来照看这些战利品和他们自己。毫无疑问，还有许多其他军营侍从为了获取食物和报酬提供各种各样的服务。人们定期尝试减少行李和侍从的数量，但由于战争是公认的获取财产的手段，因此在很多时候，侍从人数肯定超过了士兵。

攻城战

亚历山大的军队还包括一套攻城设备。这似乎是亚历山大在战争中相当发达的一个方面：投石车、攻城槌和攻城塔，拆开后装在骡车上，连同辎重队的其余部分跟在军队后面。对提尔长达7个月的围攻（公元前332年）是亚历山大大帝最著名的成就之一。这一点我们从对提尔围城战的详细描述中就可以清楚地看到，这些描述不仅出现在现存的历史学家记述中，还出现在《亚历山大传奇》（下称《传奇》）中，《传奇》是描写亚历山大生平的通俗版本，在古代和中世纪广泛流传，并不断被美化。这就是亚历山大的行为在这片土地上留下的永久印记。提尔古城建在黎巴嫩海岸附近的一个小岛上。围攻期间，亚历山大修建了一条通往该岛的堤道，虽然没有完工，但这条堤道后来导致了中间河道淤塞，因此提尔古城的遗迹现在是大陆的一部分。

战　役

说起重构亚历山大的战役，我们的出发点是现存资料中的记载。这些记载可以通过仔细剖析加以补充：现代作者曾参观过战役遗址——尽管古代对地形的描述并不总是精确，而且在某些情况下，很难确定交战地点。例如，阿契美尼德军队曾试图在"波斯之门"阻止亚历山大穿过扎格罗斯山脉到达帕萨尔加德和波斯波利斯，而"波斯之门"的位置就难以完美定位。但是，即使我们掌握了对一场战役的一些描述，了解了战役发生的地点，在进行详细的重建时，仍然面临着严峻的问题。阿里安和普鲁塔克借鉴过历史学家托勒密的著作，此人可能参加了征战中的所有主要战役。然而，这并不代表托勒密是一个很好的信息来源。从他在骑兵部队的位置来看，他只能看到一小部分行动，而行动的大部分都是混乱不堪的。但无论如何，托勒密很可能并不是主要依靠自己的记忆来重构事件的。他对战役的描述可能基于亚历山大的"史官"卡利斯提尼斯的记述，卡利斯提尼斯可能从远处目睹了这些战斗，并且能够与许多参与者交谈。

但是卡利斯提尼斯可能并不关心准确性,这一点从亚历山大在格拉尼库斯河与波斯人的第一次战役的记录中就可以看出。

格拉尼库斯河战役

据阿里安和普鲁塔克所述,在特洛伊,亚历山大参观了阿喀琉斯的陵墓,并从雅典娜神庙拿走了一块据说在特洛伊战争中使用过的盾牌,随后,亚历山大从特洛伊出发,抵达格拉尼库斯河,并在此发现了一支波斯军队,由当地总督指挥,控制着高耸陡峭的远岸。亚历山大的幕僚帕曼纽建议他推迟到早晨再进攻,但据说亚历山大回答道,如果他越过了赫勒斯滂海峡,现在却被格拉尼库斯河的细流阻挡,那么就连赫勒斯滂海峡都会感到羞愧。于是亚历山大率领军队进入河中,攻打波斯人。阿里安对接下来发生的事情给出了更多的细节,但两位作者都列出了一份波斯人的名单,亚历山大在抵达远方旱地后,接连遇见并击杀了他们。人们已经认识到,这是亚历山大的战役中最难重构的一次,因为对它的描述相当模糊,学者们评论说,对亚历山大一系列单打独斗的描述更像是荷马《伊利亚特》里的段落。事实上,与荷马的相似之处可能是有意为之,尤其是如果遵循的是卡利斯提尼斯的描述的话。荷马早在《伊利亚特》中描述阿喀琉斯一天的战斗时,就写过主人公如何跳进斯卡曼德洛斯河去追捕特洛伊人,如何与河水本身战斗。亚历山大声称自己是阿喀琉斯的后裔,而卡利斯提尼斯对这场战役的描述——首先是跳入河中,然后是单打独斗——既希望能够揭示两位英雄之间的关系,又关注其报道是否准确。狄奥多罗斯则给出了完全不同的描述:亚历山大在河边扎营过夜,次日清晨便率领军队在旱地上作战。不管狄奥多罗斯的消息来源是什么,在这种情况下,他的说法可能更接近于事实。

如果狄奥多罗斯的说法更准确,那么另一个版本中,亚历山大和帕曼纽之间关于在河对岸发动攻击的战术交流就必须被否决了。在现存记述中,两人之间有过几次这样的战术交流,而且它们有一个标准的模式:帕曼纽向亚历山大提出明智且谨慎的建议;亚历山大置之不理,结果证明亚历山大的做法是对的。通常,他们的交流充满智慧:据说,大流士致信亚历山大提出和平条件时,帕曼纽曾对亚历山大说,"如果我是你,我会接受";亚历山大回答说,"如果我是你,我也会接受"。我们没有理由像某些人那样,认为这些故事反映了两人之间的裂痕日益加深。的确,由于帕曼纽的儿子被判密谋推翻国王,亚历山大处死了帕曼纽,但直到那时,帕曼纽仍然是值得信赖的参谋,并得到了国王丰厚的奖赏。我们要认识到,这些都是特定类型的故事,是关于"智慧参谋"的故事。这些故事都描述了一个年长的人给一个年轻的统治者提供建议,因此在希罗多德的《历史》中,年轻的居鲁士大帝得到了吕底亚前国王克洛伊索斯的建议;叔叔阿尔达班时常提醒薛西斯,斯巴达前国王德玛拉图斯也给他出主意。通常情况下,如果这个年轻人足够明智,就会接受建议,迈向成功,或者,如果他愚蠢不堪,拒绝建议,就会遭遇磨难。但亚历山大却颠覆了这一模式:他拒绝了建议,却仍然取得了成功,这表明他是一个真正杰出的统治者。古代作者的叙述说明了他们自己对亚历山大性格的看法,有时牺牲了对事实的忠诚。

亚历山大在战役中取得了诸多成就,要想提高其重要性,还有其他方法。薛西斯入侵希腊的故事,尤其是希罗多德所讲述的版本，为研究亚历山大的历史学家们提供了机会，可以将两位指挥官进行比较。最明显的例子是描述亚历山大进入法尔斯省的，波斯波利斯的城市和宫殿就坐落在那里，亚历山大通过了扎格罗斯山脉的一个隘口，即波斯之门，抵达那里。

波斯之门

公元前480年，薛西斯穿过希腊向雅典进军时，唯一能阻挡他的地方是位于希腊中部山脉和大海之间的一条狭窄通道，名为Thermopylae，意思是"温泉关"，因当地有温泉而得名。希罗多德描述了斯巴达国王列奥尼达和300名斯巴达重装步兵，以及约5000名其他士兵如何保卫关隘。据他所说，斯巴达人本可以一直坚持对抗，却被一个叫厄菲阿尔特的当地人背叛了，他带领一队薛西斯的军队沿着一条鲜为人知的小路，走到了斯巴达阵地的后面。战斗的第三天，列奥尼达发现他的部队被包围，最终他死在了战场上。薛西斯的胜利打开了通往雅典的道路，不久之后他就洗劫了这座城市。这场战斗的失败本可以避免，因为列奥尼达知道这条小路，却没有充分保护它。大约50年后，由于希罗多德的描述，这个故事很快成了一个英雄自我牺牲的事例，进入大众文化。但这个故事也可以被重复使用。

历史学家们都描述了亚历山大从美索不达米亚出发穿过扎格罗斯山脉向法尔斯挺进的过程，其间会通过一条狭窄的通道，狄奥多罗斯称之为苏西安高崖，而阿里安称之为波斯之门，由波斯指挥官阿尔塔巴赞斯把守。就像列奥尼达在温泉关一样，阿尔塔巴赞斯在隘口上筑起了一堵墙来保护他的军队，但他的军队规模要大得多，狄奥多罗斯说有2.5万名步兵，阿里安则说有4

万名步兵,这些数字一如既往地不可靠,高得令人难以置信。在两位作家的描述中,亚历山大起初像薛西斯一样无法通过正面进攻突破敌军阵地,当地一名男子告诉他,山里有一条狭窄的山路可以把他带到波斯防线后面。在随后的战斗中,波斯人被打败了,但与列奥尼达不同的是,阿尔塔巴赞斯逃跑了。这是亚历山大前往波斯波利斯途中的最后一次军事遭遇,他为了报复薛西斯在温泉关之后洗劫雅典而摧毁了波斯波利斯(见第六章)。温泉关战役和波斯之门战役之间的相似之处太多,不可能是巧合,很明显,无论扎格罗斯山上发生了什么,对于记述者来说,把它作为薛西斯在希腊唯一一次胜利的恰当反转,再合适不过了。

预 兆

古代作者关注的另一个重要领域是对战争超自然方面的兴趣,这与现代作者不同。军事史作为一门现代学科,往往侧重于实际问题,即敌方部队的相对实力和素质、地形性质、后勤组织、指挥官及其下属的能力等。虽然关于亚历山大战役的古代记载有时缺乏这些细节,但它们通常都有关于预兆和先知建议的丰富记载。这种强调确实反映了古代战争的重要真理:鉴于战争的不确定性,古代军事指挥官大量使用占卜,向神寻求人力无法提供的信息。因此,好的manteis(先知),即那些不仅能够正确地建议未来行动的结果,还被记载为站在胜利一方的人,得到高度评价,并能从他们所服务的个人和群体中获得丰厚的回报。在现存的亚历山大战役记载中,尤其是在阿里安的记载中,他的先知,特密苏斯的亚里斯坦德,扮演着非常重要的角色。亚里斯坦德解释了各种各样的事情,包括献祭动物的内脏、鸟类的行为、梦境、占星事件（如日食），以及不寻常的现象（如流汗的雕像）。所有这些都是先知通常会被咨询的问题，但这些故事需要谨慎对待。预言总是以某种方式成真，这是古代叙事的一个特点，包括历史叙事。在阿里安和普鲁塔克的书中，亚里斯坦德的预言，无论多么不可能，最终都是正确的，很明显，他们在叙述中加入这些预言主要是为了证明关于亚历山大的观点。最伟大的将军应该有最伟大的先知相伴，这很合理，因此亚里斯坦德完美的预言记录反映了亚历山大自己的无敌性。亚里斯坦德并没有出现在亚历山大最后一年的记载中，大概是因为他实际上已经在征战的某个时刻去世了，但只有当亚里斯坦德离开后，亚历山大才开始目睹预示他死亡的征兆，而这些征兆在当时并不是所有人都能理解的。

征 战

亚历山大的亚洲远征可以分为两个明显的阶段。第一阶段，他作为希腊国家联盟的领袖，旨在将亚洲的希腊城市从阿契美尼德王朝的控制下解放出来，并为150年前薛西斯入侵希腊向波斯人进行报复。第一个目标，解放希腊城市，在公元前334年，也就是征战的第一年，基本实现，亚历山大向南穿过小亚细亚，然后向东进入安纳托利亚中部。第二年，波斯人重新控制了他解放的一些城市，但亚历山大派遣了一支部队来解决这个问题，到公元前332年底，波斯人在该地区的势力永远消失。出于对波斯人的报复，亚历山大摧毁了波斯波利斯城及其宫殿。亚历山大去那里的路线并不直接，但在军事上是有意义的。在某种程度上，这是由他的对手大流士保卫自己领土的行动所决定的。

亚历山大在远征开始后不久就解散了他的大部分舰队，而他需要阻止大流士使用海上力量，这是通过控制地中海东岸的主要港口实现的。亚历山大史家的叙述提供了额外的解释，即亚历山大的征战决策通常是以其个人意愿为依据的：这可能是准确的，但尚不清楚他们是通过什么途径了解到亚历山大的思想活动的。亚历山大沿着地中海海岸行军，进入了埃及，虽然这使他远离了大流士和法尔斯，但如果能把富裕的埃及王国从大流士的帝国中分离出来，那么这一迂回之路也非常值得。公元前331年上半年，亚历山大离开埃及后，直接越过幼发拉底河和底格里斯河，然后穿过美索不达米亚，经过巴比伦和苏萨的王都，穿过扎格罗斯山脉，进入法尔斯。亚历山大离开埃及不到一年就进入了波斯波利斯，几个月后就摧毁了这座宫殿。从亚历山大的下一步行动中可以明显看出，这标志着盟军战役的结束。亚历山大把盟军的队伍遣送回国，并给予他们丰厚的报酬，但他允许任何一个希腊人重新应召成为雇佣兵。因此，公元前330年夏天，从波斯波利斯出发的军队现在只关心是否能实现亚历山大自己的目标。

　　征战的第二阶段，亚历山大先是追击大流士，他已经两次击败了大流士。在大流士被他的下属贝苏斯下令暗杀后，贝苏斯成了亚历山大的新目标。在这场追逐中，亚历山大进入了帝国东北角的巴克特里亚和索格狄亚那，当地精英阶层迟迟无法接受政权的更迭。因此，亚历山大花了三年时间才使该地区平定下来。下一步，亚历山大向东南的旁遮普和印度河流域进军，最好将这视为一场新的征战。公元前334年春天，跟随亚历山大越过赫勒斯滂海峡的军队中，有多少人在8年后仍和亚历山大一起战斗，我们不得而知：在此期间，伤员和年老的士兵将被遣送回家，由马其顿派遣的增援部队取代。大多数年长的军官要么已经去世，要么留在了更西边的阵地，但亚历山大的年轻战友们仍然陪伴在他身边。印度战役把亚历山大带到了下游的印度河三角洲，这也是他第一次接触潮汐海洋。征战的最后阶段是穿过伊朗南部返回法尔斯，同时派遣一支舰队沿波斯湾向美索不达米亚南部行进。亚历山大在现在的伊朗西部和伊拉克东部度过了他生命中的最后18个月。

　　本书其余部分将不再详细叙述这次远征。虽然下面的章节大致按时间顺序排列，但它们更具主题性，并将利用当代材料来展示亚历山大如何融入他所走过的世界。了解亚历山大征战最简单的方法是使用本书前面提供的地图和大事年表。

第四章

指挥官：亚历山大和希腊人

在公元前338年的喀罗尼亚战役中，亚历山大的父亲腓力确立了马其顿在爱琴海以西希腊世界的统治地位。反对阿契美尼德帝国的征战，表面上的目的是解放爱琴海以东的希腊城市，由腓力策划，并由亚历山大执行。虽然亚历山大的成就使他远远超越了希腊人的世界，因为他控制了近东各王国，但他与这些王国的关系对他统治的稳固性仍然至关重要。关于亚历山大生平的记载可以告诉我们他对希腊城市的态度，古代演说家和现代学者一直在争论亚历山大是解放者还是压迫者。除了相关记载，当时城市本身的碑文也可以告诉我们亚力山大的行为及其影响，考虑到这一点，我们可以对这些问题有更多的了解。

自治与控制

为了理解亚历山大与希腊城市的关系，我们必须意识到两个核心问题。一个是autonomia（自治）一词的含义，这是古希腊政治词汇中的一个重要元素；另一个是派系和竞争的存在，这是几乎所有希腊城市政治生活的特征。

　　自治并不等同于独立：它意味着城市在自己的法律下运作，因此更多地涉及内部管理，而不涉及其他权力。但一座城市是否自治，可能是一个视角问题。小亚细亚的希腊城市从公元前6世纪中叶开始隶属于吕底亚人、波斯人、雅典人、斯巴达人，然后又隶属于波斯人。在公元前5世纪，作为雅典的盟友（或者从更负面的角度来看，作为雅典帝国的成员），这些城市可以称为自治城市，但是这种自治只能通过雅典的海军力量和雅典驻军的存在来保证，以保护城市的自治权（由亲雅典的政治领导层定义），免受波斯人支持的流亡者夺取政权的威胁。从这些亲波斯公民（或前公民）的角度来看，驻军是缺乏自治的标志。然而，对于这些城市来说，它们无法选择完全独立于外界干涉。只有极少数希腊城市可以被认为是真正独立的：公元前338年的喀罗尼亚战役前，雅典、底比斯和斯巴达都是这种例外，它们与马其顿国王的关系与其他城市有些不同。

　　竞争是古希腊生活的核心部分。从荷马史诗开始，对威望的竞争就成为群体中更富有、更具影响力的成员生活的驱动力。城邦制度的发展，特别是公民议会和法院的发展，并没有削弱这种竞争，而是提供了一个竞技场和一套更明确的规则，在这些规则下，这种竞争得以进行。希腊城市的政治分歧与其说是由意识形态决定的，不如说是由个人的野心决定的。甚至像"民主"和"寡头政治"这样的术语——被历史学家和哲学家们用于讨论内乱——通常指的也是更实际的区分（公元前5世纪，由雅典或斯巴达支持），正如修昔底德在戏剧性地描述伯罗奔尼撒战争早期科西拉岛爆发的内乱时所指出的那样。在小城市，雄心勃勃的未来领导人通常会从大城市寻求财政支持和间或的军事支持；即使在雅典，主要的政治家们也准备从外部势力获取资助。反对的煽动者会从腓力二世和波斯国王那里获取资金。

这种权力竞争的必然结果是政治流亡。在任何时候，失败的派系都会被判损害城市的利益，然后被逐出他们的城市，或者他们会自行离开，避免被杀害，无论这是否是司法程序的结果。他们被剥夺财产后，要么向其他城市的朋友寻求帮助，同时策划自己的回归，要么，如果他们已经不受欢迎，他们可能会寻求雇佣兵的服务。流亡是社会中富裕成员的经历，而穷人在政治生活中扮演着更被动的角色，甚至在民主城邦中也是如此。

科林斯同盟

腓力二世在喀罗尼亚战役中击败底比斯和雅典的军队后，对这两座城市的态度有些不同。在底比斯，对这个违反了协议的盟友，他安排了马其顿军队驻扎，据推测，他还流放了那些对马其顿怀有敌意的主要政客。由于演说家德马德斯的鼓吹，没有一位雅典政治家被驱逐，腓力也没有在雅典驻军；这座城市成了腓力的盟友，这一地位表明，雅典仍然是一个自治实体，尽管雅典的军事行动自由受到了限制。

第二年，腓力与希腊各城市（斯巴达除外）达成了一项更为普遍的协议，其中一些细节可从雅典的铭文中得知。这一约定被称为"科林斯同盟"，包括建立一个由腓力领导的联盟，以对抗波斯人。根据几年后在雅典发表的一篇演讲，联盟的条款始于希腊城市要自由和自治的声明，这篇演讲被认为是由德摩斯梯尼撰写的，但实际上并非如此。一篇与此相关的残缺铭文上有希腊城市作为协议一部分的宣誓条款。它们发誓不干涉盟友的宪法，不夺取其任何领土，不拿起武器攻击盟友，不推翻腓力及其继承人的王国，为任何受到攻击的盟友而战。它还提到了一个同盟委员会，如果任何成员被认为违反了协议条款，就可以召集该委员会；铭文还指出腓力被称为霸主（hegemon），即同盟的领袖；腓力和他的继任者决定去哪里，盟军都必须听从。亚历山大统治初期的一篇更为残缺的铭文描述了雅典人和亚历山大将为雅典人为征战派出的军队提供物资的细节。腓力遇刺后，亚历山大迅速采取行动，重新确立了同盟的条款，但在第二年，底比斯叛乱对同盟关系进行了考验，当时亚历山大正在保卫他的北部边境。

洗劫底比斯

狄奥多罗斯和阿里安都对底比斯叛乱有详细的描述，尽管他们之间有不同之处，但他们清楚地表明，这场叛乱的模式与公元前5世纪修昔底德所描述的反对雅典人的叛乱非常相似。叛乱的导火索是流亡者的到来，这些流亡者似乎得到了波斯人的金钱支持，他们杀掉了亲马其顿的政客，这些政客自喀罗尼亚战败以来一直掌权。这使得公民团体很难避免与亚历山大产生冲突，在新的政治领导人有机会争取其他城市的支持之前，亚历山大就来到了这座城市前。亚历山大迅速完成了攻城任务，然后把如何处置底比斯的决定权交给了同盟委员会，正如科林斯同盟的条款所表明的那样。不可避免地，代表们会支持惩罚反叛城市，尽管摧毁底比斯可能十分残酷，但这与公元前5世纪雅典对待其他希腊城市的方式并无不同。

小亚细亚的城市和爱琴海东部的岛屿

第二年春天,亚历山大率领军队进入亚洲,他的首要任务是从波斯国王手中夺取那里的希腊城市的控制权。这不是一个简单的任务,我们可以通过研究莱斯博斯岛米蒂利尼城的经历来理解它所涉及的一些东西,这些经历可以用尚存的叙述和一篇记录事件解决的铭文中的信息进行重构。恰巧,修昔底德详细描述了公元前428年至公元前427年米蒂利尼人民发动起义反抗雅典时所面临的困难:起义失败了,因为大多数公民团体对抵抗雅典舰队并无热情,雅典舰队是被派来迫使他们重新结盟的。不到一个世纪后,他们又面临着类似的情况。公元前4世纪初,希腊城市与波斯国王签订了条约,将亚洲大陆城市的控制权交给了国王,而波斯人认为这些条款仍然有效。岛屿并没有被包括在条约内,但波斯人显然打算得到或保持对这些岛屿的控制。

公元前334年,亚历山大率领军队进入亚洲,他与莱斯博斯岛的当权者达成了某种协议,派遣了一支由雇佣兵组成的驻军去支持对他友好的人,这些人现在控制着米蒂利尼。第二年春天,波斯海军抵达莱斯博斯岛,并说服其他城市站到他们一边。米蒂利尼被围困,由于波斯舰队的力量,公民们并没有什么真正的选择,他们与波斯人达成了协议,同意赶走亚历山大提供的雇佣兵,并通过摧毁记录条款的石头来废除他们与亚历山大的协议。他们还同意让流亡者回城(这些流亡者大概在亚历山大的军队到达时离开了这座城市),并归还他们离开这座城市时所拥有的一半财产。另一半可能由支持亚历山大的人占有,他们在亚历山大到来之前可能已经被放逐了。阿里安认为,波斯人重新控制了这座城市后，实际上并没有遵守协议中的条款。第二年，即公元前332年，亚历山大派遣了黑格罗库斯将军重新控制了岛屿，夺回了莱斯博斯岛的城市，包括米蒂利尼。一个新的协议的条款被记录在一篇留存下来的铭文上——这本身就表明他们可能受到了尊重。

铭文中残存的部分并没有解释流亡者现在可以返回的条件：很有可能与波斯人前一年掌权时提供的条件相同。不过，它确实非常详细地阐述了确保城内两个派系、返回的流亡者和已经在城内的流亡者之间和解的程序。它的目的是防止利用法庭对和解条款提出质疑，并建立了一个仲裁机构，从返回的流亡者和已经在城内的流亡者中平等抽调人选。亚历山大的行动究竟是解放者的，还是这些城市的新征服者的行动，现代学者对此意见不一。然而，他的现实立场并不是在解放城市还是压迫城市之间做出选择，而是要防止主要公民之间的分裂产生不稳定，杜绝波斯人卷土重来的机会。在以弗所城，亚历山大不得不出面阻止敌对派系之间的流血冲突。来自希俄斯岛和大陆的普里埃内城的同时代铭文提到了解决争端的类似尝试，并表明亚历山大进行了大量的通信和仲裁，试图为爱琴海东部城市带来持久的秩序。

亚历山大成功的一个标志是他所经过的城市给予他的荣誉。在许多地方，后来的铭文表明存在着被称为亚历山德里亚的节日，以及亚历山大巴赛勒斯（国王）和克蒂斯特斯（建城者）的祭司与祭坛。公元前6世纪末，为了纪念建城者，城市会举办一个体育节，并向他献祭，这已经成为一种惯例。按照公元前5世纪以前的惯例，如果建城者在这座新城市度过余生并在那里去世，他将被埋葬在城市中心，他的坟墓将被视为一个神圣的地方。他会被视为神话中的英雄，如斯巴达的俄瑞斯忒斯和雅典的忒修斯，人们发现了他们所谓的遗骨后，带到了各自的城市进行正式埋葬。但是，英雄的荣誉和对神的尊崇没有很明显的区别。在公元前5世纪的很多时候，城市的统治者可能会决定选择一个新人作为他们的建城者。最显著的例子是，伯罗奔尼撒战争结束时，斯巴达从雅典手中夺走了萨摩斯岛，并在岛上建立了一个新政权。据一位公元前3世纪的萨摩斯历史学家说，这位新统治者决定任命斯巴达指挥官来山德为他们的新建城者，并为他设立了一个节日，将他奉为神。与此相一致的是，各个城市都设立了亚历山大的祭仪，并在随后的几个世纪里保持着这种祭仪。当然，正是那些从亚历山大定居小亚细亚中受益的人，才更有理由引入这种荣誉。这有助于巩固亚历山大支持者的地位，例如，他们将亚历山大作为建城者，使他对城市的存在负有责任；但这并不是否认这些行为的诚意。

普里埃内城有铭文记载，亚历山大为新建的雅典娜神庙举行了献礼（图4）。亚历山大到来后，其他城市也开始修建新的神庙。在米利都的迪迪玛，公元前494年被波斯人摧毁的阿波罗神庙被修复，人们可以再次咨询神谕。这种发展不一定是即时的，但它们见证了这些希腊城市命运的重大转变。

斯巴达

有一座希腊城市与其他城市和马其顿人格格不入，那便是斯巴达。在公元前371年被底比斯将军伊巴密浓达击败之前，斯巴达一直是希腊最强大的城市之一，直接控制着伯罗奔尼撒

图4 刻在普里埃内雅典娜神庙中的石块。第一块铭文记载了亚历山大大帝为神庙揭幕的仪式

40%的领土,并领导着覆盖了其余大部分领土的联盟。但从那以后,斯巴达失去了大部分领土和所有的统治地位。斯巴达人拒绝加入科林斯同盟,也不愿跟随亚历山大,而是与大流士谈判,寻求财政支持,在希腊发动起义。斯巴达国王阿基斯于公元前333年至公元前332年在克里特岛的一次尝试失败后,于公元前331年在伯罗奔尼撒半岛发动了起义。反马其顿的政客们在伯罗奔尼撒的许多城市支持阿基斯,但雅典并没有加入他的行列,位于伯罗奔尼撒半岛南部阿卡迪亚的重要城市梅格洛波利斯也忠于亚历山大。在阿基斯围攻梅格洛波利斯时,马其顿摄政王安提帕特率领军队杀死了他,这标志着希腊各地对亚历山大的强烈反对已经结束。

雅　典

　　雅典似乎从亚历山大那里得到了比其他城市更多的荣誉。在格拉尼库斯河取得第一次胜利后,亚历山大选择将他在战场上分得的战利品送到雅典,在卫城奉上三百套盔甲,上面明确写着:"腓力的儿子亚历山大和希腊人,除了斯巴达人,从亚洲的野蛮人手中[夺得这些战利品献上]。"亚历山大占领苏萨的王宫时,发现那里有两尊雅典人为纪念弑僭主者哈莫迪乌斯和阿里斯托杰顿而竖立的雕像,这两个人暗杀了雅典最后一个僭主的兄弟,被认为是解放英雄。公元前480年,雅典被洗劫后,薛西斯把这些雕像带回了波斯,据阿里安说,亚历山大现在又把它们送了回去。亚历山大摧毁波斯波利斯的宫殿,作为科林斯同盟征战的最后行动,很明显是在报复薛西斯对雅典的洗劫。

　　正如我们所看到的,和希腊各城一样,雅典的政治家们分为支持亚历山大和不支持亚历山大的两派。亚历山大在伊苏斯第一次战胜大流士后，大流士不再有能力为他们提供财政支持，反马其顿的政客们便一直保持沉默，直到亚历山大死后一年。在演说家吕克戈斯的领导下，雅典人增加了国家财政收入，并用这笔钱修复和改善了市政建筑，包括狄俄尼索斯剧院和体育场（1896年第一届现代奥运会再次修复了它）；确立了在城市酒神节上表演公元前5世纪伟大悲剧家埃斯库罗斯、索福克勒斯和欧里庇得斯的戏剧的做法；他们还十分重视ephebeia，即对年轻人的训练。在经历了从喀罗尼亚战役前到底比斯被摧毁的紧张、危险的时期后，雅典在亚历山大东征时繁荣起来，得益于从波斯帝国归来的退伍老兵手中获得的财富。现代学者有时认为，雅典一直在寻找反对亚历山大的方法，但支持这一观点的证据很难找到。

公元前324年，亚历山大从巴基斯坦战役中胜利归来，率领军队走出格德罗西亚沙漠。这引起了他帝国中一些官员的担忧，他们利用亚历山大不在的时间从公共资金中大量敛财，但希腊城市的当权者却争相庆祝亚历山大的凯旋，他们派遣大使前往苏萨和巴比伦向他表示祝贺。雅典决定用一尊刻有"亚历山大国王，无敌之神"的雕像来纪念亚历山大。我们有理由相信，这反映了当时的流行观点：亚历山大不仅仅是一个征服的英雄；而且从当时的一篇演说的片段中可以得知，没有人明显反对这一观点。虽然亚历山大被称为神，但他的雕像并没有被设立祭坛或任命祭司，因此它与小亚细亚各城市提供的祭仪并不相同。演说中对亚历山大过于夸张的描述可能是有根据的，因为它声称，在巴基斯坦，亚历山大比狄俄尼索斯神走得更远，占领了连赫拉克勒斯都未能占领的地方。希腊其他城市可能也有类似的说法，但我们掌握的这些证据的价值值得怀疑。

流亡者

亚历山大从东方归来时最具争议的行为之一，至少在现代学者看来，是要求希腊各城市召回流亡者。正如我们所见，几乎所有希腊城市都存在流亡者问题。一般情况下，个人不可能在自己的城市以外拥有土地，因此那些长期流亡的人必须找到某种方式来养活自己。上层社会群体构成了政治流亡者的大多数，成为重装步兵或骑兵参与作战是为数不多的就业形式之一，许多曾跟随亚历山大的雇佣兵也曾在某个时刻流亡。作为他从东方归来后重组帝国的一部分，亚历山大要求他的总督们解散他们的雇佣军，并且必须找到解决办法，确保这些人有地方可去。最好的解决办法是让他们返回自己的城市，在那里定居。

亚历山大遵循惯例，利用一个主要的泛希腊节日，这里指的是公元前324年举办的奥林匹克运动会，作为他宣布决定的时机。每个希腊城市都会派出神圣的使者参加这个节日，因此它是交流重要信息的理想场所。要求城市召回流亡者是干涉它们的事务，推翻它们的法庭裁决。因此，这挑战了它们的自治权，但现存的历史记载在描述希腊城市的反对程度上存在分歧。对雅典来说，还存在一个特殊的问题，因为许多雅典人在萨摩斯岛上拥有一小块土地，而岛屿的主人已经被驱逐出境。如果之前的主人能够回来，这些雅典人可能会面临巨大的收入损失。

在伯罗奔尼撒半岛的忒格亚城，有一段残存下来的铭文与执行法令有关。这段铭文清楚地表明，各城市可以就流亡者如何返回进行谈判，同时也表明，我们在处理小亚细亚问题时，对流亡者和留下来的人之间能否和解的担忧，在这里也是一个重大问题。铭文的残余部分描述了将房屋和花园分配给返回的流亡者的过程，流亡者必须为此补偿现在的所有人。铭文还提到了一个由城外陪审员组成的特别法庭，负责处理争端。这并不代表亚历山大的行为粗暴或严厉。如果对希腊城市来说，公元前324年后的几年和前几年一样和平（至少自公元前331年阿基斯战败以来），那么就有可能判断流亡法令的影响。然而，亚历山大第二年的去世以及随后的战争——不仅在希腊，还包括前亚历山大帝国的整个范围——造成了前所未有的更大规模的混乱。

现代学者遵循古代叙事的思路，倾向于将"流亡者赦免令"的实施视为一种独裁行为，迫使城市违背自己的意愿接纳昔日的敌人。这种观点部分解释了为什么认为亚历山大是压迫者，认为他承诺的"为希腊人争取自由"只不过是一句空洞的口号。毫无疑问，有人因亚历山大的行动而蒙受损失，尤其是那些曾经与阿契美尼德统治者共事过的人，但铭文的证据表明，亚历山大希望与希腊城市建立良好的关系，而他从阿契美尼德王朝首都国库中释放的财富，在接下来的几十年甚至几个世纪里，极大地充实了小亚细亚和大陆的城市。

第五章

法老：亚历山大和埃及

公元前332年年末，亚历山大进入埃及，没有遭到当地居民或波斯总督马查西斯的反对，因为马查西斯的士兵太少，无法进行任何抵抗。这是亚历山大统治下第一个主要的近东王国，其政府体系起源于2500多年的法老统治。人们普遍认为，埃及是一个一成不变的文明，但这一点不应被夸大：在亚历山大到来之前的几个世纪里，自青铜时代晚期的新王国时期结束以来，埃及的统治发生了许多变化。新王国时期结束之后，又经历了四个世纪的"第三中间期"（公元前1069—前664），当时王国已经分裂，最终被亚述人征服。此后，第二十六王朝（公元前664—前525）统治埃及，直到波斯在冈比西斯的统治下入侵，导致阿契美尼德王朝统治埃及120年。埃及于公元前404年脱离波斯帝国，但60年后又重新被征服，此时距亚历山大到来只有12年。导致这些权力转移的冲突在埃及社会留下了印记。尽管如此，统治者们还是会采用他们成功的前任所采用的做法和表现形式，因为他们试图确认自己的权威，从而维持表面的连续性。

对于现存的亚历山大史料来说，亚历山大在埃及时期的两件事至关重要：建立亚历山大港和参观锡瓦的阿蒙神庙。据阿里安描述，亚历山大被pothos（压倒性的欲望）操控：这些行为是出于他个人的情感驱动，而不是出于任何实际考虑。这种解释在最近的学术研究中得到了广泛的遵循。古代作者对这两个事件的相对年代持不同意见，这可能会增加人们对建立亚历山大港的故事的怀疑，整个事件可能并不如我们所见的那样。

亚历山大港

在罗马帝国时期，位于尼罗河三角洲西部边缘埃及海岸的亚历山大港是世界上最重要的城市之一。公元前3世纪末，亚历山大港已经通过贸易发展成为世界上最大的城市，在古典时代只有罗马比它更大。它是一个巨大的贸易中心，也是地中海和东方之间的重要联系点。亚历山大图书馆汇集了所有希腊文献，成为科学和学术的中心。亚历山大死后大约一个世纪，人们第一次计算地球周长，就是在亚历山大港进行的；公元前3世纪，犹太《圣经》也是在这里被翻译成希腊语的，正是通过这一翻译，即众所周知的七十士译本，希伯来《圣经》文本为早期基督教作家所熟知。

所有古代的亚历山大史家都强调，亚历山大亲自参与了亚历山大港的建设，认为他决定了亚历山大港的修建地点（根据普鲁塔克的说法，他在梦中得到了建议），以及城墙和主要公共建筑的布局。他们还提供了一版关于建设亚历山大港的预言故事。他们说，这座城市的轮廓是用大麦粒勾勒出来的（要么是因为这是马其顿的常规做法，要么是因为没有白垩可用）；有些版本还提到，后来鸟儿成群结队地飞下来吃大麦。根据解释，大麦的使用意味着这座城市注定会因为土地上的果实而变得富饶，但在涉及鸟类的版本中，它们的到来预示着人们会从四面八方来到亚历山大港定居。这些记载中有多少是可信的呢？答案是，可能没有。

亚历山大死后，他的遗体被从巴比伦送到西方，在马其顿安葬。途中，遗体被托勒密截获，带到埃及，埋葬在孟斐斯，而不是亚历山大港。孟斐斯在托勒密统治下一直是埃及的行政中心，亚历山大死后，托勒密以总督的身份控制了埃及，直到公元前311年。同年，托勒密用埃及语撰写了一份文件，被称作《总督石碑》。他在其中写道，他搬到了"希腊海边亚历山大国王的堡垒，原名拉科蒂斯"。这一事件发生在亚历山大死后12年以及他离开埃及后20年，可能标志着亚历山大港真正的起点。公元前304年，托勒密宣布自己为国王，可能在那之后，这座城市才开始成为一个主要的文化中心。它最著名的建筑，图书馆和博物馆，通常与托勒密的儿子及继承人"爱手足者"托勒密二世（公元前283—前246在位）有关。从《总督石碑》上的文字来看，尚不清楚该地在托勒密一世迁到那里之前是否被命名为"亚历山大国王的堡垒"，也不清楚它是否还有一个埃及名字拉科蒂斯。考古学提供的关于该地最早的历史信息很少，因为这座古城被埋在现代城市和海洋之下，尽管挖掘工作仍在进行，未来可能会出现一些东西。目前，几乎没有同时代的证据支持这一观点，即在以亚历山大的名字命名的城市后来发展为最重要城市的过程中，他本人功不可没。

他的征战行动进入伊朗东部、阿富汗和其他地区时，亚历山大确实开始建立定居点，通常命名为亚历山大城，包括现在阿富汗的坎大哈。普鲁塔克在《论亚历山大大帝的命运和美德》一文中指出，亚历山大建立了70多座城市，并声称他这样做的目的是在"野蛮人"中传播希腊文化和知识。这个数字可能有些夸张，但至少有20个名为亚历山大城的定居点是通过铭文和文字记载而为人们所知的。并不是所有地点都能被准确定位，还有一些城市，如特洛伊附近的亚历山大·特洛阿德，原本以其创建者独眼安提柯的名字命名为安提柯·特洛阿德，是后来的统治者重新命了名。有些是对原有城市的重建，有些则是新建的城市。阿富汗东北部的阿伊-哈努姆被认为是奥克苏斯河畔亚历山大城的遗址，人们在挖掘中发现了一座希腊剧院和神庙，建于亚历山大时代后的几十年，但普鲁塔克认为它们是文化中心，这一想法显然是不现实的。这些城市大多不过是堡垒，由准备在亚洲开始新生活的马其顿老兵占领，可能还有从周围村庄来的当地居民。这些地方并不是主要的商业中心，而是在有叛乱危险的地区设置的控制点。与所有其他的亚历山大城相比，亚历山大有意在埃及建立一座新的商业城市的想法显得格格不入。他可能想在那里留下一个驻军堡垒，这就是托勒密在《总督石碑》中提到的，但亚历山大港的遗址显然不是一个军事驻点。

围绕着这座城市建设的种种预兆，首先反映了这座城市未来的成功：城市的财富越庞大，人们就越有可能把它与亚历山大本人联系起来。亚历山大早期的三部历史故事都起源于这座城市：托勒密，他的历史故事是阿里安作品的主要来源；克莱塔卡斯，他的作品在狄奥多罗斯和库尔提斯之后；还有所谓的《传奇》，这本关于亚历山大生平的虚构文学广为流传的是公元3世

第五章　法老：亚历山大和埃及

纪及以后的版本，但它起源于公元前3世纪。托勒密尤其把自己和亚历山大联系在一起，正如我们所见，他把亚历山大的头像印在他的硬币上，并把建立王城的功劳归功于亚历山大，这对他很有帮助。其他作者没有理由不公布提高自己城市地位的事实版本。古希腊城市宣称神话英雄是他们的缔造者，而亚历山大大帝是一个值得称颂的英雄，因此亚历山大港的人乐意宣称其为城市的创建者，但亚历山大亲自建立这座城市的故事更多地属于传说而不是历史。

阿蒙神谕

在现存的历史中，最受关注的埃及事件是亚历山大访问利比亚沙漠锡瓦绿洲的阿蒙神庙。除了狄奥多罗斯、库尔提斯、普鲁塔克、阿里安和查士丁的记载之外，我们还有亚历山大的"史官"卡利斯提尼斯记载的许多内容，以及地理学家斯特拉博的记录，他在奥古斯都皇帝的统治时期写作，也就是说，比狄奥多罗斯稍晚一些。现代学者根据古代资料，将亚历山大与神谕的相遇视为他认识自己的转折点。然而，与亚历山大参与宗教的其他案例一样，其证据复杂而混乱。

锡瓦的主要神庙建于法老雅赫摩斯（公元前570—前526在位）统治时期，供奉阿蒙神，阿蒙神的主要祭祀中心在底比斯。在底比斯，阿蒙神谕以埃及神谕的传统方式运作。每逢重大节日，八大祭司会扛着神像，乘着圣船列队行进。那些想请教神谕的人可以在神走近的时候询问。如果神向他们"点头"，也就是说，如果神像在经过时朝向他们摇摆，就表示肯定的回答，但如果它摇摇晃晃地离开了询问者，就表示否定的回答。另一种询问的方法是,在神所行的道路上放置两个备选的书面陈述,神倾向哪一边,就表明神的选择是哪一个。在锡瓦,神谕也以同样的方式运作。亚历山大参观圣地时,游行队伍从主神庙通往第二座较小的神庙,这座神庙由内克塔内布二世建造,游行的队伍会携带祭仪的神像沿着这条路线行进。由于神谕在内克塔内布时期之前就已经存在,所以他的神庙一定是为了增加现有游行路线的纪念性而建造的。

从雅赫摩斯建造神庙时起,希腊城市昔兰尼(靠近现代班加西)的神圣使者(theoroi)就造访了锡瓦,而阿蒙在昔兰尼以阿蒙神或宙斯阿蒙的名义接受祭拜。在描绘中,他长着公羊角,因此埃及人用公羊头代表阿蒙神。希罗多德记载了吕底亚国王克洛伊索斯对神谕的请教,如果记载准确的话,这应该发生在吕底亚历史的早期。公元前5世纪,人们在爱琴海就认可了阿蒙神,而公元前4世纪早期的铭文表明雅典人曾派遣神圣使者前往这座神庙。但是,虽然这座神庙在希腊有一定的威望,但它位于埃及领土的边缘,其威望远远低于上埃及阿蒙的古老神庙。因此,亚历山大的造访不太可能是为了给埃及人留下深刻印象,而古代作者也并没有用这些词来描述这次造访。将亚历山大的造访与他对希腊城市昔兰尼加统治权的兴趣联系起来会更有意义,昔兰尼加在大流士一世时期曾由波斯控制,但在公元前404年埃及起义后脱离了外部控制。

卡利斯提尼斯声称,亚历山大想拜访神庙,是为了效仿他的祖先珀尔修斯和赫拉克勒斯,虽然早期作者并没有提到这些英雄确实去过锡瓦。希罗多德亲自拜访了神庙,并讲述了赫拉克勒斯在埃及的冒险故事,讲述了赫拉克勒斯如何去拜访他父亲宙斯在底比斯的神庙，以及宙斯如何为了阻止赫拉克勒斯看到他的本来模样，戴着公羊头作为伪装。但他没有说赫拉克勒斯去过锡瓦。阿里安的整个描述似乎是基于卡利斯提尼斯（可能源于托勒密的历史故事），他给出了同样的解释，但补充说，亚历山大想要找出他的出生或起源（genesis）。卡利斯提尼斯和阿里安都没有记载亚历山大向神询问了什么。在其他的叙述中，只有查士丁解释了他为什么要请教神谕，详述了他想知道关于自己出生的故事，但其他四位作者都对亚历山大与祭司的对话做了更全面的描述，即使这段对话并不可靠。

古代历史学家对翻译人员在与外国人交往中的作用常常含糊不清。亚历山大访问锡瓦时，尚不清楚各方用什么语言交谈。普鲁塔克在《亚历山大传》中，几次提到语言上的笑话和双关语，他认为埃及官员说的是希腊语，但说得很差：他暗示阿蒙神祭司可能是在无意中称呼亚历山大为 Pai Dios（宙斯之子）的，因为他实际想说的是 paidion（孩子）。在普鲁塔克看来，这是一个巧妙而偶然的预兆，但其他作者都没有这样描述这些事件。他们给人的印象是，所有的交流都是直接的，可以用简单的希腊语来解释。亚历山大不大可能懂埃及语。阿蒙神祭司可能懂希腊语，因为有一个既定的模式：希腊人会参拜神庙。然而，可以肯定的是，亚历山大会有翻译人员陪同，这样他就能准确知道所说的内容。他很可能已经被认作法老，或者至少是即将被加冕为法老的人，因此对他的称呼要符合他的职位所要求的礼节。

这十分重要，因为古代作者声称，亚历山大第一次到达锡瓦时，阿蒙神祭司称呼他为神之子（狄奥多罗斯），或者具体称呼为宙斯之子（卡利斯提尼斯和普鲁塔克）、朱庇特之子（库尔提斯）或哈蒙之子（查士丁）。根据狄奥多罗斯、库尔提斯和查士丁的说法，亚历山大对此的回应是，从现在起，他将用这个头衔来称呼自己，这表明了一个过程的开始，最终亚历山大会与他的部下疏远，因为他是在否认腓力是他的父亲。然而，正如我们所见，亚历山大在埃及的头衔遵循了埃及的传统，其中包括"太阳神之子"；埃及（或利比亚）祭司这样称呼他，是礼节，而不是启示。

克莱塔卡斯的作品中有对亚历山大造访的更详细的描述。克莱塔卡斯不是亚历山大来访的目击者，但是，他在埃及写作，确实了解埃及神谕的运作：我们得到的雕像被祭司抬到船上的描述有些混乱，但基本上是真实的。但是，古代历史叙事中关于请教神谕的故事往往遵循一定的模式，亚历山大史家的读者会期待询问者和祭司之间的对话，就像希腊最著名的德尔斐神谕的模式一样（尽管德尔斐神谕因其回答含糊不清而著称）。仅仅是通过一尊雕像的动作来回应对神谕的咨询，就不那么容易戏剧化了。因此，我们得到的故事与我们所知道的埃及神谕的运作并不一致。一些学者，包括锡瓦的考古者，试图通过假设一个单独的"王家神谕"来调和这些说法，这更接近于希腊模式，但这并不能令人信服，猜测历史学家在复述中增加了戏剧性反而更为合理。这些作者声称，亚历山大提出了两个问题：杀害他父亲的凶手是否受到了惩罚，以及他是否会统治世界。在这些叙述中，第一种说法似乎是为了加强亚历山大已经接受了神圣父权的观念，据说神谕的回应是他的父亲不会被凡人伤害（但杀害腓力的凶手已经得到了报复）。第二个问题得到了积极的回应，我们将在稍后讨论这一问题的含义。

63

关于请教神谕的故事在希腊文学中很常见。德尔斐的神谕在希罗多德的《历史》中占据重要地位,《历史》是第一部书写下来的历史著作,也是最有影响力的著作之一。普鲁塔克的著作《希腊罗马名人传》中有许多关于神谕的讨论,他还写了一系列关于希腊神谕的文章。因此,在希腊和罗马的亚历山大史家的叙述中,访问锡瓦神庙引起了极大的关注也就不足为奇了。它证明了神参与了亚历山大取得的成就,并通过神谕的回应揭示了亚历山大的伟大。这些对亚历山大本质的确认对读者来说很重要,但是埃及人有自己的方式来表明亚历山大的重要性以及他与诸神的关系,首先就是承认他是法老。

法老亚历山大

如果我们阅读希腊和罗马历史,了解埃及人对一位新统治者的期望,我们可以看到亚历山大是能够达到他们的期望的。孟斐斯位于尼罗河三角洲的顶端,是下埃及的王家中心,是这一时期埃及的行政中心,也是亚历山大最先去的地方。新法老登基时的常规仪式首先是正式宣布其尊名,随后准法老将乘坐王家驳船前往王国的主要神庙,这一旅程是为了"在各省建立秩序"。王国的所有官员都要重新宣誓就职,此时外国盟友也要重新宣誓结盟。整个过程以孟斐斯的加冕仪式结束,加冕仪式最好在6月埃及新年庆典期间举行。没有一位作者真正描述了亚历山大的加冕仪式,但他们确实提到了各种仪式将要举行的场合。阿里安提到孟斐斯的两次庆典,一次发生在亚历山大抵达时,另一次在他离开前不久。库尔提斯说,亚历山大从孟斐斯乘船沿河而上,他还记载了一个悲惨的事件:一位年轻的马其顿贵族试图追上亚历山大,他乘坐的船倾覆,随后他溺水身亡。阿里安还描述了亚历山大出发前在孟斐斯接待使节和分配办公场所的情况。

希腊和罗马作家不愿提及真正的加冕仪式,这一点意义重大。同样,他们也不愿描述亚历山大在巴比伦(亚历山大肯定在这里坐上了国王的宝座)和苏萨(在这里也很可能登上了王位)的时间。这在一定程度上可能是作者选择叙事结构的结果。这些故事或多或少都把亚历山大描绘成一个因与"东方"接触而逐渐堕落的人:他对"野蛮人"的行为越来越感兴趣,并失去了对自己的控制。这一主题我们将在其他地方讨论,但如果亚历山大被认为在征战中过早地采用了被征服民族的做法,故事的情节就会被削弱。

埃及有许多庙宇,修复或扩建庙宇是法老的工作之一。最后两位埃及统治者内克塔内布一世(公元前380—前362在位)和内克塔内布二世(公元前360—前343在位)在建筑工程上一直精力充沛。内克塔内布二世很可能开始了一些工程,但波斯人在埃及独立后重新控制埃及时(公元前404—前343),这些工程还没有完工。埃及的证据表明,亚历山大准备遵循传统,修复庙宇。

在卢克索的阿蒙-拉神庙,靠近上埃及古王城底比斯,亚历山大被描绘在"圣船圣堂"的墙壁上,人们认为他修复了这座圣堂。在一系列传统埃及风格的浮雕中,亚历山大被描绘成法老的模样,面朝阿蒙-拉。随附的文字称他为"上埃及和下埃及的国王,两国的君主,Setepenre Meryamun(阿蒙的挚爱,拉神的选择),拉神之子,王冠的拥有者,亚历山大"(图5)。这是法老称

66 呼的标准形式,铭文上记载着亚历山大已经执行了他的父亲阿蒙-拉的命令。"圣船圣堂"中绘有神的圣像,立在礼舫上。在重要的节日里,神庙里的祭司们会把圣像放在船上列队行进。在卡纳克附近的另一座阿蒙神庙中,有一段铭文称亚历山大翻修

图5 亚历山大大帝(右)在卢克索的阿蒙霍特普三世神庙中被描绘成法老的模样

了图特摩斯三世（法老，公元前1475—前1429在位）的圣堂，亚历山大再次被授予完整的法老头衔。再往下游，在赫尔莫波利斯，铭文记录了亚历山大进一步的修复工作。我们从埃及纪念碑上看到的画面是亚历山大追随他前辈的足迹，正如我们所见，这幅画面与希腊和罗马对他在埃及时期的描述截然不同。

第六章

世界之王：亚历山大和波斯

历史学家阿庇安是阿里安的同时代人，他记录了罗马将军大西庇阿和他的导师，希腊历史学家波利比乌斯之间的一次谈话，这段对话发生在公元前146年的迦太基城外，当时罗马军队正在洗劫这座城市。阿庇安说波利比乌斯记录下了他听到的对话。大西庇阿目睹了这座古城的毁灭，不禁深思

城市、国家和帝国覆灭的必然性：这样的命运降临在曾经幸运的特洛伊城，亚述人、米底人和波斯人也曾遭遇这样的命运，他们的帝国曾经是最伟大的，最近马其顿的辉煌帝国也是如此。

他接着引用了《伊利亚特》中的诗句，特洛伊王子赫克托耳在其中预言了特洛伊城的沦陷，大西庇阿向波利比乌斯解释说，他在思考未来罗马沦陷的时间。

不同的国家纷至沓来，统治着世界的大部分地区，尤其是亚

洲地区，这一观点是有作品存世的亚历山大史家著书时历史学界已公认的主题。在《亚历山大远征记》最后一卷的开头，阿里安提出了一个不太可能的猜测，即亚历山大计划环游阿非利加，并从西部进攻迦太基。他补充说，在亚历山大看来，米底人和波斯人没有权利获得"伟大的国王"这一称号，因为他们只控制了亚洲最小的部分。这可能反映了阿里安自己的观点，而不是亚历山大的观点，但是在亚历山大统治前一个世纪，希罗多德对波斯帝国崛起的记载中，将波斯人奉为了米底人权力的继承者。尽管"统治亚洲"并不是一个精确定义的概念，但这是亚历山大可以期望通过击败大流士后获得的，公元前331年10月1日，他在高加米拉——靠近伊拉克北部现代城市摩苏尔——第二次也是最后一次击败了大流士。

"世界之王"

从巴比伦天文志中，我们知道了高加米拉战役的确切日期，以及前后的一些事件，比如我们在本书前面章节看到的例子，它记录了亚历山大的死亡。高加米拉天文志，涵盖巴比伦年的第六个月和第七个月，相当于公元前331年9月8日至11月6日，就像所有天文志一样，记录了每晚的观察，以及如果发生了重大事件，对应的是何种仪式：9月25日，一条狗被烧死，可能是由于一道闪电（此处黏土板有缺损）。到了第六个月，即Ulūlu月底，这块黏土板上写着在市场上一个银币可以买到多少大麦、枣、芥菜、水芹、芝麻和羊毛；然后是哪些行星运行到了哪个星座；还有幼发拉底河的水位高度。这些数据之后还有其他事件的报告，包括9月18日大流士营地爆发恐慌；马其顿军队抵达战场；

在这场战争中,大流士的军队在被打败之后的逃跑过程中抛弃了国王。这个细节很有意思,因为它有助于解决亚历山大史家之间的分歧:狄奥多罗斯和库尔提斯声称大流士在他的军队开始逃跑之前一直坚持,但普鲁塔克和阿里安认为大流士是第一个逃跑的人。这样看来,通常更可靠的阿里安可能是错误的。

书写黏土板的抄写员称大流士为"国王",但称亚历山大为"世界之王"。这个翻译有些不确切,但在现存的历史学家记载中,类似的名称都用来指代亚历山大。由于将世界划分为各个大陆是希腊地理学家的创造,巴比伦人对"亚洲"并没有明确的概念,"世界之王"可能是巴比伦人对"亚洲之王"一词的理解方式。普鲁塔克将亚历山大在高加米拉的胜利作为他战役的高潮,他指出:"随着战争出现结果,波斯人的统治被完全推翻了,亚历山大被宣布为亚洲之王,他大规模地祭祀诸神,并以财富、地产和省份奖励他的朋友。"这就是巴比伦抄写员在选择名称时所面对的情况。

"世界之王"这一头衔首次出现在讲述亚历山大战役的戈尔迪乌姆之结的故事中。在弗里吉亚的古都戈尔迪乌姆,亚历山大看到一辆用复杂的结与轭相连的手推车,并被告知谁能解开这个结,谁就会成为"亚洲统治者"(根据阿里安和库尔提斯的说法)或"世界之王"(根据普鲁塔克的说法)。据记载,亚历山大对此的反应有两种版本,其中比较流行的是他直接用剑把结割断,而另一种说法是他拔出了一个把结固定在一起的钉子。无论哪种情况,他都被认为实现了预言。普鲁塔克、狄奥多罗斯和库尔提斯(但不是阿里安)记述亚历山大在锡瓦请教神谕的版本中,也提到了神谕告诉亚历山大他将统治世界。在这些记载中，没有任何迹象表明亚历山大误解了神谕的含义，或者说它是不可靠的。这些反应可以理解为预示着亚历山大离开埃及后，在高加米拉与大流士相遇的结果。

苏　萨

　　在高加米拉战败后，大流士三世向东逃走，亚历山大率领军队南下，穿过美索不达米亚，直抵波斯。他来到的第一个大城市是巴比伦，我们会在后面讨论他与这座城市的关系。然后，他又去了苏萨，和巴比伦一样，苏萨也是阿契美尼德王朝的首都。两位亚历山大史家记载了一个关于亚历山大访问苏萨宫殿的奇怪故事，这可能掩盖了亚历山大生平中的一个重要事件。根据狄奥多罗斯和库尔提斯的说法，亚历山大在宫殿里巡视，他到达正殿后，坐在了王座上。由于亚历山大个子不高，他的脚够不到宝座前的地板，于是一个侍从拿来一张矮桌子作为脚凳。这时，宫殿里的一个太监开始号啕大哭，最后解释说，这是大流士以前吃饭的桌子：看到大流士命运的转变，太监无法保持沉默。亚历山大起初想把这张桌子搬走，但他的朋友菲罗塔斯告诉他，要把这种情况看作亚历山大胜利的预兆。

　　这个故事告诉了我们什么？这不太可能是真的。对阿契美尼德国王坐在王座上的描绘通常显示他们有一个脚凳，而我们所知道的关于"国王的桌子"的一切都表明，大流士用餐的任何桌子都不适合充当脚凳。亚历山大也不太可能表现出故事中所暗示的那种麻木不仁。对这段插曲的一种可能的解释是，这是对亚历山大即位并加冕为伟大国王的混乱描述。普鲁塔克在《亚历山大的命运》一文中提到，一个名叫狄马拉图斯的古希腊老人看到亚历山大坐在苏萨的大流士宝座上，便高兴地哭泣起来。苏萨是阿契美尼德国王加冕的地方。普鲁塔克在《阿尔塔薛西斯传》中描述了阿尔塔薛西斯二世在帕萨尔加德举行的不同的继承仪式，但很明显，阿契美尼德国王在不同的地方有不同的仪式。亚历山大史家可能不太愿意描述亚历山大自愿参加阿契美尼德仪式，因此把这些事件作为预兆故事来讲述，但我们不应该假设亚历山大也有同样的顾虑。

这就提出了一个问题：亚历山大的终极目标是什么。一些历史学家将亚历山大描述为"最后的阿契美尼德人"，暗示他视自己为大流士三世的继承人。基于这一观点，亚历山大计划将他的王国中心从马其顿转移到位于苏萨和巴比伦的阿契美尼德王国中心。与这一举动有关的是他采用了波斯服装和波斯宫廷礼节，这令他的马其顿同伴感到不安。另一种观点认为，这些做法对管理亚历山大帝国东部地区很有必要，并认为，如果亚历山大活得更久，他会把注意力转向西方，可能会回到马其顿。

要想在这种不确定性中找到出路，我们必须首先思考亚历山大征战现存叙事的目标读者。对于读过亚历山大历史的罗马读者来说，波斯人仍然是他们的敌人。罗马人面对的是幼发拉底河对岸的帕提亚帝国，而不再是阿契美尼德的国王们。几位罗马统帅曾率领远征队横渡幼发拉底河与帕提亚人交战，结果喜忧参半。阿里安在心中把哈德良皇帝作为他的读者，哈德良曾与他的前任图拉真在亚美尼亚和美索不达米亚征战，后来，他成为皇帝，就撤出了幼发拉底河以东的领土。阿里安试图把亚历山大塑造成一个值得罗马读者仿效的人物，因此，他尽可能地淡化任何关于亚历山大可能愿意将自己树立为伟大国王的说法。但正如我们所见,我们有充分的理由认为,马其顿的宫廷习俗借鉴了一些波斯模式。波斯王权对于亚历山大和他的马其顿人来说,远没有对于从存世文献中了解亚历山大的罗马人来说那么奇怪。

波斯波利斯的大火

亚历山大明白姿态的重要性。他采用了阿契美尼德的仪式,帮助他维护自己的权威,但他的阿契美尼德前辈们有时会通过破坏性行为来展示自己的力量。亚历山大在征战中最臭名昭著的行为之一就是烧毁了波斯波利斯宫殿。这座宫殿由大流士和薛西斯建造,他们曾率领军队进入希腊,而现存的资料记载中更为流行的故事是,这座宫殿是在一次喝醉的聚会后被烧毁的,在那次聚会上,一个名叫泰伊思的雅典妓女鼓动亚历山大摧毁薛西斯建造的宫殿,以此来报复他曾经毁灭雅典。这个故事在现存的几乎所有版本中都有讲述,除了阿里安的版本。阿里安说亚历山大故意焚毁了宫殿,而阿里安本人似乎不赞成这种行为。物证倾向于支持阿里安更冷静的观点,并表明宫殿里的东西和建筑一样都是目标(尽管黄金和白银首先被带走了)。残存的石雕被焚烧的证据表明,家具被堆放起来,然后被放火焚烧。

为什么亚历山大要摧毁波斯波利斯,却没有破坏其他王室中心,如苏萨和巴比伦?这个问题一直困扰着学者们。这样做并不能使他的新臣民波斯人喜爱他。最有可能的解释是,这确实是对薛西斯毁灭雅典的象征性报复。这是希腊城邦参与这场战役的部分理由,亚历山大很难忽视这一点。他可以在其他王室中心统治他的帝国,不需要波斯波利斯。后来的波斯传说放大了大火的影响,声称亚历山大连同宫殿一起摧毁了古代琐罗亚斯德教的宗教著作,但这是不可信的。

穿波斯服装

对亚历山大史家来说,在伊朗的活动导致了亚历山大名声的无情衰落,因为他越来越被"东方"的行为方式所吸引。他们描述了亚历山大如何开始采用波斯(或米底)的服饰和宫廷仪式,包括残害他的对手,并要求他的朋友们俯伏在他面前。与此同时,他们认为亚历山大变得越来越暴虐:他以前的朋友要么因莫须有的罪名被处决,要么在暴怒中被杀。现代学者虽然修改了关于腐败和衰落的叙述内容,但他们倾向于认为这种说法大体上是正确的。这是一个错误。亚历山大的堕落和衰落被道德家视为东方诱惑与腐败的最明显的例子。这种对他生平的解读成为传记作家和历史学家的惯用手法,但它掩盖了一些重要的事实。马其顿国王是包括西部波斯总督在内的一个网络的一部分,总督宫廷(其本身受波斯国王宫廷的影响)的许多做法被马其顿人和爱琴海的其他国王采用或改编:亚历山大来到"东方"时是熟悉其做法的。我们也看到了,在埃及和苏萨,亚历山大毫不费力地扮演了法老或国王的角色。现存的故事显示,亚历山大逐渐开始采用波斯服装,后来又开始"试用"正式的宫廷礼节,在此过程中,他面临着马其顿同胞的怀疑甚至敌意。但在普鲁塔克的书中,还有一些更有利于亚历山大的故事,描写了他的马其顿朋友们沉沦于奢华的生活之中,而亚历山大却为他们树立了节俭和自制的榜样。这两个版本都不具有说服力:两者都更关心为读者提供道德榜样,让他们仿效或抵制,而不是准确地报道实际发生的事情。罗马作家和读者可能会假装对亚历山大在伊朗气候下穿波斯服饰感到震惊，而不是对他的马其顿同胞。因此，我们可以理所当然地认为，从他在巴比伦和苏萨的时期开始，或者更早，亚历山大的移动宫廷就采取了适合当时情况的规程，国王本人也完全保留了他的智力。

宫廷礼仪

古代作者和许多现代学者最关心的问题是，亚历山大是否希望他的同伴们在他面前行跪拜礼。亚历山大史家似乎都相信，波斯人拜倒在伟大国王面前是寻常的做法，尽管事实并非如此：只有战败的敌人才会这样做。更为复杂的是，历史学家们还提出，跪拜是承认波斯国王神性的一种方式。他们描述了亚历山大如何试图将这种做法引入他的宫廷礼仪，利用社交场合作为实验，并声称他的成就值得崇拜。然而，在这些故事中，亚历山大的史官卡利斯提尼斯成功地领导了反对这些变革的行动，这种做法被放弃了。

然而，令人难以置信的是，卡利斯提尼斯会是一位反抗的领袖。他的亚历山大征战史以奉承而著称。它可能是亚历山大效仿他英勇的祖先阿喀琉斯、赫拉克勒斯和珀尔修斯的故事的来源，也可能是将亚历山大远征描绘成一系列神定的胜利故事的来源。在记载亚历山大沿着小亚细亚南海岸行进时，他描述了海浪在亚历山大面前翻滚。卡利斯提尼斯本人也不受欢迎：亚历山大同伴的回忆录中讲述了一些关于他的故事。故事中，他在社交场合脾气暴躁，举止粗鲁。但在公元前327年，他卷入了一场反对亚历山大的阴谋，因此被逮捕，并在被捕期间死亡。在他死后的几十年里,他被重新塑造成一个有原则的反对者,反对亚历山大采用波斯习俗,反对亚历山大声称自己拥有神圣血统。关于跪拜的实施和卡利斯提尼斯的反对,很可能都是为了使卡利斯提尼斯的死符合哲学家反抗暴君的既定故事模式。从希罗多德描写的公元前6世纪雅典哲学家、政治家梭伦和吕底亚国王克洛伊索斯的会面开始,哲学家和君主的会面就成了希腊作家的常见话题。后来的历史也产生了影响:在库尔提斯、普鲁塔克和阿里安开始写作前不久,哲学家塞涅卡被尼禄皇帝下令自杀,塞涅卡曾被任命为皇帝的导师。因此,当亚历山大史家们开始写作时,卡利斯提尼斯已经成为一名哲学殉道者,因为向专制政权说出真理而被杀害,他反对跪拜的故事也广为人知,不容忽视。然而,它们与我们所知道的亚历山大时代及更早时期的波斯习俗并不一致,因此它们不是解决亚历山大对宫廷礼仪感兴趣这个问题的最佳方式。

我们可以更有信心地说,亚历山大任命人担任礼仪职位,这是阿契美尼德宫廷生活的正常组成部分。他有一个宫廷大臣或礼宾官,这个职位来自希罗多德对大流士一世统治时期宫殿组织的描述,他控制着接近国王的途径;他的朋友赫费斯提翁得到了另一个头衔——辅政大臣(chiliarch),这个职位在波斯宫廷里很常见。他的随从中有位高权重的波斯人,包括他的对手大流士三世的儿子。在高加米拉胜利后把土地分给他的朋友们时,亚历山大表现得像一个波斯国王,有效地将这些朋友培养成了他新帝国的贵族。在他统治后期,他为大量波斯和马其顿领袖组织宴会,对宴会的描述与早期阿契美尼德王朝波斯波利斯的文献中所知的非常相似。亚历山大史家顺便提到了这些事实,但他们并不认为这些事实导致了亚历山大和其他马其顿人之间的矛盾。

亚历山大的王后们

亚历山大的婚姻证明了他是如何融入他的新王国的。如我们所见，他的父亲腓力有好几个妻子，他利用婚姻来维持与马其顿邻国的关系。波斯国王也以同样的方式把有权势的贵族束缚在自己身上，尤其是在没有直接继承权的情况下，他们会娶前任统治者的前妻或女儿。在亚历山大帝国东北部的殖民地，他娶了一位伊朗贵族的女儿罗克珊娜。公元前324年，他从东方回来，又娶了两个女人：阿尔塔薛西斯三世的女儿、阿尔塔薛西斯四世的妹妹帕里萨蒂斯和大流士三世的女儿斯妲特拉。这些婚姻使他与波斯最后两位国王的家族联系在一起，如果亚历山大活得更久，可能会从中产生亚历山大的王位继承人，此人将是阿契美尼德先王的直系后代。伊苏斯战役后，斯妲特拉和帕里萨蒂斯，连同大流士家族的其他成员，在大马士革被马其顿人俘虏。亚历山大史家称，亚历山大对待这些被俘的妇女，包括大流士的妻子和母亲，非常尊重。他本可以更早地和斯妲特拉结婚。所有亚历山大史家都提到了大流士在高加米拉战役前给亚历山大的信件，信中大流士向亚历山大提亲，并以幼发拉底河以西领土的控制权作为嫁妆。这样的协议实际上会使亚历山大与大流士成为共同统治者，并可能使亚历山大的某个儿子最终继承整个帝国。亚历山大的军事胜利使这一提议变得多余，但斯妲特拉的孩子仍可能是亚历山大的潜在继承人。也许正是出于这个原因，罗克珊娜急于保护她（尚未出生的）孩子的地位，很可能在亚历山大死后不久就杀害了斯妲特拉和帕里萨蒂斯。

对亚历山大婚姻的讨论不可避免地引起人们更广泛地思考他对性的态度。这是古代作者不可忽视的一个话题，也引起了现代学者的兴趣，并影响了对亚历山大的现代表现。但是古代作者提出的问题与最近争论的问题有很大的不同。亚历山大史家并没有给出亚历山大性关系的大量细节，尽管普鲁塔克简短地提到巴西妮曾是他的情妇，巴西妮是波斯首领之一阿尔塔巴左斯的女儿，也是大流士的海军统帅罗得岛的门农的遗孀，在伊苏斯战役之后，门农和大流士家族的其他人一起被俘。他们更感兴趣的问题是亚历山大的自我控制和性节制，从他对待大流士的被俘妻子和女儿的方式可以看出。这种克制被古代作者视为一种特别男性化的美德，他们没有从性取向的角度讨论性。小说家克劳斯·曼和玛丽·瑞瑙特以及电影导演奥利弗·斯通等现代作者关注的问题是，亚历山大是否与男性和女性都发生过性关系，他们重点关注亚历山大与赫费斯提翁的友谊，以及关于一个叫巴戈阿斯的波斯太监的故事。虽然在现存的文本中没有明确提及这种关系，但它们并非不可想象。然而，如果亚历山大的同性恋倾向完全集中于双方自愿的性关系上，那么就有可能像提及他的性节制一样，把他浪漫化。亚历山大成年后的大部分时间都是在军事行动和宫廷中度过的，在那里，展示权力是维持秩序的一种手段。也许应该进行辩论的，不是关于亚历山大是否曾经和一个男人发生过性关系，而是关于他是否或多久与一个不情愿的伴侣强行发生性关系，无论男性还是女性。亚历山大在世时，这种行为不会被书写其生平的人注意，但这是所有宫廷和军队的特点，因此如果这并不是亚历山大经历的一部分，那将会是非常了不起的。

第七章

旅行者：亚历山大的阿富汗和巴基斯坦之行

公元前330年春末，亚历山大离开波斯波利斯，开始在他所赢得的帝国的东部展开一场新的征战。过了五年多他才回来。从一开始，这趟东征就比他生平中任何其他部分吸引了更多的奇怪故事和更多的说教评论，近几个世纪来，它一直是令历史学家着迷的源泉。对古代作者来说，这是亚历山大被东方的奢华所诱惑，失去了对激情的控制的时期。也正是在这个时候，他的士兵们拒绝继续前进，最终使他永不止息的向前迈进的欲望停歇了。对于现代作者来说，亚历山大在处理阿富汗及其周边地区的叛乱时所遇到的困难最早地证明了他不可能统治这个国家；他杀害宫廷成员的行为表明他正在成为一个偏执的暴君；他对待印度河流域人民的方式简直不亚于种族灭绝。直到最近，几乎都没有确凿的证据表明亚历山大的东征涉及了什么，但考古学家的发现，以及巴克特里亚（位于现在的阿富汗）的波斯总督辖地发现和出版的文献，为古代作者的观点提供了一些重要的修正。

亚历山大和亚马逊女王

有一个故事特别说明了亚历山大在东方活动的奇妙故事是如何在很早之前就流传开来了。库尔提斯详细描述了亚马逊女王塔勒斯特里斯造访过里海附近的亚历山大营地。她有300名女战士陪同,她此行的目的就是怀上亚历山大的孩子。为此,她与国王共度了13个夜晚,然后回到了她的族人身边。普鲁塔克提供了关于这个故事来源的细节,他说他读过的大多数作者都记载了这个故事,并列举了其中五位作者,但同时也列出了其他九位没有提到这个故事的作者。两份名单中都有陪同亚历山大的人,但普鲁塔克又讲了一个故事,使人对这一事件产生了怀疑。几年后,历史学家奥涅西克里图斯给亚历山大征战时的同伴利西马科斯读书。当他读到亚马逊女王的故事时,据说利西马科斯微笑着问:"当时我在哪里?"

库尔提斯把这个故事与亚历山大采用波斯服饰和宫廷礼仪联系在一起,他认为这是亚历山大完全失去自制力的标志。其他历史学家也在叙述这一点时提到亚历山大采用波斯服装,尽管,如我们所见,马其顿宫廷很可能在亚历山大统治前就已经受到波斯礼节的影响,而且亚历山大在埃及、巴比伦和苏萨就已经按照当地的期望行事了。

进军阿富汗

亚历山大最初的目标是阻止大流士三世在他的帝国东部地区建立新的势力。然而,到了公元前330年夏天,大流士因他的将军贝苏斯背叛而死,贝苏斯自封为王,登基为阿尔塔薛西斯五世。此时，亚历山大能够声称，作为合法的国王，他是在为大流士的死报仇。他的行军路线经过现在的伊朗北部到达阿富汗，在那里他向南绕过多山的内陆，然后沿着从坎大哈到喀布尔的现代公路路线，再向西北转向巴克特拉（今巴尔赫），越过奥克苏斯河，这条河现在是阿富汗和乌兹别克斯坦的边界，在亚历山大时代则是巴克特里亚和索格狄亚那的边界。此时，贝苏斯已经失去了波斯人的信任，波斯人背叛了他，把他交给了亚历山大。那是公元前329年的春天，但在亚历山大离开索格狄亚那和巴克特里亚之前，又经历了两年的战斗：他面临着后方的叛乱，以及塔奈斯河或雅克萨提斯河另一边的敌对邻居。

希腊和罗马的记载从马其顿军队和宫廷的角度呈现了这几年发生的故事。其中有小规模的战斗，城市被洗劫，亚历山大的随从不时出现麻烦。很少有人提到他们的对手。因此，人们很容易想象，亚历山大正面临着与19世纪英国、20世纪俄国和21世纪北约部队所面临的同样困难。历史学家乔治·格罗特在19世纪中叶提到了"巴克特里亚和索格狄亚那粗鲁但充满活力的部落"。小说家史蒂芬·帕斯菲尔德用当代美国士兵的语言和态度描述了亚历山大的步兵。但在亚历山大时代，这个地区并不是一片孤独的荒野。最近，一些可以追溯到阿尔塔薛西斯三世和亚历山大大帝统治时期的文件显示，这一地区在很大程度上融入了波斯帝国的其他部分。

这些文件包括写在皮革上的信件，其中几封是公元前353年至公元前348年期间由可能是巴克特里亚总督的阿赫瓦马兹达寄给另一位官员巴加万的。信中说，阿赫瓦马兹达必须处理有关巴加万行为的投诉，并让巴加万继续完成他布置的任务。

图6 公元前324年用阿拉姆语写成的一份来自巴克特里亚的文件,列出了在总督辖地分发的物资

两人的职责都延伸到了索格狄亚那和巴克特里亚。还有其他关于分发物资的信件和记录。其中一些记录在形式上与公元前5世纪在波斯波利斯发现的文件非常相似。所有的巴克特里亚文献都是用阿拉姆语书写的,到了公元前4世纪,阿拉姆语已经成为整个帝国的行政语言(图6)。很明显,亚历山大到达时,巴克特里亚是一个组织良好的地区,与帝国的其他部分融为一体。他在控制该地区时所面临的困难并不是因为该地区落入了纷争不休的军阀之手,而是在于它的管理可以被他的对手有效利用,尤其是叛军斯皮达迈尼斯,他把贝苏斯交给了亚历山大,然后又反过来反对他。

帝国边界

索格狄亚那和阿契美尼德帝国的北部边界是雅克萨提斯河,希腊人也称它为塔奈斯河,它被认为是亚洲和欧洲的分界线。对岸是斯基泰，阿里安和库尔提斯都有关于亚历山大如何渡河去对付对岸的斯基泰人的记载。这两人的说法截然不同，尽管都是以亚历山大的祭祀开始的，提到他意图渡河，且收到不祥的预兆。在阿里安的版本中，当随后的祭祀也出现不利的结果时，亚历山大决定无视这些预兆。他过了河，起初是成功的，但后来喝了一些受污染的水，得了重病，不得不返回河对岸。在库尔提斯的故事中，第二次祭祀是非常积极的；这些不祥的预兆预示着亚历山大的部下遭到了伏击，但尚未向亚历山大报告，不过渡过雅克萨提斯河的战役是会取得圆满成功的。这两个故事中的哪一个是正确的，我们无法确定，但这两个故事都表明亚历山大穿越雅克萨提斯河的象征意义是相当大的。

约公元前518年，大流士一世在该地区征战，后来大流士在贝希斯敦刻下了关于他的统治的记载，还描述了他如何穿越"海洋"与斯基泰人作战。大流士和他的继任者认为他们的帝国从一片海洋延伸到了另一片海洋，在这个概念中，他们认为雅克萨提斯河是一片北方的海洋。在穿越雅克萨提斯河时，亚历山大并没有试图占领其北部的领土，而是遵循了阿契美尼德先辈的做法，宣示他从一片海到另一片海的权力范围。而他后来在巴基斯坦的希发西斯河上的行动很可能也是为了达到同样的目的。

亚历山大最终得以解决索格狄亚那和巴克特里亚的事务。其间，他遵循阿契美尼德的惯例，通过婚姻将自己与当地波斯贵族联系起来。他的新婚妻子是罗克珊娜，是索格狄亚那领袖奥克夏特斯的女儿，亚历山大后来任命他为巴克特里亚南部地区总督。希腊和罗马历史学家似乎不愿意承认罗克珊娜的重要性，他们认为这场婚姻是爱情的结晶，而在库尔提斯的描述中，罗克珊娜的社会地位远不如亚历山大。然而，很明显，正是这段婚姻巩固了亚历山大对该地区的控制。之前讨论的巴克特里亚文献中有一份很长的物资清单，涵盖了亚历山大统治的第七年，也就是公元前324年的三个月，当时总督的政府运作顺利。在接下来的几个世纪里，巴克特里亚成为亚历山大帝国最繁荣的地区之一。

宫廷阴谋

除了军事活动的危险外，亚历山大还面临着来自宫廷内部的袭击。尽管这些威胁不是来自他的密友，但有两次，它们导致了高级朝臣的死亡。对于亚历山大和他的同时代人来说，阴谋是宫廷生活中不可避免的一部分。亚历山大的父亲曾被一名从前的护卫暗杀，仍不清楚这是否属于一个更大的阴谋。但对于后来的作者，尤其是那些生活在罗马皇帝统治下的作者来说，这些事件是一个机会，让他们思考朝臣在专制政体中应该如何行事。20世纪的独裁政权反过来又为现代学者撰写亚历山大宫廷的文章提供了范本，有时又为他们的叙述增添了一层时代错乱的色彩。

公元前330年秋，一场暗杀亚历山大的阴谋被揭发，涉及他的随行人员中的一些次要人物。据说亚历山大的一个同伴，帕曼纽的儿子菲罗塔斯，要么牵涉其中，要么知情不报。菲罗塔斯被判处死刑，亚历山大还下令杀死帕曼纽，当时他正留在米底的埃克巴坦那指挥。距离如此之远，我们不可能判定菲罗塔斯和帕曼纽是否有罪，他们的死亡很可能是由于王室成员为争夺国王恩宠而相互争斗所导致的。阿里安简单地叙述了菲罗塔斯的罪行。另一方面，库尔提斯对菲罗塔斯的审判做了非常详细的描述，包括审判双方的指控。他对事件的描述与提比略皇帝统治下的罗马元老院议员的审判记载有些相似，对此，塔西佗的《编年史》中有过描述。这种方式可以将早期统治者变得越来越专制和多疑的事件生动地呈现给罗马读者。

　　第二个阴谋导致了另一位朝臣的死亡。公元前327年春，大约是亚历山大与罗克珊娜结婚时，一群王室成员密谋暗杀他。在一次狩猎中，一个名叫赫莫拉尔斯的侍从遭到了羞辱。这些侍从很容易接近国王，所以他们可以很好地针对国王实施阴谋，这就是赫莫拉尔斯的计划。阴谋当天，亚历山大刚好熬夜，因此得救，第二天阴谋就被发现了。在随后的调查中，亚历山大的史官卡利斯提尼斯卷入了这起阴谋并被捕。和其他阴谋一样，我们不知道他是否有罪，在这起特殊的案件中，我们甚至不知道他遭遇了什么。阿里安说，当时在场的历史学家对他的命运给出了相互矛盾的描述：托勒密说他被处决了，而亚里斯多布鲁斯说他在关押期间死于疾病。在现存的记述中，卡利斯提尼斯死亡的真正原因是他反对亚历山大声称的神圣地位，并反对亚历山大要求他的同伴们跪拜；侍从的阴谋只是为逮捕他提供的借口。大多数现代学者都接受了这种说法，但是，正如我们所见，这种说法有其问题。

　　另一起重大的朝臣死亡事件发生在菲罗塔斯和卡利斯提尼斯被捕之间：亚历山大在一次醉酒的晚餐后用长矛刺死了他的同伴克雷图斯。克雷图斯是亚历山大父亲腓力手下的骑兵将领，并一直在亚历山大手下担任这一职务。据说公元前334年，他在格拉尼库斯河战役中救了亚历山大的命。公元前328年秋，亚历山大任命他为巴克特里亚总督。根据现存的所有叙述，在这之后不久的一次晚宴上，两人发生了争执。关于这场争论的实质内容，以及两人实际所做的事情的叙述并不一致，甚至可能不可靠，但当晚亚历山大确实杀死了克雷图斯。两个人可能都喝醉了。罗马道德家把克雷图斯和卡利斯提尼斯的死做了比较，认为这是国王杀害朋友的两个例子，而现存记载的作者则称两人都提出了相似的指控——尤其是亚历山大声称自己是宙斯的儿子，这是对他父亲腓力的侮辱。这是后来对亚历山大的标准指控，并给予克雷图斯的死更大的意义，因为他的死亡是由于亚历山大越来越意识不到自己终有一死。但竞争和野心是王室的特征，很有可能在这种氛围中，男人一旦接近酒精和武器最能解释当时发生了什么。

进入印度河流域

亚历山大从阿富汗向东南行进，穿过兴都库什山脉，进入印度河流域北部，即现在的巴基斯坦。根据希罗多德《历史》一书的记载，大流士一世曾在这个地区征战，他所说的印度河以西的部分地区曾向波斯国王进贡。在大流士一世和亚历山大统治期间，人们对该地区了解不多，因此不清楚后来的阿契美尼德国王的统治范围向东延伸了多远，尽管据阿里安记载，在高加米拉战役中，一支与巴克特里亚接壤的印度人小分队曾与巴克特里亚人并肩作战。对于希腊和罗马的历史学家来说，这无论如何都不是一个重要的问题。他们的叙述更多地集中在亚历山大向东远行的想法上，而不是他的英雄前辈们的。亚力山大占领了一座貌似坚不可摧的堡垒,奥尔努斯岩山,据说连赫拉克勒斯都无法攻破这座堡垒,他和他的同伴们曾在尼萨城待过一段时间,狄俄尼索斯也曾造访过尼萨城,那里有常春藤(一种与酒神特别相关的植物)的存在就证明了这一点,这显然是在该地区其他地方找不到的。

四条主要支流从喜马拉雅山流下,从西流入印度河:从西到东依次为海达斯佩斯河(今杰赫勒姆河)、阿塞西尼斯河(今奇纳布河)、海德拉奥特斯河(今拉维河)和希发西斯河(今比阿斯河)。这些河流之间的领土由一些相互敌对的印度王公控制。亚历山大在这里采取了与在帝国其他地区不同的控制模式。他没有任命总督和地方军事指挥官,而是任命那些同意接受他权威的王公担任统治者。第一个这样的重要统治者是塔克西莱斯,他的领土位于印度河和海达斯佩斯河之间。因此,亚历山大面临着塔克西莱斯的邻居波鲁斯的反对,波鲁斯位于海达斯佩斯河的东侧。

亚历山大在快速渡河之后击败了波鲁斯,这是他征战亚洲的第四次也是最后一次重大战役。为了纪念胜利,人们铸造了一系列大银币或奖章,被称为"波鲁斯德卡德拉克马"或"大象奖章",奖章一面绘着一名骑士正在独自攻击两个骑着大象的高个子骑兵,其中一个骑兵正朝骑士投掷长矛,一般认为这指代的是亚历山大和波鲁斯,另一边是亚历山大本人,全副武装,手控雷电,头戴有胜利之翼的花环(图7)。这些特征可能与"不可战胜的神"这一头衔有关,这是雅典人在两年后亚历山大从这场战役归来时授予他的称号。这些硬币或奖章可能是颁发给亚历山大的士兵作为他们征战的奖励的。他们向亚历山大展示了他心目中的军队,无所不能,所向披靡。希腊城市也会以同样的方式

图7 亚历山大为庆祝他在印度战役中的胜利而发行的硬币或奖章。正面是一个骑士正在攻击骑在大象背上的武士,可能代表亚历山大和波鲁斯。反面是身穿盔甲的亚历山大手持雷电,加冕胜利

认可他的成功。但这些硬币不应被视为亚历山大在声称自己拥有任何"神圣地位"。

亚历山大在战后对波鲁斯的处理成了热门话题,尤其是在一系列歌剧中十分流行,这些歌剧使用的是18世纪意大利诗人梅塔斯塔西奥的剧本。1941年苏赫拉布·莫迪导演的《昔干答儿》是第一部关于亚历山大的完整电影,电影中也有相关的情节。波鲁斯宣誓效忠亚历山大,亚历山大恢复了他的地位,甚至扩大了他的领土面积。

折返?

此后,亚历山大继续向东越过亚辛河和海德拉奥特斯河,一直到希发西斯河,这里发生的事情成为亚历山大最常被讲述的故事之一。根据传说,在希发西斯河岸边,亚历山大的士兵们最终拒绝继续跟随他。据说亚历山大把自己关在帐篷里,拒绝见任何人,然后说他会一个人去。但即使这样也不能使他的士兵

改变主意,他还是顺从他们的意愿,折返了。这个故事可以在现存的所有记载中找到,因此它的真实性很少受到怀疑,但这种一致性证明的是,这个故事在现存最早的叙事形成之前就已经流传开来了:这是一个令人难忘的故事,因此任何后来的叙述者都无法忽视它。我们有充分的理由认为这个故事是虚构的。从海达斯佩斯河向东进军之前,亚历山大已经下令建造一支运输船舰队,带领他的军队顺流而下,到达下游。希发西斯河很可能被认为是波斯帝国与印度的边界,就像雅克萨提斯河是索格狄亚那的北部边界一样。事情可能是这样的:亚历山大打算越过希发西斯河来维护自己的权威,然后再回到西岸,就像他于统治初期在雅克萨提斯河和多瑙河所做的那样。如果是这样的话,那么根据托勒密的说法,正如阿里安所记载的,是不祥的预兆阻止了他的前行,而不是他的士兵。亚历山大在帝国东部的活动更有意义,因为他巩固了对从大流士三世手中赢得的领土的统治,而不是无休止地寻求新的征服。亚历山大历史的记述者对阿契美尼德帝国的现有疆界并不感兴趣,因此他们认为亚历山大的一举一动都是为了赢得新的领土,但只有亚历山大本人才知道得更清楚。到达亚历山大声称的领土东部边缘后,他准备转向南方,向大海进军。他还不想折返回家。

到达印度洋

关于亚历山大穿过印度河流域到达印度洋的故事,我们完全依赖于亚历山大历史学家的记载。希腊人或印度人的铭文都没有保存下来,大河不断变化的河道抹去了可能存在的任何考古遗迹。亚历山大沿着海达斯佩斯河而下,他的军队沿着河两岸齐头并进。他的目的似乎是，通过确认那些地方统治者承认他的主权，并大力反对那些抵制他的人，来维护自己的权威。这与他在其他地方的政策没有什么不同，但现代学者倾向于将这一阶段的行动描述为特别暴力和具有破坏性的。当然，亚历山大确实在一些地方遇到了抵抗，他最严重的一次受伤是在围攻旁遮普南部的一座城市的时候。在旁遮普南部，虽然他的军队在印度河东侧的领土上行军，必要时还进行战斗，但亚历山大并不关心在这片领土建立直接统治，他可能跟大流士一世一样，把这条河作为他帝国的东部边界。事实证明，这是亚历山大帝国最早被他人占领的地区之一。据普鲁塔克记载，在旁遮普，一位年轻的印度王公（普鲁塔克称他为安德罗科都斯）拜访了亚历山大的宫廷。这位王公就是旃陀罗笈多·孔雀，他在公元前322年左右掌权，并迅速控制了印度北部从恒河三角洲到印度河的大部分地区。到他公元前298年退位时，孔雀王朝已经囊括了南亚的大部分地区，包括印度河西岸的各邦国。

很明显，对亚历山大来说，他到达印度洋标志着他战役的成功结束，他通过在海上向众神献祭来庆祝他的胜利。但他征战的最后阶段成为他所有行军中最声名狼藉，也可能是最被误解的部分。

格德罗西亚沙漠

亚历山大从旁遮普带了一支舰队到印度洋，他打算派这支舰队沿着波斯湾向上到达底格里斯河和幼发拉底河的河口，再从那里逆流而上到巴比伦。拥有一条从美索不达米亚几乎到阿富汗的海军航线将具有巨大的价值，但它依赖于舰队沿着基本不适宜居住的伊朗南部海岸航行时得到补给。正是由于这个原因，亚历山大率领一支陆军穿过伊朗南部的格德罗西亚地区，从印度河三角洲返回帕萨尔加德。根据阿里安的描述，亚历山大的目的是确保舰队在海湾航行时有淡水和粮食供应。毫无疑问，这是一项艰巨的任务，因为这片土地大部分是沙漠，而且海岸上几乎没有好的停泊点。这次陆地远征花了两个月的时间，但可以说是成功的，因为在克里特指挥官尼阿库斯的领导下，舰队顺利地完成了它的旅程。

亚历山大时代之后的古代作者将穿越格德罗西亚的行军形容成了一场源于亚历山大的傲慢和愚蠢的灾难。在冷静地讲述了亚历山大如何克服重重困难实现自己的目标后，阿里安叙述了一系列关于沙漠之旅的艰难故事，他在主要资料中没有找到这些故事，但肯定地认为这些故事"值得一提，而且并非完全不可信"。普鲁塔克声称，亚历山大在格德罗西亚沙漠中失去了四分之三的军队，尽管他带进格德罗西亚的军队远远少于一半。现代学者可能已经准备好相信这些可怕的故事了，甚至认为穿越沙漠的行军是亚历山大在报复他的士兵，因为他们迫使亚历山大在希发西斯河折返。这不是古代作家的想法。阿里安称，亚历山大试图超越他的著名前辈，居鲁士大帝和传说中的巴比伦女王塞米拉米斯，他们都穿过了沙漠，失去了几乎所有的军队。我们应该认识到，在沙漠之旅的故事中，人们对亚历山大的兴趣不是他的愚蠢，而是他超人的耐力。

一旦他率领军队走出沙漠，道路首先通向帕萨尔加德和波斯波利斯，然后通往苏萨和埃克巴坦那，直到亚历山大人生的最后一章在通往巴比伦的道路上开启。

第八章

终有一死：亚历山大在巴比伦

亚历山大生命的最后阶段是在巴比伦度过的。他在征战初期曾在那里待过一段时间，这是他造访的第一个阿契美尼德王室中心。我们已经看到了巴比伦天文志的片段，其中记载了亚历山大在高加米拉战役中的胜利，并称他为"世界之王"。这份天文志还记录了他与巴比伦总督的谈判，他承诺要恢复马杜克神的埃萨吉拉神庙，以及他于公元前331年10月20日进入巴比伦城。亚历山大在将近八年后，也就是公元前323年春天，回到了巴比伦，他就是在那里去世的。巴比伦文献可以说明亚历山大在这座城市中的行为以及他与学者-祭司关系的重要方面。文献还可以帮助我们理解希腊和罗马一些令人费解的故事。

巴比伦学者

编撰天文志的学者也负责撰写巴比伦王家编年史。像天文志一样，它记录了重要的历史事件，但没有对其进行评论，因此它们不同于王家铭文，王家铭文是为公共消费设计的，强调国王的美德和权力。编年史的顺序始于那布·那西尔国王（公元前747—前734在位）即位，并至少延续到公元前2世纪后期。亚历山大在位的八年，虽然在巴比伦历史上很重要，但在这种背景下，也只是短暂的一段时间。

除了记录当下，巴比伦学者还根据过去的事件创作了指导作品。其中包括《征兆结集》，它列出了天体事件，特别是日食，并指出了它们预示着什么。这一切的目的都是要扶持国王，使他的统治长久，巴比伦城也能因此受益。因此，除了记录天体事件和确定对国王的潜在威胁外，学者-祭司还会建议国王采取什么行动来避免预测到的危险。

亚历山大进入巴比伦，公元前331年

亚历山大在高加米拉获胜后进入巴比伦时，是在追随先前胜利的新统治者的路线，包括亚述的萨尔贡二世（公元前722—前705在位）和波斯的居鲁士大帝。库尔提斯对亚历山大进入巴比伦的记载遵循了这些早期国王的官方文件中的模式。在描述中，这座城市的人民欢欣鼓舞，而新国王则向诸神献祭，并承诺恢复他们的庙宇。恢复庙宇的承诺并不一定表明庙宇之前被破坏了，砖砌的大型建筑需要不断修缮，国王可以改善它们，保持它们屹立不倒：国王对城市结构的关心体现了他的美德。阿里安声称薛西斯摧毁了巴比伦神庙，但在任何巴比伦文献中都没有提到这一点。

所有现存的故事都没有提到亚历山大在巴比伦加冕，但他在到达巴比伦的时候就已被承认为国王，并且在当时和后来的巴比伦文献中也是这样描述的。普鲁塔克称，亚历山大与巴比

伦预言家联系紧密,这表明他正陷入迷信之中,但这是他作为国王的必然结果,城市的宗教-行政组织将被派去为他提供建议和支持。这一次,他没有在巴比伦停留太久,而是前往位于苏萨和波斯波利斯的其他波斯王室中心。但亚历山大将在他生命的最后时期回到巴比伦,他要再一次听从巴比伦祭司的指引。

公元前331年9月20日,巴比伦历法Ulūlu月的第13天,也就是高加米拉战役前11天,发生了一次月食。土星在天空中,木星已经落下。这记录在上文所述的天文志里,并且在现存的亚历山大史家记载中提到过。《征兆结集》中解释了那天发生的日食的意义,它不仅预示着现任国王的死亡,而且还预示着他的儿子将无法继承他的王位,一位新的统治者将从西方而来,统治8年。公元前331年9月日食之后的那场战争确实导致大流士统治的结束,以及之后他生命的结束。他的继任者确实是一位来自西方的统治者,亚历山大。但公元前323年10月将标志着亚历山大8年统治的结束。除非命运可以避免,否则亚历山大的未来将一片暗淡。

亚历山大进入巴比伦,公元前323年

公元前323年年底,亚历山大从印度战役中归来。次年,亚历山大在米底的埃克巴坦那度过了夏天,秋冬在扎格罗斯山脉北部与科萨人展开了斗争,并于公元前323年春天前往巴比伦。据阿里安和狄奥多罗斯所述,巴比伦祭司劝阻他不要进入城市,理由是这对他很危险。他们可能受到了前一个5月发生的月食和日食的影响。那一天月食的意义是"世界之王将死,他的王朝

将终结"。这类预测本应在100天内实现,但偶尔也会在稍后生效。公元前323年4月和5月,祭司们也很有可能期待着日食的出现,尽管这些日食最后都没有显现。阿里安说,祭司建议亚历山大不要从西边进入这座城市,他补充说,据当时与亚历山大在一起的亚里斯多布鲁斯的说法,国王试图听从这一建议,但因为地面被水和沼泽淹没,他无法绕过这座城市。在涉及不幸预言的记述中,主人公试图避免厄运,却被不可抗力所阻止,这种情况是很常见的,阿里安显然意识到了这个故事给出的信息,但这并不意味着这不是一个基本准确的叙述。

要么是在亚历山大不听劝告进入巴比伦之后,要么在他等待进城的时候,祭司很可能又举行了另一个仪式来保护他免遭厄运。这就是"代王仪式",这是从亚述文献中得知的。这个仪式包括国王临时退位,通常为100天,由罪犯或疯子代替他成为国王。他们的想法是,任何不幸都会降落在替代国王,而不是真正的国王身上。一旦预测的风险期结束,替代者将被处决,真正的国王将恢复他的统治。巴比伦文献中没有提到这一仪式,但希腊作家金嘴狄翁,普鲁塔克的同时代人,曾提到这一仪式,他将其与波斯习俗混淆了。巴比伦人可能从亚述人手中继承了这一仪式,并在波斯时期及后期经常使用。在狄奥多罗斯、普鲁塔克和阿里安的叙述中,都有一个疯子或狂人坐在王座上,穿着亚历山大的礼服,戴着他的王冠。在故事中,这被认为是亚历山大即将死亡的预兆,而且有人认为这个疯子是自愿登上王位的。然而,它与代王仪式太过相似,不可能是巧合,因此,这或许可以作为证据,证明亚历山大在公元前323年举行过这种仪式。不过,他显然在6月前又回到了王位上。

死 亡

　　普鲁塔克和阿里安都详细描述了亚历山大生命中的最后几天。他们依据的是所谓的"王室日志",他们认为这上面真实记录了亚历山大的日常活动。虽然这样记录的存在也并非不可能,但大多数学者怀疑,公元2世纪的作家所能得到的东西与它们能有多大的关系。根据这些日志的记载,普鲁塔克和阿里安描述了亚历山大如何患上热病,在生命的最后几天,他主要躺在床榻上,主持作为国王所要求的宗教仪式,并向他的军官们下达入侵阿拉伯计划的指示。他的身体逐渐衰弱,在他死前的一段时间甚至失去了说话的能力。所有这些都是可信的。虽然亚历山大年仅32岁,但他曾多次受伤,包括在旁遮普的一次胸部严重受伤。他还大量饮酒。他的同伴赫费斯提翁上一年在埃克巴坦那也死于类似情况,没有被谋杀的嫌疑。

　　然而,不可避免的是,在他死后的几年内,有关亚历山大被毒死的故事开始流传。大多数亚历山大史家的记载称,亚历山大在希腊的摄政王安提帕特组织了这次暗杀,他把自己的儿子卡桑德和伊奥拉斯送到巴比伦,带着亚里士多德提供的毒药。这个故事极有可能是为了在亚历山大死后立即爆发的继任者冲突中破坏安提帕特和卡桑德的声誉而编造的。亚历山大大帝的母亲奥林匹娅斯为了保护孙子,罗克珊娜的幼子亚历山大四世的利益,与安提帕特和卡桑德对立,可能就是这个故事的来源。

　　然而,流传最广的关于亚历山大之死的故事是他所谓的临终遗言。阿里安根据所谓的"王室日志"记载,亚历山大在去世前几天失去了说话的能力，但因为这个故事太广为人知而不可忽视，他还指出，一些作者说，亚历山大的同伴问他把王国留给谁，亚历山大的回答是"给最强的人"。亚历山大死后的几年里发生的事件使得这种反应似乎具有预见性。在接下来的几十年里，亚历山大的将军们互相争斗，试图控制整个帝国，或者最终为自己开辟王国。即使他死了，亚历山大仍然是这场冲突的一部分。正如我们所见，他的遗体被送回马其顿，准备埋葬在维尔吉纳的王陵中，后来却被转移到埃及，托勒密是埃及的第一个总督，后来又成为埃及的法老，他利用亚历山大的遗体使自己的统治合法化。

亚历山大建立的帝国甚至在他的遗体尚未妥善埋葬之前就已开始瓦解。由于本书的篇幅限制，无法继续讲述接下来几年的故事，不过这些故事早在之前就多次被讲述了。我们透过支离破碎的当代证据，透过后来历史传统的扭曲镜头，得以窥探历史上的亚历山大，剩下的就是看看他是如何在现代世界的想象中达到他所占据的位置的。

第九章

亚历山大死后

本书试图以亚历山大时代的证据为基础,展示亚历山大大帝及其世界。这通常意味着要挑战人们对他行为的普遍看法,比如他怎么做,为什么要这样做,甚至要质疑有些事情是否真的是他所为。但是,如果人们长期以来对亚历山大的看法是不可靠的或错误的,那么这些看法最初是从何而来的呢?在最后一章中,我们将探讨亚历山大的身后事,以及亚历山大的一些形象是如何在大众的想象中产生的。

罗马的亚历山大效仿者:尤利乌斯·恺撒及其他

公元前45年,罗马元老院投票决定在罗马奎里努斯神庙中竖立一尊尤利乌斯·恺撒的雕像,其头衔是 Deus Invictus("不可战胜的神")。恺撒于次年被暗杀,但此时他仍是罗马的独裁者,在罗马拥有绝对的政治权力。"不可战胜的神"(希腊语 Theos Aniketos)这一头衔与雅典人在公元前324年投票给亚历山大雕像的名称相同,讽刺的是,这也发生在亚历山大去世的前一年。名称的选择不太可能是巧合。在为这座雕像投票表决时，著名政治家（有时也是哲学家）西塞罗正试图给恺撒写一封建议信，建议他如何统治，故意模仿亚历山大旧日的导师亚里士多德写给他的信。最后，西塞罗放弃了这个想法，他在给朋友阿提克斯的一封信中写道："他的气质和自制力都是最好的，但即使是亚里士多德的学生，一旦被称为国王，也会变得傲慢、残忍和放纵。"这很符合罗马共和国的道德家的想法，他们反对君主制，认为亚历山大夺取大流士的王位是走向暴政的开始。

尤利乌斯·恺撒和亚历山大这两位他们的时代最伟大的军事人物之间的相似之处很容易被勾画出来。普鲁塔克的《亚历山大传》与《恺撒传》相互映照，还有几位作家讲述，在恺撒的事业起飞之前，他曾在西班牙看到了一尊亚历山大的雕像，并为自己在亚历山大去世的年龄取得的成就如此之小而哭泣。他并不是唯一一个将亚历山大视为潜在模范的罗马人。他同时代的老对手庞培为罗马吞并了地中海东部的领土，而这些领土曾经是亚历山大帝国的一部分，庞培采用了 Magnus 这个家族名，意为"伟大的"，他的雕像发型还模仿了亚历山大。所以亚历山大可以为雄心勃勃的人提供一个榜样。庞培出生时，在庞贝城委托制作亚历山大镶嵌画的人（见引言中的图1）大概也认为亚历山大是一个值得放在家中公共场所的人物。其含义是，来访者可能会把亚历山大的美德与主人自己的美德联系起来。

公元前44年2月15日，在牧神节上，恺撒的副官马克·安东尼向他献上一顶王冠，恺撒拒绝了。当时的一些人怀疑，恺撒安排这次的活动似乎是为了要求国王的头衔，就仿佛要顺应民众的要求；另一些人则解释说，他把王冠放在他旁边的王座上，是要求大家将他作为神来崇拜，因为在罗马游行中，众神通常以宝座上的象征物来代表。这两种解释很可能是同时存在的。在这一时期，王权被认为是波斯和希腊化的东方特征，罗马人认为，在这一地区，国王被当作神来崇拜。不管到底发生了什么，人们认为，这一王冠事件是一个月后恺撒被自称捍卫共和国的人暗杀的导火索。正是在这次暗杀事件之后的几年里，关于亚历山大生平最早的叙事作品，狄奥多罗斯《历史丛书》第17卷，诞生了。而关于恺撒生死的记忆一定影响了他和他的读者解读亚历山大生平的方式。它还影响了狄奥多罗斯同时代的庞培乌斯·特洛格斯，他的历史记录现在以缩略的形式保存下来，一个约300年后由查士丁创作的缩略版本。

恺撒是在政治混乱和内战时期掌权的，内战导致了罗马共和国的崩溃。他的养子奥古斯都结束了战争，声称要恢复对元老院和罗马人民的统治，并确立自己为第一位罗马皇帝。对于奥古斯都和他的继任者来说，如何调和对单一领袖的需要与罗马共和制的传统是一个持续的问题，这是我们在塔西佗、苏维托尼乌斯以及卡西乌斯·狄奥的叙事中发现的一个潜在主题。塔西佗和苏维托尼乌斯与普鲁塔克和阿里安在同一时期进行创作，而卡西乌斯·狄奥则创作于公元3世纪早期。据记载，有些皇帝并不太成功，尤其是公元37年即位的卡利古拉。据说卡利古拉曾像他之前的恺撒和奥古斯都一样，在亚历山大港参观亚历山大大帝的陵墓时拿起亚历山大的胸甲来穿。据说他还要求罗马元老院的元老们跪倒在他面前，伸出脚而不是手，让他们亲吻。库尔提斯对亚历山大的总体负面描述可能部分受到了对卡利古拉的记忆和描绘的影响：库尔提斯要么是在卡利古拉的继任者克劳狄乌斯统治时期，要么是在几十年后韦斯巴芗统治时期进行的创作。

普鲁塔克和阿里安写作时，在成功的统治者图拉真皇帝（公元98—117在位）和哈德良皇帝（公元117—138在位）的统治下，人们已经接受了罗马帝国是一个专制政体。亚历山大被认为是正确的王权典范：这些作家强调他的智慧和自制力，同时警告仿效东方统治者习惯的潜在危险。两位皇帝都曾跟随亚历山大的脚步，率领军队越过幼发拉底河进入美索不达米亚，因此当时的作家把亚历山大作为军事成功的象征和对奢侈无度的危险警告是十分恰当的。

古代历史叙事中流传下来的亚历山大是在特定的环境下成长起来的。他是由罗马作家（虽然其中有几个是用希腊语写作的）为罗马读者创作出来的。罗马人关心的是如何成为统治者，以及如何在独裁统治下作为一个主体生活，这是罗马历史记录的中心主题，同样也出现在亚历山大大帝的历史记录中，他们对东方邻国的怀疑和敌意也是如此。最近，这些担忧有时会再次出现：20世纪上半叶欧洲的独裁统治时期，以及"9·11"事件后"文明冲突"观念的重生，都对亚历山大研究产生了影响，罗马人的偏见似乎已经预先呼应了20世纪和21世纪的政治。

中世纪的亚历山大

今天，如果我们想了解亚历山大，我们会向罗马时期的亚历山大史家寻求信息。然而，在亚历山大死后到现在的大部分时间里，还有另一种更为突出的故事传说。乔叟在《僧侣的故事》

中简要介绍了亚历山大的功绩,并指出:

> 艾莉莎恩德的故事广为流传,
> 每一个谨慎的人
> 都能从他手中分得一份财产。

僧侣所指的故事被称为《传奇》,讲述了亚历山大的生平,起源于公元前3世纪的埃及,并在随后的几个世纪中不断发展,翻译成多种语言,从冰岛到印度都有它的译本。

我们能读到的最早版本的《传奇》来自公元3世纪。它讲述了亚历山大的生平,其中的虚构元素在后来的版本中变得更加夸张。亚历山大据说是埃及最后一位法老内克塔内布的儿子,内克塔内布也是一位魔术师,他来到腓力的宫廷,以蛇的形态伪装成阿蒙神,引诱奥林匹娅斯。内克塔内布是亚历山大的第一个导师,但亚历山大发现他是自己的父亲后就杀了他。在后来的波斯传说中,如约公元1000年的《列王纪》中所记载,亚历山大变成了伊斯坎达尔,名义上是腓力的儿子,但实际上是波斯国王达拉卜的儿子,因此是他的对手达拉(大流士三世)同父异母的兄弟。这些不同的亲子关系使亚历山大与他所统治的王国更加紧密地联系在一起。他早年生活中的其他元素则被赋予了更多幻想色彩:例如在《传奇》中,他最喜欢的马比塞弗勒斯不仅除了亚历山大外谁也驯服不了,而且还吃人。另一个故事讲述了年轻的亚历山大在开始他的征战之前乔装去刺探波斯国王的宫廷。7世纪阿拉伯征服之后的故事版本中,据说亚历山大乔装去了信奉伊斯兰教的安达卢西亚的宫廷,王后立刻识破了他的伪装。

在亚历山大功绩中记载的许多事件在《传奇》中都有所描述，尽管顺序不同。书中详细描述了亚历山大对提尔的围攻。后来的版本包括了更多的神奇故事：亚历山大坐着狮鹫拉的战车飞到了空中，然后坐着玻璃潜水钟潜入大海深处；他去了天堂，并预言了自己的死亡。随着时间的推移，《传奇》中的故事越来越多地讲述亚历山大对智慧的追求，而在中世纪西欧流传下来的版本中，亚历山大成为骑士精神和善良的象征。

正是通过《传奇》中的故事，亚历山大，以亚历山大大帝（o Megalexandros）之名，在古典历史和神话知识遗失的几个世纪里，继续在希腊广为人知。1670年，《传奇》的早期现代希腊语版本，《亚历山大大帝之书》在威尼斯出版，此后一直在发行。亚历山大也成为卡拉吉奥兹皮影戏中的一个角色，这在古典时代的人物中是独一无二的。这种流行的娱乐形式源于奥斯曼土耳其的传统，在19世纪发展出了希腊特色，并在20世纪上半叶达到了流行顶峰。亚历山大大帝出现在许多剧本中，最有名的是在《亚历山大大帝和被诅咒的蛇》中，剧中随着他的性格发展，亚历山大大帝成为一个勇于纠正错误的战士，他杀死了一条威胁整个王国的龙：他已经成为圣乔治的一个变体。

在希腊流行文化中，亚历山大扮演了一个很大程度上被基督教化了的武士英雄的角色，这可能是现代希腊对亚历山大形象的应用反应强烈的部分原因。在希腊和（前南斯拉夫的）马其顿共和国之间的关系中，这是一个特别的问题。2006年，马其顿共和国决定以亚历山大大帝的名字命名斯科普里机场，并在机场上竖立了一座巨大的亚历山大大帝骑马雕像，这一决定引发了希腊政府的抗议。

亚历山大、启蒙运动和帝国

《传奇》中具有骑士精神的亚历山大很适合中世纪的世界，也很适合像路易十四和叶卡捷琳娜大帝这样的专制君主的宫廷。新的亚历山大出现在17世纪末到19世纪初的启蒙运动时期。最初在法国，后来在苏格兰和英格兰，最终在德国和其他地方，哲学家和历史学家在研究古代历史，尤其是亚历山大大帝时，引入了一种更具批判性的方法。希腊和拉丁语的亚历山大史家著作都有了新的版本和译本，其可靠性受到了严格的审查。与此同时，亚历山大被重新视为模范统治者。一些作家选择强调他的负面特征，他的残酷，尤其是他对史官卡利斯提尼斯等学者的迫害。但这是欧洲向海外扩张的时期，对其他人来说，亚历山大的征战被视为给懒惰和不变的东方带来了活跃与进步的欧洲文明。对于这些作家来说，大流士三世的帝国和他们同时代的奥斯曼帝国实际上没有什么区别。在伏尔泰的一些文章和孟德斯鸠男爵《论法的精神》中也可以发现对亚历山大最积极的评价：他们认为亚历山大最大的成就是通过他的城市基础和他组织的海上航行，打开了东方的贸易和商业。

对于英格兰和苏格兰的作家来说，英国在独立战争中失去美洲殖民地，是重新研究古希腊历史的动力。1786年，苏格兰历史学家约翰·吉利斯出版了两卷本的《古希腊历史、殖民地和征战》。这本献给国王乔治三世的书是针对美国发生的事件而写的，其明确意图是展示民主或共和主义的危险以及君主立宪制的优越性。两年前，英国保守党议员威廉·米特福德出版了《希腊史》八卷本的第一卷。他出版最后一卷时，法国大革命已经发生了，这给人们提供了一个更加清晰的教训，让人们认识不受约束的人民统治的危险。对于吉利斯和米特福德来说，民主的雅典在公元前5世纪就被斯巴达国王打败，在公元前4世纪又被腓力国王统治下的马其顿打败，这代表了民主的一切都是错误的，相比之下，亚历山大的职业生涯是君主制所能做到的最好的例子。对吉利斯来说，亚历山大是"一个非凡的人，他的天才可能改变并改善了古代世界的状态"。

亚历山大的"文明使命"是一个用来证明英国介入印度的主题，在失去美国领土后，印度成为殖民扩张的主要焦点。帝国主义的拥护者仿效早期法国作家，把英国人描绘成亚历山大的继承人，把欧洲的活力和文明带到了无生气的亚洲。但亚历山大的遗产也可能被其他人继承。亚历山大·伯恩斯爵士是英国驻喀布尔的政治代理人，直到1841年他被暗杀，此后不久英国军队被赶出喀布尔，喀布尔在第一次英阿战争（1839—1842）结束时被摧毁。亚历山大·伯恩斯爵士曾于19世纪30年代在中亚到处游历。他随身带着亚历山大历史学家的著作，去寻找他们提到的遗址。但他也指出，在中亚的部分地区，亚历山大被认为是一位伊斯兰教先知，并在他的回忆录中提到，当地统治者（主动）声称自己是亚历山大的直系后裔。亚历山大的这些思想很可能是通过波斯语版本的《传奇》传播出来的。

英雄抑或恶徒

也许这一时期对亚历山大的研究中最有影响力的要数德国历史学家约翰·古斯塔夫·德罗伊森的研究，其《亚历山大大帝史》于1833年出版（从未被译为英文）。德罗伊森曾在柏林学习，受到哲学家黑格尔和地理学家亚历山大·冯·洪堡的影响。德国的启蒙学者将德国与古希腊紧密联系在一起，尤其是因为这两个国家都是由许多被大国包围的小国组成的。德罗伊森支持德国的统一事业，他笔下的亚历山大也是一个统一者，不仅统一了交战的希腊城邦，而且统一了整个西亚。在他看来，亚历山大死后的这段时期，直到当时还被视为希腊世界的衰落时期，实际上是一个胜利的时期，因为希腊文化在他的军队经过的地区蓬勃发展。此外，德罗伊森认为，亚历山大欢迎来自不同文化的人进入他的宫廷，鼓励他们思考共同的东西，包括单一神的想法，因此，他也许为基督教铺平了道路。

政治哲学家约翰·斯图尔特·密尔的朋友，激进的议员乔治·格罗特在他广受欢迎的《希腊史》12卷中，对亚历山大对文明的贡献没有那么正面的描述。在格罗特看来，亚历山大代表了专制和帝国主义最糟糕的一面：

> 只要我们能够大胆地预测亚历山大的未来，我们就看不到任何前景，除了多年来不断的侵略和征服，直到他横越并征服了全世界，征战才有可能结束……现在，这样一个无边无际、异类纷呈的帝国，怎么能够好好管理，对臣民有利呢？这很难证明。

现代关于亚历山大的争论始于启蒙运动时期。历史学家仍在试图判断他是一个浪漫的英雄还是一个嗜血的暴君，以及他的征战是否利大于弊。这是因为，在很大程度上，这些论据是基于我们在本章开始时所考虑的亚历山大史家的有限文集。在这本通识读本的结尾,我无意对亚历山大或他的遗产提出我自己的看法。现存的叙述可以解释为支持各种评价。然而,我的目的是要表明,这些说法不一定足够可靠,我们根本无法利用它们得出任何明确的结论。正如我们所见,亚历山大时代的材料,如希腊和埃及铭文,雅典政治家的演说,巴比伦学者-祭司的日志,可以提供一些有限的替代视角。在问出"我们应该如何看待亚历山大大帝"这个问题之前,我们也许应该问,"他的同时代人如何看待亚历山大大帝"。这个问题还没有得到令人信服的回答,但本书是朝着这个方向的一个开始。

索 引

（条目后的数字为原书页码，见本书边码）

A

Acesines River 阿塞西尼斯河 88, 89

Achaemenid empire 阿契美尼德帝国 3, 9, 10—17, 22, 30, 32, 40, 43, 55, 56, 69, 71—73, 82, 83, 84, 87, 90

Achilles 阿喀琉斯 36, 75

Aegae 埃盖 17, 28, 29, 30

Aegean 爱琴海
  Area 爱琴海地区 12, 13, 15, 16, 21, 61, 74
  sea 爱琴海 10, 11, 22, 43, 47, 49

Aeschines (Athenian orator) 埃斯基涅斯（雅典演说家）25, 26

Aeschylus (Athenian playwright) 埃斯库罗斯（雅典剧作家）52

Afghanistan 阿富汗 3, 32, 58—59, 80, 82, 87, 92

Africa 阿非利加 11, 68

Agis III (king of Sparta) 阿基斯三世（斯巴达国王）50, 54

Ahura Mazda 阿胡拉·马兹达 12

Ai-Khanoum 阿伊-哈努姆 59

Akhvamazda (satrap of Bactria) 阿赫瓦马兹达（巴克特里亚总督）82

Akkadian 阿卡德帝国 6

Alexander I Philhellene (king of Macedon) 亚历山大一世，"爱希腊者"（马其顿国王）10, 17, 18

Alexander II (king of Macedon) 亚历山大二世（马其顿国王）18, 25, 26

Alexander III (Alexander the Great) 亚历山大三世（亚历山大大帝）passim

Alexander IV (son of Alexander the Great) 亚历山大四世（亚历山大大帝之子）28, 98

Alexander of Epirus (uncle and brother-in-law of Alexander the Great) 伊庇鲁斯的亚历山大（亚历山大大帝的舅舅和妹夫）26, 30

Alexander Mosaic 亚历山大镶嵌画 1, 3, 5, 100

Alexander Romance《亚历山大传奇》103—104, 105

Alexandreia (festival) 亚历山德里亚（节日）49

Alexandria (in Egypt) 亚历山大港（埃及）57—60, 101

Alexandria-on-the-Oxus 奥克苏斯河畔亚历山大城 59

Alexandria Troas 亚历山大·特洛阿德 59

Amasis (king of Egypt) 雅赫摩斯（埃及法老）60, 61

Amazons 亚马逊人 81

America 美国 105, 106

Ammon (*or* Hammon) 阿蒙（或哈蒙）61, 63, 103
  参见 Amun

Amphipolis 安菲波利斯 20, 25

Amphissa 安飞沙城 22

Amun 阿蒙 7, 27, 57, 61, 62, 65, 66, 67
  oracle of 阿蒙神谕 60—64

Amyntas I (king of Macedon) 阿敏

塔斯一世（马其顿国王）10, 13, 17
Amyntas III (king of Macedon) 阿敏塔斯三世（马其顿国王）18, 19, 25, 26
Anatolia 安纳托利亚 11, 15, 26, 32, 40
Andalusia 安达卢西亚 103
Andracottus 安德罗科都斯 *see* Chandragupta Maurya 见旃陀罗笈多·孔雀
Anshan 安善 10
Antigonus the One-Eyed (Macedonian commander) 独眼安提柯（马其顿统帅）59
Antipater (regent of Greece) 安提帕特（希腊摄政王）28, 50, 97, 98
Aornus 奥尔努斯 88
Apollo 阿波罗 22, 50
Appian (historian) 阿庇安（历史学家）68
Arabs, Arabia 阿拉伯 97, 103
Aramaic 阿拉姆语 83
Arcadia 阿卡迪亚 50
Archelaus I (king of Macedon) 阿奇劳斯一世（马其顿国王）18, 27
Archelaus (half-brother of Philip II) 阿奇劳斯（腓力二世的异母兄弟）19
argyraspids 银盾步兵队 34
Ariobarzanes (Persian commander) 阿尔塔巴赞斯（波斯统帅）38—39
Aristander of Telmessus (seer) 特密苏斯的亚里斯坦德（先知）3, 40
Aristobulus (historian) 亚里斯多布鲁斯（历史学家）86, 96
Aristogeiton (Athenian tyrantslayer) 阿里斯托杰顿（弑僭主者）52

Aristotle (philosopher) 亚里士多德（哲学家）23, 97, 100
Armenia 亚美尼亚 72
Arrhabaeus (Lyncestian noble) 阿里哈贝斯（林塞斯蒂斯贵族）31
Arrhidaeus (half-brother of Alexander the Great) 阿里哈贝斯（亚历山大大帝的异母兄弟）19
Arrian of Nicomedia (historian) 尼科美底亚的阿里安（历史学家）4, 5, 16, 28, 32, 35, 36, 38, 39, 40, 46, 48, 52, 57, 59, 60, 62, 65, 68, 69, 70, 72, 73, 76, 84, 86, 87, 90, 92, 94, 95, 96, 97, 98, 101, 102
Artabanus (uncle of Xerxes) 阿尔达班（薛西斯的叔叔）37
Artabazus (father of Barsine) 阿尔塔巴左斯（巴西妮的父亲）78
Artaxerxes I (king of Persia) 阿尔塔薛西斯一世（波斯国王）15
Artaxerxes II (king of Persia) 阿尔塔薛西斯二世（波斯国王）16, 71
Artaxerxes III (king of Persia) 阿尔塔薛西斯三世（波斯国王）16, 21, 22, 77, 82
Artaxerxes IV (king of Persia) 阿尔塔薛西斯四世（波斯国王）16, 77
Artaxerxes V 阿尔塔薛西斯五世 见 Bessus
Asia 亚洲 10, 15, 22, 32, 33, 40, 47, 52, 59, 68, 69, 70, 83, 88, 106, 107
Asia Minor 小亚细亚 30, 40, 44, 47—50, 53, 54, 55, 75
Assyria, Assyrians 亚述 11, 30, 56, 68, 94, 96

asthetairoi 伙友步兵的一种 34
astronomical diary 天文志 6, 69, 93, 95
Athena 雅典娜 36, 50
Athenaeus of Naucratis (writer) 瑙克拉提斯的阿忒纳乌斯（作家）29
Athens, Athenians 雅典 8, 14, 15, 18, 19, 21, 22, 25, 38, 39, 44, 45, 46, 47, 49, 50, 52, 53, 54, 61, 73, 88, 99, 106, 108
Attalus (Macedonian noble) 阿塔罗斯（马其顿贵族）22, 30
Atticus (friend of Cicero) 阿提克斯（西塞罗的朋友）100
Audata (wife of Philip II) 奥妲塔（腓力二世之妻）19
Augustus (emperor of Rome 27 bce-ce 14) 奥古斯都（罗马皇帝，公元前27—公元14在位）60, 101
Axios River 阿克西奥斯河 17

B

Babylon, Babylonians 巴比伦 6, 7, 11, 12, 41, 53, 58, 65, 70, 71, 72, 73, 75, 81, 91, 92, 93—98, 108
Bactra 巴克特拉 82
Bactria 巴克特里亚 41, 80, 82, 83, 84, 85, 87
Bagavant (Persian official) 巴加万（波斯官员）82
Bagoas (lover of Alexander) 巴戈阿斯（亚历山大的情人）78
Bagoas (murderer of Artaxerxes III and IV) 巴戈阿斯（杀害阿尔塔薛西斯三世和四世的凶手）16—17

Balkh 巴尔赫 82
Bardiya (king of Persia 522) 巴迪亚（波斯国王，公元前552在位）11
Barsine (widow of Memnon of Rhodes) 巴西妮（罗得岛的门农的遗孀）78
Beas River 比阿斯河 88
Behistun 贝希斯敦 84
Benghazi 班加西 61
Berlin 柏林 107
Bessus (Persian commander) 贝苏斯（波斯统帅）41, 81, 82, 83
Bible《圣经》57
Black Sea 黑海 10, 11, 21
Bodrum 博德鲁姆 13
Boeotia 维奥蒂亚 20, 21
Bosporus 博斯普鲁斯 10, 11, 21
British 英国 82, 106
British Museum 大英博物馆 5
Bubares (son-in-law of Amyntas I) 布巴雷斯（阿敏塔斯一世的女婿）10
Bucephala 比塞弗勒斯 24
Bucephalas (Alexander the Great's horse) 比塞弗勒斯（亚历山大大帝的马）24, 103
Bulgaria 保加利亚 3
Burnes, Alexander (British official) 亚历山大·伯恩斯（英国官员）106
Byzantium 拜占庭 21, 22

#

Cadmeia (daughter of Alexander of Epirus) 卡德梅亚（伊庇鲁斯的亚历

山大之女）26

Caligula (emperor of Rome) 卡利古拉（罗马皇帝）101, 102

Callisthenes (historian) 卡利斯提尼斯（历史学家）36, 60, 61, 62, 63, 75—76, 86, 87, 105

Cambyses (king of Persia) 冈比西斯（波斯国王）11, 14, 56

Caria 卡里亚 13

Carthage 迦太基 68, 69

Caspian Sea 里海 81

Cassander (son of Antipater) 卡桑德（安提帕特之子）28, 97, 98

Cassius Dio (historian) 卡西乌斯·狄奥（历史学家）101

Catherine the Great (empress of Russia) 叶卡捷琳娜大帝（俄国女皇）105

cavalry 骑兵 33, 53

Cersobleptes (king of Thrace) 塞索布勒普提斯（色雷斯国王）20, 21

Chaeronea, battle of 喀罗尼亚战役 22, 43, 44, 45, 47, 52

Chalcidice 哈尔基季基 17, 18, 20, 23

Chandragupta Maurya (ruler of India) 旃陀罗笈多·孔雀（印度统治者）91

Chaucer (poet) 乔叟（诗人）102

Chenab River 奇纳布河 88

Chios 希俄斯 49

Christianity 基督教 107

Cicero, Marcus Tullius (Roman politician) 马库斯·图利乌斯·西塞罗（罗马政治家）99, 100

Claudius (emperor of Rome 41–54 ce) 克劳狄乌斯（罗马皇帝，公元41—54在位）4, 102

Cleisthenes (Athenian politician) 克里斯提尼（雅典政治家）14

Cleitarchus (historian) 克莱塔卡斯（历史学家）59, 63

Cleitus (Macedonian commander) 克雷图斯（马其顿统帅）86, 87

Cleopatra (wife of Philip II) 克莉奥帕特拉（腓力二世之妻）19, 30

Cleopatra (sister of Alexander) 克莉奥帕特拉（亚历山大的妹妹）25, 26, 27

Coins 钱币 7, 8, 12

Corcyra 科西拉 45

Corinth 科林斯 22

Corinth, League of 科林斯同盟 22, 33, 45—46, 47, 50, 52

Cossaeans 科萨人 95

Crenides 克里尼德斯 20

Crete 克里特 50

Croesus (king of Lydia) 克洛伊索斯（吕底亚国王）11, 14, 37, 61, 76

Ctesias of Cnidus (historian) 尼多斯的克特西亚斯（历史学家）16

Curtius Rufus, Quintus (historian) 昆图斯·库尔提斯·鲁夫斯（历史学家）4, 59, 60, 63, 69, 70, 71, 76, 81, 84, 86, 94, 101

Cyprus 塞浦路斯 11, 14

Cyrenaica 昔兰尼加 11, 61

Cyrene 昔兰尼 61

Cyrus (son of Darius II) 居鲁士（大

索引

流士二世之子) 15, 16

Cyrus the Great (king of Persia) 居鲁士大帝(波斯国王) 10—11, 12, 14, 37, 92, 94

D

Damascus 大马士革 77
Danube 多瑙河 11, 21, 90
Darics 大流克 12
Darius I (king of Persia) 大流士一世(波斯国王) 10, 11, 12, 14, 15, 30, 61, 73, 76, 84, 87, 91
Darius II (king of Persia) 大流士二世(波斯国王) 15, 72
Darius III (king of Persia) 大流士三世(波斯国王) 1, 3, 16, 31, 33, 37, 41, 50, 52, 69, 70, 71, 76, 77, 78, 81, 82, 90, 100, 103, 105
Datis (Persian commander) 达蒂斯(波斯统帅) 15
Delphi 德尔斐 22, 63, 64
   sanctuary of Apollo 阿波罗的圣所 20, 21
Delphic Amphictyony 德尔斐近邻同盟 21, 22
Demades (Athenian orator) 德马德斯(雅典演说家) 45
Demeratus (king of Sparta) 德玛拉图斯(斯巴达国王) 37
Demeratus of Corinth (courtier of Alexander the Great) 科林斯的狄马拉鲁斯(亚历山大大帝的廷臣) 71
Demosthenes (Athenian orator) 德摩斯梯尼(雅典演说家) 22, 46

Didyma, Temple of Apollo 迪迪玛, 阿波罗神庙 14, 50
Dio Chrysostom (writer) 金嘴狄翁(作家) 96
Diodorus of Sicily (historian) 西西里的狄奥多罗斯(历史学家) 4, 37, 38, 39, 46, 59, 60, 63, 69, 70, 71, 95, 96, 101
Dionysus 狄俄尼索斯 27, 53, 88
divinations 预言 39
Droysen, Johann Gustav (historian) 约翰·古斯塔夫·德罗伊森(历史学家) 106—107
Dynastic Prophecy 王朝预言 16

E

Ecbatana 埃克巴坦那 12, 85, 92, 95, 97
Egypt, Egyptians 埃及 3, 8, 11, 16, 27, 41, 56, 58, 59, 60, 61, 62, 63, 64, 66, 67, 70, 74, 81, 98, 103, 108
Elam 埃兰 11, 12
Elimiotis 以利米欧提斯 19
England 英格兰 105
Enūma Anu Enlil《征兆结集》94, 95
Epaminondas (Theban commander) 伊巴密浓达(底比斯统帅) 50
Ephesus 以弗所 39
   temple of Artemis 阿耳特弥斯神庙 23
Ephialtes (betrayer of Greeks at Thermopylae) 厄菲阿尔特(温泉关的希腊叛徒) 38
Epirus 伊庇鲁斯 17, 26, 27
Eretria 埃雷特里亚 14, 15

Esagila 埃萨吉拉 93
Euboea 优卑亚 14
Euphrates River 幼发拉底河 41, 69, 72, 77, 91, 102
Euripides (Athenian dramatist) 欧里庇得斯（雅典剧作家）18, 27, 52
Europe 欧洲 10, 12, 22, 30, 83, 102, 104, 105, 106
Eurydice (mother of Philip II) 欧律狄刻（腓力二世之母）25—26, 27, 28
exile, exiles 流亡 45, 46, 48, 53—55

F

Fars 法尔斯 12, 38, 41, 42
France 法国 105
French Revolution 法国大革命 106

G

Ganges River 恒河 91
Gaugamela, battle of 高加米拉战役 3, 32, 33, 69, 70, 71, 76, 77, 87, 93, 94, 95
Gedrosia 格德罗西亚 53, 91, 92
George III (king of Britain) 乔治三世（英国国王）105
Germany 德国 105, 107
Gillies, John (historian) 约翰·吉利斯（历史学家）105, 106
Gordium 戈尔迪乌姆 70
Granicus River, battle of 格拉尼库斯河战役 32, 36, 50, 87
Greece, Greeks 希腊 3, 8, 9, 14, 30, 31, 33, 34, 38, 39, 40, 41, 43, 44, 46, 47, 50, 52, 53, 54, 55, 59, 60, 61, 62, 64, 70, 73, 82, 84, 87, 89, 93, 104, 105, 107, 108
Grote, George (historian) 乔治·格罗特（历史学家）82, 107
Gygaea (daughter of Amyntas I) 吉盖娅（阿敏塔斯一世之女）10

H

Hadrian (emperor of Rome 117–138 ce) 哈德良（罗马皇帝，公元117—138在位）4, 72, 102
Haliacmon River 阿利阿克蒙河 17
Halicarnassus 哈利卡尔那索斯 13
Harmodius (Athenian tyrantslayer) 哈莫迪乌斯（雅典弑僭主者）52
Hegel, Georg Wilhelm Friedrich (philosopher) 格奥尔格·威廉·弗里德里希·黑格尔（哲学家）107
Hegelochus (Macedonian commander) 黑格罗库斯（马其顿统帅）48
Hegesander (historian) 黑格桑德（历史学家）29
Helen of Alexandria (painter) 亚历山大港的海伦（画家）3
Hellespont 赫勒斯滂 14, 21, 22, 36, 42
Hephaestion (companion of Alexander) 赫费斯提翁（亚历山大的同伴）76, 78, 97
Heracles 赫拉克勒斯 7, 53, 62, 75, 88
Hermolaus (Macedonian page) 赫莫拉尔斯（马其顿侍从）86
Hermopolis 赫尔莫波利斯 67
Herodotus (historian) 希罗多德（历

索引

史学家）14, 17, 37, 38, 61, 64, 69, 76, 87
Heromenes (Lyncestian noble) 希罗门尼斯（林塞斯蒂斯贵族）31
Himalayas 喜马拉雅 88
Hindu Kush 兴都库什 87
Hippias (Athenian tyrant) 希庇亚斯（雅典僭主）14
Homer (poet) 荷马（诗人）24, 36, 44
  Iliad《伊利亚特》36, 68
Hoplites 重装步兵 34, 53
House of the Faun 农牧神之家 1, 4, 7
Humboldt, Alexander von (geographer) 亚历山大·冯·洪堡（地理学家）107
Hydaspes River 海达斯佩斯河 88, 90, 91
  battle of 战役 32
Hydraotes 海德拉奥特斯 88, 89
Hypaspists 持盾卫队 34
Hyphasis River 希发西斯河 84, 88, 89, 90, 92

I

Iceland 冰岛 103
Illyria, Illyrians 伊利里亚 17, 18, 19, 25, 30
India 印度 42, 87, 90, 91, 92, 103, 106
Indian Ocean 印度洋 90, 91
Indus Delta 恒河三角洲 42, 92
Indus River 印度河 11, 87, 88, 91
Indus Valley 印度河流域 32, 42, 80, 90
Iollas (son of Antipater) 伊奥拉斯（安提帕特之子）97

Ionian revolt 爱奥尼亚人起义 14
Iphicrates (Athenian commander) 伊菲克拉特斯（雅典统帅）25
Iran 伊朗 3, 5, 11, 12, 24, 42, 58, 74, 75, 82, 92
Iraq 伊拉克 3, 11, 42, 69
Isagoras (Athenian politician) 伊萨戈拉斯（雅典政治家）14
Islam 伊斯兰教 103, 106
Israel 以色列 3, 11
Issus, battle of 伊苏斯战役 3, 32, 52, 77, 78
Italy 意大利 26

J

Jaxartes River 雅克萨提斯河 82, 83, 84, 90
Jhelum River 杰赫勒姆河 88
Jordan 约旦 3, 11
Julius Caesar (Roman politician) 尤利乌斯·恺撒（罗马政治家）4, 99, 100, 101
Jupiter (god) 朱庇特（神）63
Jupiter (planet) 木星 95
Justin (historian) 查士丁（历史学家）4, 26, 31, 60, 62, 63, 101

K

Kabul 喀布尔 82, 106
Kandahar 坎大哈 59, 82
Karagiozis 卡拉吉奥兹 104
Karnak 卡纳克 67

亚历山大大帝

114

L

Larissa 拉里萨 20
Lebanon 黎巴嫩 3, 11, 35
Leonidas (king of Sparta) 列奥尼达（斯巴达国王）38, 39
Lesbos 莱斯博斯 47, 48
Levant 黎凡特 32
Libya 利比亚 3, 7, 11, 60
Louis XIV (king of France) 路易十四（法国国王）105
Luxor, temple of Amun-Re 卢克索，阿蒙-拉神庙 65
Lycurgus (Athenian orator) 吕克戈斯（雅典演说家）52
Lydia, Lydians 吕底亚 11, 12, 14, 37, 44, 76
Lyncestis 林塞斯蒂斯 31
Lysander (Spartan commander) 来山德（斯巴达统帅）49
Lysimachus (Macedonian commander) 利西马科斯（马其顿统帅）81

M

Macedonia, Macedonians 马其顿 1, 9, 10, 11, 13, 14, 17, 18, 24, 25, 27, 28, 29, 30, 32, 33, 42, 43, 44, 45, 46, 50, 57, 58, 59, 65, 68, 69, 72, 73, 74, 75, 77, 81, 82, 98, 106
Macedonia (former Yugoslav), Republic of 马其顿共和国（前南斯拉夫）104
Macedonia, Upper 上马其顿 31
Macedonian phalanx 马其顿方阵 33
manteis, 见 seers

Mann, Klaus (novelist) 克劳斯·曼（小说家）78
Marathon, battle of 马拉松战役 15
Mardonius (Persian commander) 马多尼乌斯（波斯统帅）14, 15
Marduk 马杜克 93
Mark Antony (Roman politician) 马克·安东尼（罗马政治家）100
Marmara, Sea of 马尔马拉海 10, 21
Mausolus (satrap of Caria) 摩索拉斯（卡里亚总督）13
Mazaces (satrap of Egypt) 马查西斯（埃及总督）56
Meda (wife of Philip II) 美妲（腓力二世之妻）19
Medes, Media 米底 11, 12, 68, 69, 85, 95
Mediterranean 地中海 41, 57
Megabazus (Persian commander) 梅加巴佐斯（波斯统帅）10
Megalopolis 梅格洛玻利斯 50
Memnon of Rhodes (commander of Greek mercenaries and Persian fleet) 罗得岛的门农（希腊雇佣兵与波斯海军统帅）78
Memphis 孟斐斯 58, 64, 65
Mesopotamia 美索不达米亚 11, 12, 38, 41, 42, 71, 72, 91, 102
Metastasio, Pietro (poet) 彼得罗·梅塔斯塔西奥（诗人）89
Miletus 米利都 14, 50
Mill, John Stuart (philosopher) 约翰·斯图尔特·密尔（哲学家）107
Mitford, William (historian) 威廉·米特福德（历史学家）105, 106

Modi, Sorab (film director) 索拉布·莫迪（电影导演）89
Sikandar《昔干答儿》89
Molossia 摩罗西亚 28
Montesquieu, Baron de (philosopher) 孟德斯鸠男爵（哲学家）105
Mosul 摩苏尔 69
Mount Athos 阿索斯山 15
Mytilene 米蒂利尼 47, 48

N

Nabonassar (king of Babylon) 那布·那西尔（巴比伦国王）94
Nabonidas (king of Babylon) 那波尼德斯（巴比伦国王）11
Nabopolassar (king of Babylon) 那波帕拉萨（巴比伦国王）11
National Archaeological Museum, Naples 国家考古博物馆，那不勒斯 1
NATO 北约 82
Nearchus (Cretan commander) 尼阿库斯（克里特统帅）92
Nebuchadnezzar (king of Babylon) 尼布甲尼撒（巴比伦国王）11
Nectanebo I (king of Egypt) 内克塔内布一世（埃及法老）65
Nectanebo II (king of Egypt) 内克塔内布二世（埃及法老）61, 65, 103
Neoptolemus (son of Alexander of Epirus) 涅俄普托勒摩斯（伊庇鲁斯的亚历山大之子）26
Neoptolemus of Molossia (father of Olympias) 摩罗西亚的涅俄普托勒摩斯（奥林匹娅斯之父）27
Nero (emperor of Rome) 尼禄 76
Nicepolis (wife of Philip II) 尼塞波利丝（腓力二世之妻）19, 20
Nile 尼罗河 57, 64
Nysa 尼萨 88

O

Olympias (mother of Alexander the Great) 奥林匹娅斯（亚历山大大帝之母）19, 20, 24, 26, 27—28, 31, 98, 103
Olympic Games 奥林匹克运动会 20, 23, 52, 54
Olynthus 奥林索斯 20
Omens 预兆 39—40
Onesicratus (historian) 奥涅西克里图斯（历史学家）81
Opis 俄庇斯 11
oracles 神谕 见 Amun; Delphi; Didyma
Orestes 俄瑞斯忒斯 49
Orpheus 俄耳甫斯 27
Ottoman Empire 奥斯曼帝国 104, 105
Oxus River 奥克苏斯河 82
Oxyartes (Sogdian commander) 奥克夏特斯（索格狄亚那统帅）84

P

Paeonia 帕埃尼亚 19
Pakistan 巴基斯坦 3, 11, 32, 53, 84, 87
Palestine 巴勒斯坦 3, 11
Parmenion (Macedonian commander) 帕曼纽（马其顿统帅）22, 23, 36, 37, 85

Parthia, Parthians 帕提亚 72
Parysatis (daughter of Artaxerxes III) 帕里萨蒂斯（阿尔塔薛西斯三世之女）77, 78
Pasargadae 帕萨尔加德 12, 35, 71, 92
Pausanias (killer of Philip II) 帕萨尼亚斯（刺杀腓力二世者）31
Pausanias (pretender) 帕萨尼亚斯（觊觎王位者）25
Pella 佩拉 18, 23, 28, 29
Peloponnese 伯罗奔尼撒 50, 54
Peloponnesian War 伯罗奔尼撒战争 15, 45, 49
Pentheus 彭透斯 27
Perdiccas II (king of Macedon) 佩尔狄卡斯二世（马其顿国王）18
Perdiccas III (king of Macedon) 佩尔狄卡斯三世（马其顿国王）18, 25, 26
Persepolis 波斯波利斯 12, 35, 38, 39, 41, 52, 73, 77, 80, 83, 92, 95
Perseus 珀尔修斯 61, 75
Persia, Persians 波斯 10, 12, 14, 16, 22, 30, 31, 33, 36, 38, 40, 41, 44, 45, 46, 47, 48, 49, 50, 52, 56, 61, 65, 68—79, 80, 81, 82, 84, 94, 95, 96, 101, 103, 106
Persian Gates 波斯之门 35, 38
Persian Gulf 波斯湾 42, 91
pezhetairoi 伙友步兵 34
Pherae 费莱 20
Phila (wife of Philip II) 菲拉（腓力二世之妻）19
Philinna (wife of Philip II) 费里娜（腓力二世之妻）19, 20
Philip II (king of Macedon) 腓力二世（马其顿国王）18—22, 23, 24, 25, 26, 27, 28, 29, 30, 33, 43, 45, 46, 52, 63, 64, 77, 85, 86, 87, 103, 106
Philippi 腓力皮 20
Philotas (companion of Alexander the Great) 菲罗塔斯（亚历山大大帝的同伴）71, 85, 86
Philoxenos of Eretria (painter) 埃雷特里亚的斐洛克塞诺斯（画家）3
Phocians 福基斯 21
Phocis 佛西斯 20
Phrygia 弗里吉亚 70
Phyllada《亚历山大大帝之书》104
Pieria 皮埃里亚 27
Plataea, battle of 普拉塔亚战役 15
Plutarch of Chaeronea (biographer and philosopher) 咯罗内亚的普鲁塔克（传记作者和哲学家）4, 8, 23, 24, 27, 28, 31, 35, 36, 40, 57, 59, 60, 62, 63, 64, 69, 70, 71, 74, 76, 78, 81, 91, 92, 95, 96, 97, 100, 101, 102
Polybius (historian) 波利比乌斯（历史学家）68
Polygamy 一夫多妻制 17
Pompeii 庞贝 1, 4, 100
Pompeius Trogus (historian) 庞培乌斯·特罗格斯（历史学家）4, 26, 101
Pompey (Roman politician) 庞培（罗马政治家）100
Porus (Indian ruler) 波鲁斯（印度统治者）32, 88, 89
Pressfield, Steven (novelist) 史蒂芬·帕斯菲尔德（小说家）82
Priene 普里埃内 49, 50

索引

Ptolemy (regent of Macedon) 托勒密（马其顿摄政王）18, 25, 26
Ptolemy I (historian and king of Egypt) 托勒密一世（历史学家，埃及法老）3, 35, 58, 59, 60, 62, 86, 90, 98
Ptolemy II Philadelphus (king of Egypt) 托勒密二世，"爱手足者"（埃及法老）58
Punjab 旁遮普 24, 42, 91, 97
Pydna 彼得那 20
Pylaea (festival) 皮莱节 21

R

Rakotis 拉科蒂斯 58
Ravi River 拉维河 88
Renault, Mary (novelist) 玛丽·瑞瑙特（小说家）78
Rhoxane (wife of Alexander the Great) 罗克珊娜（亚历山大大帝之妻）77, 78, 84, 86, 98
Rome, Romans 罗马 5, 7, 57, 68, 72, 73, 75, 82, 84, 85, 86, 87, 93, 99, 100, 101, 102
Russians 俄罗斯 82

S

Salamis, battle of 萨拉米斯战役 15
Samos 萨摩斯 49, 54
Sardis 萨迪斯 12
Sargon II (king of Assyria) 萨尔贡二世（亚述国王）94
Saturn (planet) 土星 95
Scamander River 斯卡曼德洛斯河 36

Scipio Africanus (Roman politician) 大西庇阿（罗马政治家）68
Scotland 苏格兰 105
Scythia, Scythians 斯基泰 11, 84
Seers 先知 39, 40
Semiramis (queen of Babylon) 塞米勒米斯（巴比伦国王）92
Seneca (tutor of Nero) 塞涅卡（尼禄的导师）76
Seven Wonders of the World 世界七大奇迹 13
Shahnameh《列王纪》103
Siwa 锡瓦 7, 57, 60, 61, 62, 63, 64, 70
Skopje 斯科普里 104
Sogdiana 索格狄亚那 41, 82, 83, 84, 90
Solon (Athenian politician) 梭伦（雅典政治家）76
Sophocles (Athenian playwright) 索福克勒斯（雅典剧作家）52
Spain 西班牙 100
Sparta, Spartans 斯巴达 14, 15, 20, 21, 22, 37, 38, 44, 45, 46, 49, 50, 52, 106
Spitamenes (Sogdian commander) 斯皮达迈尼斯（索格狄亚那统帅）83
Stateira (daughter of Darius III) 斯妲特拉（大流士三世之女）77, 78
Stone, Oliver (film director) 奥利弗·斯通（电影导演）78
Strymon River 斯特里蒙河 17
Suetonius (biographer) 苏维托尼乌斯（传记作家）101
Susa 苏萨 12, 15, 41, 52, 53, 65, 71, 72, 73, 74, 75, 81, 92, 95

Susian Rocks 苏西安高崖 38
Syria 叙利亚 3, 11

T

Tacitus (historian) 塔西佗（历史学家）86, 101
Tajikistan 塔吉克斯坦 3
Tanais 塔奈斯 82, 83
Taxiles (Indian ruler) 塔克西莱斯（印度统治者）88
Tegea 忒格亚 54
Thais (Athenian courtesan) 泰伊思（雅典妓女）73
Thalestris (queen of the Amazons) 塔勒斯特里斯（亚马逊女王）5, 81
Thebes (Egypt) 底比斯（埃及）7, 60, 62, 65
Thebes, Thebans (Greece) 底比斯（希腊）18, 22, 27, 32, 44, 45, 46, 47, 50, 52
  sack of 洗劫底比斯 46—47
Thermopylae 温泉关 15, 20, 21, 38, 39
Theseus 忒修斯 49
Thessaly 色萨利 18, 19, 20, 21
Third Sacred War 第三次神圣战争 20
Thrace 色雷斯 11, 13, 14, 17, 19, 21, 30
Thucydides (historian) 修昔底德（历史学家）45, 46, 47
Tiberius (emperor of Rome) 提比略（罗马皇帝）86
Tigris River 底格里斯河 11, 41, 91
Trajan (emperor of Rome) 图拉真（罗马皇帝）72, 102
Trojan War 特洛伊战争 36

Troy 特洛伊 36, 59, 68
Turkey 土耳其 3
Tuthmosis III (king of Egypt) 图特摩斯三世（埃及法老）67
Tyrannicides 弑僭主者 52
Tyre 提尔 35, 104

U

United States of America 美国 82
Uzbekistan 乌兹别克斯坦 3, 82

V

Venice 威尼斯 104
Vergina 韦尔吉纳 28, 29, 98
Vespasian (emperor of Rome) 韦斯巴芗（罗马皇帝）4, 102
Voltaire (writer) 伏尔泰（作家）105

X

Xenophon (historian) 色诺芬（历史学家）16, 30
Xerxes (king of Persia) 薛西斯（波斯国王）10, 12, 14, 15, 16, 20, 22, 30, 37, 38, 39, 52, 73, 94

Z

Zagros Mountains 扎格罗斯山脉 35, 38, 39, 41, 95
Zeus 宙斯 7, 20, 27, 61, 62, 63, 87
Zoroastrians 琐罗亚斯德教 74

索引

Hugh Bowden

ALEXANDER THE GREAT

A Very Short Introduction

For Isabel and Clare

Acknowledgements

The inspiration for writing this book came from many years teaching a course on Alexander the Great to students in the Department of Classics in King's College London. I have learned a great deal from them, and I hope that they will appreciate the results. The course was usually co-taught with Dr Lindsay Allen, who opened my eyes to the importance of the Near Eastern material. I am particularly grateful to her, and to all my colleagues at King's. I have learned much also from colleagues with whom I have discussed Alexander at conferences and lectures across the world, including Sulochana Asirvatham, Elizabeth Baynham, Philip Bosman, Brian Bosworth, Peter Green, Waldemar Heckel, Tim Howe, Robin Lane Fox, Sabine Müller, Daniel Ogden, Frances Pownall, Joseph Roisman, Andrew Stewart, Richard Stoneman, Pat Wheatley, Josef Wiesehöfer, and Ian Worthington. Most of the writing was done while I was Margot Tytus Fellow in the Department of Classics at the University of Cincinnati: I am grateful for the wonderful generosity and hospitality of the faculty and staff there. Thanks are due to all those at Oxford University Press involved in the production of the book, including Carol Carnegie, Kay Clement, Carrie Hickman, Andrea Keegan, Emma Ma, Joy Mellor, and Subramaniam Vengatakrishnan. Finally, as always, I want to acknowledge the support of my family—my wife Jill and my daughters, to whom this book is dedicated.

Contents

List of illustrations i

Timeline of Alexander's life iii

Map of Alexander's campaigns vi

Introduction 1

1 Before Alexander 10
2 Prince: Alexander in the Macedonian court 23
3 Warrior: Alexander's army 32
4 Commander: Alexander and the Greeks 43
5 Pharaoh: Alexander and Egypt 56
6 King of the world: Alexander and Persia 68
7 Traveller: Alexander in Afghanistan and Pakistan 80
8 Doomed to die: Alexander in Babylon 93
9 After Alexander 99

References 109

Further reading 111

List of illustrations

Map 1 Map of Alexander's campaigns **vi**
From Arrian, *Alexander the Great* (Oxford World's Classics, 2013). Oxford University Press

1 The Alexander Mosaic **2**
© Araldo de Luca/Corbis

2 A fragment of an astronomical diary from Babylon **6**
© The Trustees of the British Museum

3 Alexander depicted with ram's horns, the symbol of the Egyptian god Amun, on a silver coin **8**
© The Trustees of the British Museum

4 Inscribed blocks from the temple of Athena at Priene **51**
© The Trustees of the British Museum

5 Alexander the Great depicted as pharaoh in the temple of Amenhotep III at Luxor **66**
© The Art Archive/Alamy

6 A document from Bactria, written in Aramaic in 324 **83**
The Nasser D. Khalili Collection of Islamic Art, [IA17] © Nour Foundation. Courtesy of the Khalili Family Trust

7 A coin or medallion issued by Alexander to celebrate victory in his Indian campaign **89**
© The Trustees of the British Museum

Timeline of Alexander's life

A note on dates

The surviving ancient narratives about Alexander do not always give precise chronological information. Events mentioned in Babylonian astronomical diaries can be dated precisely, but for events mentioned by Greek writers, even if they give precise dates, we can only provide approximate equivalences, because Greek and Macedonian calendars did not work with a 365-day year, and thus were often out of alignment with the solar calendar. Therefore most dates here are given by season, but even these must be considered approximate.

356	Summer	Birth of Alexander
338	Summer	Battle of Chaeronea
337	Spring	'League of Corinth' created
336	Spring	Macedonian forces under Parmenion cross into Asia
336		Assassination of Philip II: Alexander becomes king
335	Spring	Alexander campaigns in Thrace and Illyria
	Autumn	Sack of Thebes

334	Spring	Alexander crosses the Hellespont into Asia
		Alexander at Troy
		Battle of the Granicus
	Summer	Alexander liberates Greek cities of Asia
	Autumn	Alexander in Caria
	Winter	Alexander in Lycia
333	Spring	Alexander at Gordium
	Summer	Alexander in Cilicia
	Autumn	Battle of Issus
	Winter	Siege of Tyre begins
332	Summer	Siege of Tyre ends
	Autumn	Siege of Gaza
	Winter	Alexander enters Egypt
331	Spring	Alexander visits the oracle of Amun in Siwa
		Alexander marches from Egypt to Tyre, then to the Euphrates
	1 October	Battle of Gaugamela
	20 October	Alexander enters Babylon
	Winter	Alexander enters Susa
330	Spring	Alexander enters Persepolis
		Alexander burns the palace of Persepolis
	Summer	Death of Darius III; Bessus declares himself king (as Artaxerxes V)
	Autumn	Trial and execution of Philotas and execution of Parmenion
329	Spring	Alexander enters Bactria and Sogdiana
		Capture of Bessus
	Autumn	Alexander crosses the Jaxartes River
328	Autumn	Killing of Cleitus

Year	Season	Event
327	Spring	Alexander captures the Sogdian Rock
		Alexander marries Rhoxane
		'Pages Plot'; arrest of Callisthenes
	Summer	Alexander enters the Hindu Kush
326	Spring	Alexander captures the Rock of Aornus
		Alexander crosses the Indus River
		Alexander defeats Porus on the Hydaspes River
	Summer	Alexander reaches the Hyphasis River, then returns to the Indus
	Winter	Alexander is wounded fighting the Malli
325	Summer	Alexander reaches the Indus Delta
	Autumn	Alexander marches through Gedrosia
	Winter	Alexander returns to Pasargadae and Persepolis
324	Spring	Alexander reaches Susa and rewards soldiers for the Indian campaign
		Alexander marries Stateira and Parysatis, as part of a mass wedding
		Alexander punishes satraps who abused their positions in his absence
	Summer	Alexander reorganizes his army
		Alexander decrees the return of Greek exiles to their cities
	Autumn	Death of Hephaestion
	Winter	Alexander campaigns against the Cossaeans
323	Spring	Alexander enters Babylon
	June 11	Death of Alexander

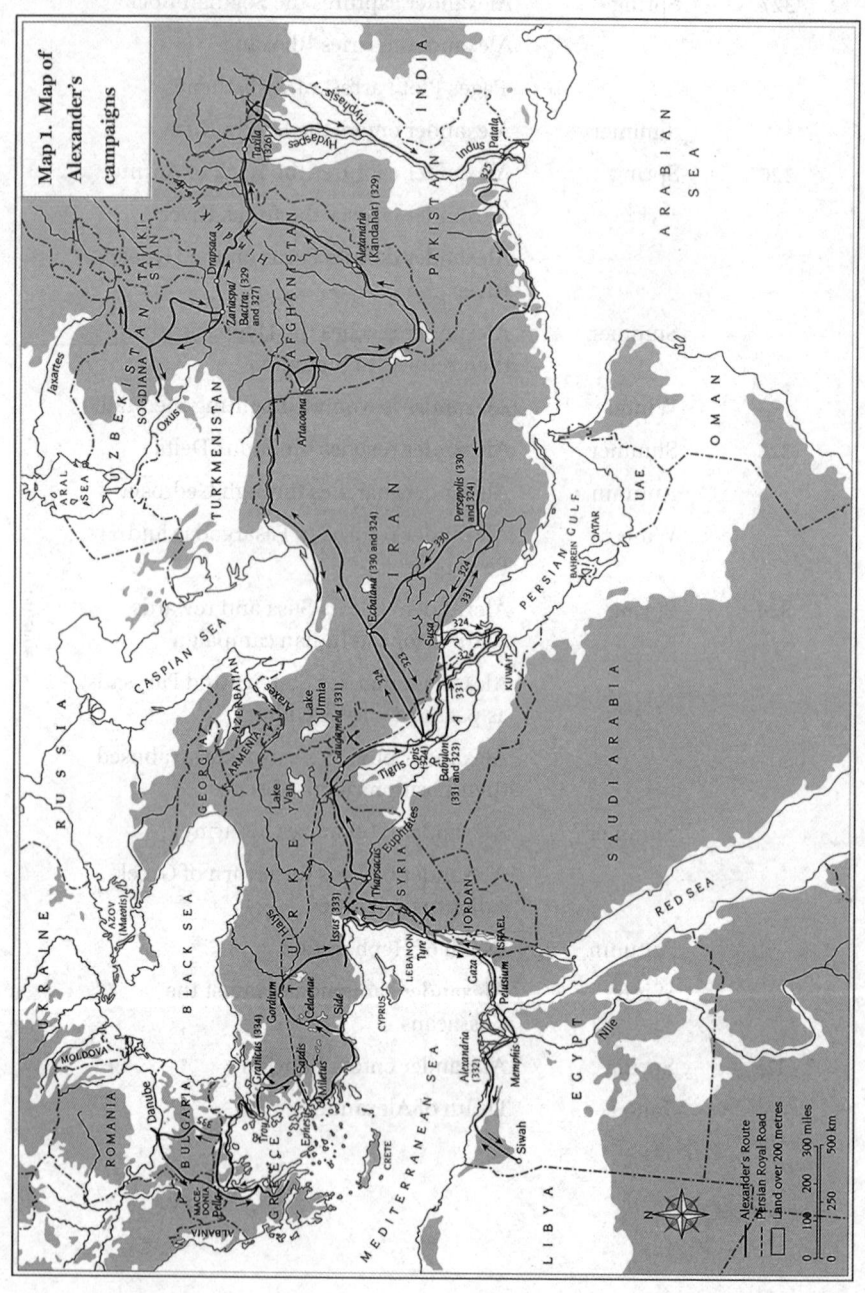

Introduction

On the mezzanine level of the National Archaeological Museum in Naples is a large mosaic depicting a battle (Figure 1). Although the left-hand part of it is quite damaged, it is easy to pick out the figure of Alexander the Great, bare-headed, on his horse, looking intently at Darius III, who rises above the rest of the mass of horses and men, standing in his chariot, looking and pointing at Alexander in obvious alarm. Just behind Darius his charioteer is whipping his team of horses to drive him away from the imminent danger: Alexander has just run his lance through the last Persian horseman to stand between him and his opponent. Behind, the skyline is bristling with Macedonian pikes, while the foreground is littered with abandoned weapons and fallen Persians. A Macedonian victory is inevitable. The mosaic, which is nearly 6 metres long and over 3 metres high, was created not long before 100 BCE, for the owner of the House of the Faun in Pompeii. This was one of the largest private houses in Pompeii, built probably by a leading Italian aristocrat, and the mosaic occupied a prominent place in it, covering the floor of an *exedra*, a reception area where every important visitor to the house would see it. The owner clearly considered that he benefited from association with the image of Alexander as heroic warrior king.

Alexander the Great was born in 356, and was king of Macedon from 336 to his death in 323. As king, he led an army into the

1. The Alexander Mosaic: an Italian view of Alexander the Great, based on an earlier Greek painting, and depicting his victory at the battle of Issus, or possibly Gaugamela

territory of the Achaemenid Persian empire, and took control of a territory that consisted of what is now Modern Greece, parts of Bulgaria, Turkey, Syria, Lebanon, Israel, Palestine, Jordan, Egypt, parts of Libya, Iraq, Iran, Afghanistan, parts of Uzbekistan and Tajikistan, and most of Pakistan. The story of his campaigns was constantly retold after his death and, almost uniquely among figures from classical antiquity, he was never absent from the popular imagination across Europe and the Near East, from his lifetime until the present day. It is not surprising then that Alexander should be the subject for a piece of Italian art made some two centuries after his death. But asking some questions about the mosaic will help us to think about Alexander himself, and what we really know about him. It will turn out that Alexander is a rather more enigmatic figure than he might appear.

So what is the Alexander Mosaic, and what does it represent? It is agreed that the mosaic itself was created sometime between 120 and 100, but many scholars have argued that it was a copy of an older Greek painting, probably painted in the late 4th century, not long after the event it portrays. Attempts have been made to attribute it to a named painter, with candidates including Philoxenos of Eretria, or a woman, Helen of Alexandria. Since no certainly ascribed work by any ancient painter survives, these attributions do not get us very far. There is debate about which battle the mosaic depicts: Alexander encountered Darius twice, at the battles of Issus (333) and Gaugamela (331). Most scholars prefer Issus, but there is again no possibility of certainty. Does it in any case depict the battle accurately, or is it largely a work of artistic imagination? And what of other figures in the picture? Who is the man in the distinctive white helmet with a gold wreath just to the left of Alexander himself? Is it his personal seer, Aristander of Telmessus, or perhaps one of his bodyguards, Ptolemy, who went on to become ruler of Egypt, and may possibly have commissioned the picture on which the mosaic is based? Some people have rightly raised the question of whether it is appropriate to treat the Alexander Mosaic simply as a 'Roman copy' of a Greek original, and then treat the image as if it actually were a 4th century painting. What we have is an Italian artwork, and attention should be paid to the context of its creation in Pompeii in the late 2nd century: what did it mean to the man who commissioned it, and the artists who worked on it, and indeed to the men and women who saw it when they visited the House of the Faun? These questions are no easier to answer, but at least they are questions about the work of art we have, rather than its imagined original.

Such concerns may not seem crucial when we are dealing with an artistic representation of one moment in Alexander's life. But very similar questions can be asked about the literary evidence for Alexander's career. The surviving narratives of Alexander's life and deeds date from between 30 BCE and the 2nd or 3rd centuries CE. The earliest surviving account that has come down to us is the work of Diodorus of Sicily, who wrote a massive *Library of History* in 40 books, starting in mythical times and extending to the death of Julius Caesar. Much of the work has been lost, but most of the seventeenth book, which is devoted to Alexander, has survived. Then there is the *History of Alexander the Great of Macedon* by the Roman, Quintus Curtius Rufus, who wrote in the reign either of Claudius or Vespasian, in the 1st century CE, and a biography of Alexander written by the Greek Plutarch of Chaeronea sometime around 100, and an account of his campaigns by another Greek, Arrian of Nicomedia, a friend of the emperor Hadrian, writing in the first third of the 2nd century. Finally, at some point after this, another Roman writer, Justin, produced an epitome, that is an abbreviated version, of the *Philippic Histories* of Diodorus' contemporary, Pompeius Trogus, which included an account of the reign of Alexander. These writers are collectively referred to as the Alexander historians. Their narratives are clearly directly or indirectly based on accounts written in the decades following Alexander's death, in several cases by men who accompanied Alexander on his campaigns, but how faithfully the authors of the surviving texts transmitted what they read is not certain. It is clear that, to a greater or lesser extent, the surviving accounts have been shaped to appeal to a contemporary readership, that is to say a readership of Greeks and Romans living in a world governed by powerful emperors, for whom Alexander might serve as a model for how to rule, or how not to rule. Fundamentally, the Alexander of the narrative sources is a Roman Alexander.

Like the Alexander Mosaic, the narrative accounts of Alexander's career probably preserve much material that goes back to Alexander's time, but what we have is in part fragmentary, and as a whole transmitted through the work of people from later centuries, who have transformed the material to suit new techniques and changed tastes. Finding effective ways to interpret these narratives is a challenge that faces anyone trying to tell the story of Alexander's life and campaigns. In many places the Alexander historians provide conflicting versions of the same set of events—and indeed Arrian notes that sometimes even eye-witness sources disagree with each other. On the other hand, when the same story appears in several different narratives, we cannot be certain that it is true: some stories about Alexander were invented in or soon after his lifetime, for example that he met, and slept with, the mythical Queen of the Amazons, and these stories rapidly became part of the narrative tradition. Some stories about him became so popular that no author could afford to ignore them, even if they could not be found in the accounts of the earliest writers. Despite decades of research into the sources of the Alexander historians (sometimes referred to by the German word *Quellenforschung*) we still have no reliable way of determining how much, if any, of their accounts can be trusted.

We can, however, make some progress in determining what is more or less likely to have happened by trying to build up a fuller picture of the world around Alexander, and to do this we need to look at more material evidence. In a case in the Ancient Iran gallery of the British Museum is displayed a small fragment of greyish terracotta, 4–5 cm wide and 6 cm high, inscribed with neat lines of cuneiform script (Figure 2). The fragment, written in Akkadian, is part of a Babylonian astronomical diary referring to the second month of the fourteenth year of the king's reign. Towards the bottom of the fragment the following can be read: 'On the 29th [day] the king died; clouds [...] the sky'. The date corresponds to 11 June 323, and the king was Alexander the Great. This small piece of clay is a near-contemporary piece of evidence for Alexander, but this is a very different Alexander from the one on the mosaic. We have texts of astronomical diaries like this covering the period from 652 to 60 BCE. Every night men would stand on the roof of the king's palace in Babylon to observe the heavens. When it was not cloudy, they would note down the position of the planets, and any other unusual phenomena (comets, eclipses, and so on). These observations would then be

2. A fragment of an astronomical diary from Babylon recording events in the second month of year fourteen of Alexander's reign, including the king's death

recorded in diaries, and after each month's observations there would be a report on the prices of staple goods in the market, and notes of any significant events that had occurred. The aim of these observations was to establish the attitude of the gods to the city and to the king in particular: if signs in the sky indicated that the king faced danger, steps could be taken to protect him. Alexander first entered Babylon on 20 October 331, and was almost certainly recognized as its new king at that time. He returned to the city in the Spring of 323, and died there a few months later. While he was in the neighbourhood of Babylon, the whole system of the Babylonian scholar-priests was focused on his well-being, and his actions were recorded in royal chronicles and other kinds of text. There was a Babylonian Alexander as well as a Roman one.

A further vision of Alexander can be found on coins issued in the period after his death by the men who took control of the various parts of his empire. Alexander himself did not issue coins with his portrait on at all: instead he followed an earlier Macedonian practice of putting the head of Heracles on his silver issues. His successors started the practice of issuing coins with his portrait on them, which indicates that, like the owner of the House of the Faun somewhat later, they saw an association with Alexander as being advantageous to them. But the Alexander of these coins had unusual attributes. Some coin portraits show Alexander with ram's horns around his ears (Figure 3). These horns were the symbol of the Egyptian god Amun, whose temples in Thebes Alexander restored, and whose oracular shrine at Siwa in the Libyan desert he visited in the Spring of 331. According to the Alexander historians, it was after this visit that Alexander began to claim that he was the son of Amun (or of Zeus, with whom Amun was identified), and these claims were a major cause of resentment from Alexander's soldiers, and his companions; and most modern scholars have accepted this idea. But the coins indicate that some of these same companions actually chose to advertise the relationship between Alexander and Amun themselves. It is possible that their attitude to Alexander's claims changed after his

3. Alexander depicted with ram's horns, the symbol of the Egyptian god Amun, on a silver coin of one of his successors, Lysimachus

death, but it is also possible that the coins, which date from the late 4th century, are telling a truer story than the narratives written hundreds of years later.

There are other images of Alexander that can help us build up a better picture of how he was seen by his contemporaries or near-contemporaries. Greek cities inscribed and erected copies of decrees he made about them; Athenian orators referred to his activities in their surviving speeches. His name and his image, in pharaonic style, were carved into the walls of the temples of Upper Egypt where restoration work was done in his name. Still other contemporary documents and artefacts can help us get a fuller picture of the world in which he operated, even when they do not mention him by name.

While it does not ignore the narratives provided by the Alexander historians, this *Very Short Introduction* to Alexander the Great attempts to give greater weight than has been customary to these contemporary documents, and to indicate what we do not know, as well as what we do. Although it is broadly chronological in its structure, it is not intended to provide a straightforward narrative of Alexander's life and his campaigns. As it happens, Plutarch's *Life of Alexander*, which is the only one of the ancient narratives to provide an account, not necessarily to be trusted, of Alexander's childhood as well as his actions as king, is about the length of a *Very Short Introduction*, and would make a suitable companion to this one. However, the timeline provided here, along with the map showing Alexander's progress (Map 1), should be enough to prevent the reader getting lost. The next chapter, 'Before Alexander', will give a brief history of the Achaemenid Persian empire and the kingdom of Macedon, before they came into conflict, while the last chapter will explore the way Alexander's memory has continued to haunt the world in the millennia following his death. In between, we will examine Alexander in his own world: not just Greece and Macedonia, but the whole complex web of places that made up the ancient Near East.

Chapter 1
Before Alexander

In around 513 BCE the Persian king Darius I (522–486) built a great bridge across the Bosporus, the narrow strait that links the Black Sea with the Sea of Marmara, and led an army from Asia into Europe. Darius himself crossed back into Asia the following year, but he left his commander Megabazus with the task of subduing the territories on the north coast of the Aegean Sea. Among the local rulers who gave earth and water to the Persians as a sign of their submission was Amyntas, a Macedonian. He was rewarded with the position of *satrap* of Macedonia, that is governor of what was now a province of the Achaemenid Persian empire, and he married his daughter Gygaea to a leading Persian called Bubares. When Amyntas died in around 495, he was succeeded by his son Alexander I, who remained a loyal subject of Darius and his son and successor Xerxes. In this way the Persians themselves established in power the family that would, 180 years later, bring down their own empire. Alexander I's great-great-great-grandson was Alexander III, generally known as Alexander the Great.

The rise of Achaemenid Persia

The Achaemenid empire was the creation of Cyrus the Great (*c*.559–530), who began as king of Anshan. This title indicated his rule over the ancient kingdom of Elam in what is now southwest Iran. Soon after coming to power around 559, Cyrus started a campaign of conquest, defeating his northern neighbours the Medes (550), and then spreading his power east over the Iranian plateau, and west into Anatolia, where he defeated Croesus, king of Lydia (546), and as a result extended his empire to the shores of the Aegean Sea. He then turned his attention to Babylon in Mesopotamia, at the time the most powerful city in the Near East. Under their kings Nabopolassar (626–605) and Nebuchadnezzar (604–562), the Babylonians had overthrown the Neo-Assyrian empire, which had dominated Mesopotamia and the territory to its west (that is roughly modern Iraq, Syria, Lebanon, Israel, Palestine, and Jordan), for several centuries, and made an empire for themselves. In 539 Cyrus defeated a Babylonian army at Opis, on the Tigris River, and entered Babylon, where he deposed its king, Nabonidus (556–539), installing his own son Cambyses in his place. Cyrus' campaigns continued until his death, and Cambyses (530–522) expanded the empire further, with the annexation of Cyprus and then Egypt (525).

Cambyses died on his journey back from Egypt—it is unclear from what cause—and was apparently succeeded by his brother Bardiya (522). At this point, however, there was a coup, and Darius, a Persian noble perhaps distantly related to the family of Cyrus, made himself king. He was able to put down a number of revolts, and, once established in power, continued his predecessors' policy of expansion. In the east he extended the empire as far as the Indus River in modern Pakistan, and he also increased his territory in north Africa, annexing the area of Cyrenaica (in modern Libya). He crossed the Bosporus in order to campaign against the Scythians on the shores of the Black Sea (*c.*513), and although this was not successful, it left Darius in control of the lands between the north Aegean coast and the Danube, consisting of Thrace and, as we have seen, Macedonia.

Ruling the empire

To maintain hold over so large and disparate an empire required effective organization. Central to the Achaemenid system was the person of the king himself. Persian royal inscriptions emphasize the identity of the king, his right to rule, and the fact that he has the support of the chief of the gods, Ahura Mazda. He is shown in sculptured scenes in royal palaces and elsewhere seated on his throne or standing, always larger than other people, and often with the flying disk that represented Ahura Mazda above him. Achaemenid iconography adopted features of Assyrian royal representations, for example showing the king hunting lions. These images were used on seals, and so were disseminated across the empire. Once Darius had entered Europe he and his successors started to mint coins in the Lydian capital Sardis, gold 'Darics' depicting the king as a warrior armed with bow and spear, which circulated in the Aegean area.

The empire had several royal capitals: Cyrus ruled from Ecbatana in Media, Babylon, and Pasargadae, created by him in Fars; Darius built himself a palace at Susa in Elam, and another new creation, Persepolis, not far from Pasargadae. The king and his court moved slowly from capital to capital during the year, partly in response to the climate (Ecbatana on the Iranian plateau was cooler in the summer months, while Babylon and Susa were more appropriate for the winters). The royal progress took the form of a grand procession, and the king spent much of the time living in tents rather than stone or brick buildings, as he also did when on military campaign. This nomadic style was distinctively Persian, in contrast to the urban focus of his Mesopotamian predecessors. Palaces in the capitals were also places where royal power could be displayed. The ruins of Persepolis, the palace built by Darius I and extended by his successor Xerxes (486–465) are the most spectacular surviving example. Sculptured friezes on the outside of its *apadana* (audience hall) depict the king's subjects from across the empire bringing him tribute. Each group is distinguished by their clothes and hairstyles, and the gifts they are carrying. Non-perishable items, including large quantities of gold and silver, were stored in the palaces (when he captured them, Alexander found in the storerooms precious metals worth, at a minimum, the equivalent of 2,500 tonnes of silver, according to the ancient authors). As well as receiving tribute kings gave gifts to their courtiers and subjects, although the reciprocity was not even. For example when the king dined, he oversaw at the same time the feeding of his family, his retainers and courtiers, and his guard, through the institution of 'the king's table'.

The provinces of the empire were ruled by satraps appointed by the king. These were often leading Persian nobles, but as we have seen, local dynasts like Amyntas of Macedon could be put in charge. They were connected to the king and to each other through marriages, and although some satrapies would be passed down through families, personal bonds to the king remained important. Satraps were required to collect taxes and tribute for the king as well for themselves, and to raise troops when called upon for the king's military campaigns. These men (and occasionally women) had palaces in their own satrapal capitals, where they kept their own courts. Some had summer palaces and lodges built within great hunting parks called 'paradises' where they could imitate the king by hunting lions and other animals. Monuments like the tomb of Mausolus, satrap of Caria (377–353), built at Halicarnassus (modern Bodrum), which was included in the list of the Seven Wonders of the World, demonstrate the ambition of local dynasts who served as satraps. The courts and palaces of the western satrapies were frequently visited by leading men from beyond the edge of the empire, and acted as models for royal courts in the Aegean area, in particular in Thrace and Macedonia. For the king to oversee the activities of the satraps required good communications, and the road system of the Achaemenid empire was admired in antiquity. It made possible the rapid movement of couriers ('neither snow, nor rain, nor the heat of the sun, nor the night prevents them from completing their appointed course at greatest speed' said Herodotus, writing in the 5th century), the progresses of the royal court, and the movement of armies—both those of the king and those of invaders.

Persia and the Greeks

The Achaemenid empire reached its greatest extent, if only briefly, under Darius' son and successor Xerxes, who conquered most of northern and central Greece, including Athens, in 480. When Cyrus had defeated Croesus of Lydia 66 years earlier, and taken over his kingdom, its territory had included a number of major Greek settlements on the east coast of the Aegean, and more Greek cities had been incorporated into the empire through Cambyses' conquest of Cyprus. These cities were governed by individuals or small groups who were kept in power by the satraps and served their interests. In 499 many of them had risen in revolt from Persian rule, and they had been supported by a fleet of 20 ships sent from Athens, and five from Eretria, on the island of Euboea. The revolt had been put down by 494, and one of the largest Greek cities, Miletus, had been sacked. Included in the destruction was the major oracular shrine and temple of Apollo at Didyma.

Some years before the Ionian revolt, in the period c.511–506, Athens had gone through a period of civil unrest, involving the 'tyrant' Hippias, and two other men, Isagoras and Cleisthenes, who went on to establish the Athenian democracy. In the course of the struggle Isagoras had called in aid from Sparta, and in response Cleisthenes had opened negotiations with the Persians, through the satrap of Lydia, and possibly had gone as far as offering submission to the king. In Darius' eyes, therefore, Athens was a rebellious subject as much as the Ionian and Cypriote cities. In 492 the Persian general Mardonius had led a combined army and fleet across the Hellespont and through Thrace and Macedonia, with the intention of marching south to Eretria and

Athens, but the expedition had been called off when much of the fleet was wrecked off Mount Athos. Two years later Darius had sent another force, under Datis, across the Aegean. Many of the Greek islands had offered submission to the king, and Eretria had been sacked, but the army had been defeated by the Athenians at the battle of Marathon (490), bringing the campaign to an end.

After Darius' death, Xerxes had inherited his father's plans, and in 481 he marched with Mardonius along the same route that the general had previously taken. This time the campaign was a success in that Xerxes accepted the submission of all the Greek cities along his path, routed a small Spartan-led army at Thermopylae, and was able to sack Athens and carry trophies back from there to Susa. This success, however, was short-lived. Xerxes' fleet (which included significant numbers of Greek ships) was defeated by a Greek fleet at Salamis in 480, and his army was defeated at Plataea the following year and retreated back to Asia.

In the next few years the remaining Persian forces were driven from the north Aegean, and the Greek cities of western Anatolia were, for a few decades, liberated from Persian control, becoming instead members of an Athenian-led alliance. It was not long, however, before Persian authority was restored on the east Aegean coast. Increasing distrust between the Greek cities led eventually to the Peloponnesian War between Athens and Sparta and their respective allies (431–404), and the real victor of that conflict was the Achaemenid empire. Both sides had tried to win support from the Kings Artaxerxes I (465–424) and Darius II (423–405), and it was the intervention in particular of Darius' younger son Cyrus on the side of the Spartans that gave them the naval power they needed to force the Athenians to surrender. In return for that support the Spartans had agreed to give up the Greek cities on the Asian mainland to the Persians.

Relations between the Spartans and the Persians broke down on the death of Darius II, as Spartan officers with a body of mercenary soldiers supported Cyrus in an unsuccessful attempt to take the throne from his elder brother Artaxerxes II (405-359). This campaign was described by the Athenian writer Xenophon, who took part in it, in his *Anabasis*, a work that provided a model for Arrian's *Anabasis* of Alexander. Artaxerxes finally settled affairs in the Aegean area in 386 by an arrangement that was known as the King's Peace, in which Achaemenid rule over the cities of the Asian mainland was recognized, and the king threatened to intervene with troops or money if the Greeks of the islands and the European mainland did not respect the settlement and each other's autonomy. In the following decades Persian money was provided to leading Greek politicians to ensure that they advocated policies that did not conflict with the king's interests, and there was little direct conflict between Greeks and the forces of the Achaemenid empire.

The Achaemenid empire in the 4th century

Xerxes' successors put up few royal inscriptions, and as a result we know much less about events elsewhere in the empire than we do for earlier periods. A Greek historian, Ctesias of Cnidus, spent time at the court of Artaxerxes II, and wrote a history of Persia now known only through quotation from other authors, but this does not tell us much. The empire remained mostly intact, although Egypt broke away from Achaemenid control in 404, and was only reconquered in 343, by Artaxerxes III (359-338). We know about the events of the last years of the empire from a number of Babylonian documents including the so-called *Dynastic Prophecy*, which reports some episodes of intrigue in the Achaemenid court. On the death of Artaxerxes III, possibly by poison but probably from natural causes, most of his relatives were murdered at the instigation of a court eunuch, Bagoas, and his one surviving son was installed as Artaxerxes IV (338-336). Two years later Bagoas had him too killed, and with the rest of the family already dead Bagoas installed a distant relative, Darius III (336-331), on the throne. Darius had been a successful military leader, and turned out to be the wrong choice for Bagoas, who was killed on the king's orders. This was the man who was to face Alexander the Great.

Macedonia: the first 150 years

Meanwhile, in Macedon Amyntas' son, Alexander I ($c.495$–454), was able to hold on to his position after Xerxes' defeat in the Aegean. He became known as Alexander Philhellene ('Friend of the Greeks'), and Herodotus reports stories which present him as having secretly worked against the Persians all along. His kingdom faced challenges from all sides, and at times from within. The Macedonian heartland was the substantial plain at the northwest corner of the Aegean, through which the rivers Haliacmon and Axios flowed, known as Lower Macedonia, with its royal capital, Aegae, at the southern edge of the plain. Alexander I had extended his rule into the higher ground to the west and north (Upper Macedonia), and also eastwards to the valley of the Strymon, to control a territory of over 17,000 km^2 (that is a little larger than the historic county of Yorkshire in the UK, or a little smaller than the state of New Jersey in the USA). As well as including large amounts of fertile land for agriculture and stock rearing, the area had forests and deposits of silver and gold. It was, however, hemmed in on all sides by potential enemies. To the east were the kingdoms of Thrace while to the northwest and west lay Illyria and Epirus. On the Aegean coast, and in particular on the Chalcidice peninsula, there were Greek cities that had been established in the 7th and 6th centuries.

Macedonian kings sometimes made multiple marriages, and as a consequence tended to produce several sons with different mothers. This practice of polygamy allowed the king to make considerable use of marriage-alliances to seal diplomatic arrangements, and it meant that there was no shortage of male heirs. On the other hand it meant that the death of a king of Macedon more than once led to a period of instability as his heirs fought each other for the throne. This happened on the death of Alexander I, and his successor Perdiccas II (454–413) took several years to establish himself in power. His reign was characterized by frequent threats from his neighbours, dealt with by a combination of limited military action, not always successful, and negotiation.

His successor Archelaus (413–399) is credited with strengthening Macedonian military effectiveness, building roads and fortifications, and possibly introducing new infantry formations. He also built a new capital at Pella, in the Macedonian plain, and established a court which attracted Greek artists and writers, including the Athenian tragedian Euripides, to move there. After Archelaus' death there was more fighting amongst his successors until his cousin Amyntas III (393–369) was able to establish himself in power. His reign coincided with increased expansionism from Illyria and growing hostility from the Greek cities of Chalcidice. These pressures continued after his death, and new ones were added, as Macedonia started to be more directly involved in the affairs of the Greek cities further south. After Amyntas' death, his son Alexander II (369–368) campaigned in Thessaly before he was assassinated, and his successor, Ptolemy (368–365), who was probably acting as regent for Alexander's younger brother Perdiccas, allied the kingdom with the Greek city of Thebes, sending hostages, including the future Philip II, another brother of Alexander and Perdiccas, to Thebes as a sign of good faith. Under Perdiccas III (365–360) Macedon found itself for a while allied with Athens instead of Thebes, but the arrangement was short-lived, as was Perdiccas himself, who was killed in battle against an invading Illyrian army, leaving the throne to his brother Philip II (360–338), the father of Alexander the Great.

Philip II

It took Philip less than three years to transform the fortunes of Macedonia through a combination of diplomacy, military reorganization, and skilled generalship. As well as having to deal with the advancing Illyrian army, he faced the threat of an uprising in Paeonia in Upper Macedonia and the possibility of a challenge for the throne from three half-brothers and two other pretenders, backed by Athens and Thrace. He was able to negotiate with the Athenians and bribe the Thracians to nullify this last danger, and he had his half-brother Archelaus executed. He also induced the Paeonians to end their threat by offering money, and was able to negotiate a temporary truce with the Illyrians. This gave him time to improve the training and organization of his army. There is some debate about how far Philip was responsible for innovations in the Macedonian way of fighting, and how much was achieved by his predecessors or left to his son Alexander to complete. Since this is a book about Alexander, it makes more sense to look at the army as it was under Alexander, and this will be described in Chapter 3. It is generally recognized, however, that Philip increased the effectiveness of the Macedonian armed forces by recruiting larger numbers of both infantry and cavalry, and instituting more regular and more thorough training. By 358 he was able to march against the Illyrians and to drive them out of Upper Macedonia.

Philip secured his relationship with his neighbours through a series of marriages. The first of his seven wives was Phila, from Elimiotis in Upper Macedonia; she was joined by Audata, a member of the Illyrian royal family, and two women from leading families from Greek cities in Thessaly, Nicepolis and Philinna, and then in 357 by Olympias, a member of the Epirote royal family. Later in his reign he married Meda, daughter of a Thracian king, and finally Cleopatra, a member of a high-ranking Macedonian family. Philip's father Amyntas III had six sons through two marriages. In contrast Philip's wives, who produced several daughters, bore him only two sons: Philinna gave birth to Arrhidaeus, who was for some reason considered unfit to rule, and Olympias was the mother of Alexander the Great. Royal wives who did not have sons had little influence at court, and little is known about these various women. Olympias, however, lived through Alexander's reign, and wielded considerable influence. We will learn more about her in the next chapter.

Philip's activities after this make it clear that he saw aggression as the most effective way to secure Macedonian interests, but he accompanied it with other activities which demonstrated that he could work with the Greeks as well as against them. In the period 357–354 he took control of all of the Greek cities in the region outside Chalcidice, from Amphipolis in the east to Pydna in the south. He also took over the city of Crenides, which controlled very productive gold and silver mines, and renamed it Philippi. In 356 he entered a chariot in the Olympic Games, and won. This was more than mere display: Olympic victors were recognized in Greece as having the favour of Zeus, and were treated with particular respect, so Philip's victory made him more difficult to ignore.

In 356 a war broke out in central Greece between Phocis and Boeotia, partly over control of the sanctuary and oracle of Apollo at Delphi. Modern scholars know it as the Third Sacred War. The cities of Thessaly, which lay between Macedonia and Phocis, became involved in the war, and Philip was called on by Larissa, the home city of his wife Philinna, to defend it against the Phocians who supported its rival Pherae (home city of another of his wives, Nicepolis—it is possible that the marriage took place after these events). In 352 Philip defeated the Phocians, and was elected commander of the whole of Thessaly. Gradually he was being drawn into the affairs of the major Greek cities.

Involvement in the south alternated with aggressive advances to the east. Philip returned to Macedonia, and went to war with king Cersobleptes of Thrace, and then moved against Chalcidice, capturing the most powerful Greek city there, Olynthus, in 348. Then in 346 he marched back south into Phocis, occupied the pass of Thermopylae, where Xerxes had defeated the Spartans, which controlled land routes between central Greece and the north, and brought the ten-year war with the Boeotians to an end. The sanctuary of Apollo at Delphi, along with the area around Thermopylae, was overseen by a council of Greeks known as the Delphic Amphictyony, made up of delegates mainly from the area around the sanctuary (*'amphictyon'* means 'neighbour'). It was not entirely clear before this date who was entitled to membership of the council, but as part of the settlement after the war, the Phocians were expelled from it, and Philip took their place. It is also unclear what influence the council had—its main task was to oversee the festival of the Pylaea, celebrated twice a year at Thermopylae, and to protect the sanctuary at Delphi—but, like his Olympic victory, membership of the Delphic Amphictyony made Philip an honoured individual in the eyes of many, if not all, Greeks. Following this he returned to Thrace, annexing Cersobleptes' kingdom by 342, and marching north as far as the Danube.

What Philip's ultimate aims were at this point is something that modern scholars disagree about, and it was unclear to his contemporaries as well. The larger Greek cities of the south, including Athens and Sparta, had interests in the natural resources of the north Aegean area, and at times formed alliances with both the northern Greek cities and the Thracian kingdoms: the growth of Macedonia could be seen to threaten their interests. The Athenians in particular were dependent on supplies of grain from the Black Sea, and so could not have a hostile power controlling the Bosporus or Hellespont. Philip's advance eastwards was also a potential threat to the Persian king. By 340 Philip was besieging cities on the north shore of the Sea of Marmara, including Byzantium, and Artaxerxes III sent supplies and mercenary troops to support them. He also, like his predecessors, sent money to politicians in Athens and elsewhere to encourage them to oppose Philip wherever possible. On the other hand Philip had been invited to intervene in Thessaly and central Greece by the leaders of Greek cities who saw him as someone who could protect them against their rivals. It is quite possible that, having secured control of the areas around Macedonia, he wanted to maintain peaceful relations with the other Greeks. Some Athenian politicians and pamphleteers, probably the recipients of gifts from him, argued for supporting Philip in a campaign against the Persians; others, equally probably receiving money from Artaxerxes, took an opposite view.

Events at opposite corners of the Aegean led to the final confrontation between Philip and Athens that brought his campaigns in Greece to completion. In 340 the Athenians made an alliance with Byzantium, which was under siege by Philip. He responded by seizing the Athenian grain fleet, and the Athenians declared war. Later that year the Delphic Amphictyony accused the city of Amphissa, just west of Delphi, of cultivating land sacred to Apollo, and began a military campaign against it. When the first season's campaign did not lead to a settlement, Philip was called down to deal with the problem. He marched against Amphissa, and then turned west to threaten Athens. Demosthenes, Athens' most effective orator, and one of the recipients of gifts from the Persian king, encouraged the Athenians to march out against Philip, and persuaded the Thebans to join them. The two sides met at Chaeronea in August 338, and Philip was the victor. He installed a garrison in Thebes, but made no attempt to punish the Athenians. Instead, he started to organize his next campaign.

In the Spring of 337 representatives of all the Greek cities except Sparta gathered at Corinth and swore oaths of allegiance to Philip, establishing an organization called by modern scholars the League of Corinth. At the meeting Philip announced a planned invasion of the Achaemenid empire, with the avowed aims of punishing the Persians for the destruction caused by Xerxes, and of once more liberating the Greek cities of Asia. To muster all the troops required for the campaign would take time, but in March 336 a Macedonian advance force of 10,000 men, led by Philip's generals, Parmenion and Attalus, crossed the Hellespont from Europe into Asia.

Chapter 2
Prince: Alexander in the Macedonian court

Alexander the Great was born in July 356, in the royal palace in Pella, while his father Philip II was campaigning against the Greek cities in the Chalcidice peninsula. As is to be expected in the case of a man whose achievements were to be so impressive, stories of omens surrounding his birth later circulated widely. The temple of Artemis at Ephesus supposedly burned down on the day Alexander was born, and it was suggested that Artemis, who was associated with child-birth among other things, had neglected her temple because she was attending the Macedonian prince's birth. It was also said that Philip received the news of Alexander's birth on the same day that he also learned that his chariot had won the Olympic Games, and that his general Parmenion had defeated the Illyrians. On the basis of this coincidence, seers were said to have predicted that Alexander would be 'invincible' or 'unconquered' (the Greek word is *aniketos*). This is a word that was frequently used to describe him by later writers.

Of the Alexander historians only Plutarch has anything to say about his childhood. Some of what Plutarch says is supported by other writers, in particular his account of Alexander's education under the guidance of the philosopher Aristotle, but several of the more dramatic stories seem to be included because they foreshadow Alexander's later achievements rather than because they are reliable. These include the story of how Alexander came to master his horse, Bucephalas, which was considered to be impossible to control, after he made a bet with his father that he could do this. Alexander does appear to have had particular affection for this horse, and is said to have offered a huge reward for its return when it was stolen in northern Iran. After the horse died during Alexander's campaigning in the Punjab, he named a city that he founded in the region Bucephala in its memory. The question of whether the story of his taming Bucephalas explains this affection, or whether the story was inspired by Alexander's later actions, remains open.

Royal women

For the Greeks and Macedonians of Alexander's time, and the Greeks and Romans of the time of the Alexander historians, an orderly society was one where decisions were taken by men. It was acceptable for women to protect the interests of their children, particularly their sons, by appealing to the male members of their families, but not to act on their own behalf. Greek literature as far back as the poems of Homer offered positive images of women who could influence their husbands to show kindness to strangers, or respect to the gods, but it also presented negative images of dangerous women who challenged the proper order of things. In democracies women's influence was necessarily limited, but in monarchies the women of the royal family could have considerable indirect power, and would be expected to use it on their children's behalf. Macedonia was no exception.

Plutarch tells a number of stories about Alexander's mother Olympias, with whom he had a close relationship throughout his life. Even while he was on campaign they corresponded by letters, and he sent gifts back to her from the spoils of his victories. Plutarch's stories are not favourable to Olympias: she is presented as jealous and suspicious in her relationship with Alexander's father Philip, and also as wild and dangerous. Part of the explanation for this is that Olympias was involved in the competition and conflict between Alexander's successors after his death, and various individuals had reasons to present a negative picture of her. It is difficult to know where the truth behind these depictions lies, but it is possible to get a more balanced understanding of the place of women in the Macedonian court by looking at the experience of other royal women. What we can say about Alexander's grandmother Eurydice and his sister Cleopatra can help us understand more about his mother.

Eurydice

The career of Eurydice, wife of Amyntas III and mother of Philip II, who may well have been alive during Alexander's early childhood, demonstrates what women could achieve, and what they might have to endure, both in life and in reputation. Eurydice was either Illyrian or Lyncestian, and Amyntas married her to maintain good relations with potentially dangerous neighbours. She bore him three sons, and this, more than anything else, will have raised her status in the Macedonian court. When Amyntas died, Eurydice was forced to enter the world of diplomacy. Her eldest son Alexander II was at this point already dead or else on the frontier fighting against the Illyrians, while a pretender, Pausanias, was making a rapid advance into Macedonia. Eurydice took her younger sons, Perdiccas and Philip, and went to the Athenian general Iphicrates, who was in the region trying to take control of the Greek city of Amphipolis. Iphicrates had been adopted by Amyntas, so Eurydice could claim him as her own step-son. According to the Athenian orator Aeschines, Eurydice put her sons into Iphicrates' lap, and begged him to protect them as his brothers. The appeal to family ties made what might otherwise have been an inappropriate action for a woman acceptable, and Iphicrates drove Pausanias out of Macedonia. A less reliable story has Eurydice, not long after this, marrying a man called Ptolemy, who had successfully installed himself as regent for Perdiccas, so that she could continue to protect her sons' interests. Who this Ptolemy was is uncertain, but it has been suggested that he was her son-in-law, who had killed her son Alexander II. If so, then Eurydice was marrying the killer of one of her sons to protect the others. An even more lurid version of events is told by Justin: he claims that Eurydice, out of a desire to marry Ptolemy, had attempted unsuccessfully to murder Amyntas, and that after his death she herself had first had Alexander and then Perdiccas killed. Aeschines' sympathetic story was told less than 30 years after the events, whereas Justin's source, Pompeius Trogus, was writing over 300 years later, with a Roman's distaste for women intervening in political affairs, but Justin's version of events was, until recently, accepted as fact. The way in which Eurydice was transformed by ancient and modern scholars from a mother relying on family connections to protect her sons into an ambitious schemer prepared to kill them should give us pause when we consider the accounts of her daughter-in-law, Olympias, mother of Alexander the Great.

Cleopatra

It was at the wedding of Alexander's sister to her uncle, Olympias' brother, generally referred to as Alexander of Epirus, that their father Philip was assassinated. Cleopatra, like Olympias, received gifts from Alexander's spoils, and at some point she interceded with him on behalf of a local dynast in Anatolia, not an inappropriate action for a sister. Alexander of Epirus died on campaign in Italy, leaving a son Neoptolemus, and a daughter, Cadmeia, and Cleopatra acted as regent for them: Neoptolemus did become ruler of Epirus some 30 years later. As Philip's daughter Cleopatra became a potentially valuable wife for the generals competing for power after Alexander's death, but she was eventually killed under uncertain circumstances in 308 BCE, when she was around 50 years old. Her life, like that of her grandmother, for all that it gave her important responsibilities, was defined by her relationships to the male members of her family.

Olympias

Olympias' career was not very different from those of her mother-in-law and her daughter. She was the daughter of Neoptolemus of Molossia, in Epirus, and her marriage to Philip was, as usual, arranged for diplomatic reasons. As the mother of Alexander her standing in the court will have been high, but little is reported about her in the period before Alexander became king—and that little is likely to be fantasy rather than fact. The story of the birth of Alexander became associated with miraculous events, and over time even stories about his conception grew up. A tradition, probably originating in Egypt in the 3rd century, claimed that Alexander was the son of Zeus, or the Egyptian god Amun, who came to Olympias in the form of a snake. Plutarch reports this story, but offers what appears to be a rationalizing explanation for it: Olympias was, he says, like most women in the region, a devotee of Orphic and Bacchic rites—that is the ecstatic worship of the god Dionysus—and she provided large snakes for these rites. It is true that the story of the death of Orpheus, torn apart by maenads or bacchants, devotees of Dionysus, was traditionally associated with Macedonian Pieria, and that Euripides' tragedy, *Bacchae*, in which the king of Thebes, Pentheus, is killed by his mother and other women in a maenadic frenzy, was first performed in Macedonia at the court of Archelaus. It is also the case that Dionysiac imagery is found on some of the magnificent vessels buried in 4th-century Macedonian tombs. But even if Olympias did take part in Bacchic rituals, which is by no means certain, and even if they did involve handling snakes, which is less likely, the resulting image of Olympias as snake-obsessed is pure invention. In those places where we have clear evidence of women taking part in Bacchic activities (and they do not include Macedonia in this period), the women who acted as priestesses were not seen as deviant in their behaviour.

After Philip's death, Olympias, as queen mother, continued to have an important role at the court in Macedon, while Alexander was on campaign. Plutarch and Arrian both refer to correspondence between Alexander and Olympias, although the texts they had access to are generally reckoned not to be genuine. It is probable that she did not have a good relationship with Alexander's regent, Antipater, and she moved back to Molossia around 330. After Alexander's death, Olympias' position became dependent on the fortune of Alexander's infant son, Alexander IV, and she was part of his entourage when she was killed by Cassander, Antipater's son, in 315. Like her mother-in-law, Eurydice, Olympias is depicted negatively in the surviving narratives; but attempts to invert these accounts to present Olympias as a powerful and independent woman are not necessarily any closer to the truth. Her position, like Eurydice's, depended on her son, and later her grandson. If we could get to a true picture behind the misleading representation of the surviving ancient narratives, which we cannot, it is likely that we would find that she was neither heroine nor monster, but that she fulfilled the expected role of a woman in Macedonian society, dutifully working for her children, at whatever cost.

The life of a prince

Archaeological excavation at the royal sites of lower Macedonia in the last few decades has done more than anything else to cast light on the world in which Alexander grew up. Although Alexander was born in Pella, which had been the royal centre of Macedon since the end of the 5th century, it is the excavations at the palace and tombs at Aegae, near modern Vergina, that have expanded the understanding of Macedonian public life in his time.

The palace at Aegae was probably built by Philip II. It stood on an outcrop of rock on the slope of the hill that formed the acropolis of the ancient city of Aegae, dominating the city below it with a monumental entrance facing the city. At the centre of the palace was an open area surrounded by a peristyle. In this open court the king could address his courtiers, and in the rooms that opened off the peristyle they could dine in groups of up to 30. Some of the mosaic floors of the palace survive, showing that it was richly decorated, but inevitably the wall decorations and the contents of the building have not survived. However, something of their wealth and splendour can be guessed at from what was found in the most famous archaeological discoveries at the site of Vergina-Aegae, the Macedonian royal tombs. These tombs, one of which may be that of Philip II, contained rich grave goods including furniture decorated with gold and ivory, as well as jewellery and other ornaments of gold and silver. Elsewhere in Macedonia other rich burials have been excavated, packed with vessels of gold, silver, and bronze. The royal tombs were painted with scenes from myth and from court life, and the palace will have been decorated in the same way. One theme of Macedonian art is particularly worth noting, and that is the Royal Hunt.

Hunting

There is no doubt that hunting was an important part of Macedonian elite life. In his collection of texts about eating and drinking, *The Learned Banqueters*, the writer Athenaeus of Naucratis includes the statement from a 3rd-century historian Hegesander, that no Macedonian was permitted to recline at dinner unless he had killed a wild boar without the use of nets. One of the plots against Alexander from within his court started after Alexander had one of his pages flogged, because, during a hunt, he killed a boar which Alexander was about to claim for himself. A successful boar hunt marked a transition between boy and man, and so for Alexander to dishonour a youth who had just made that transition by beating him was a particularly humiliating act. Hunting was a frequent subject of Macedonian art. Mosaics from Pella, and the largest painting from the royal tombs at Vergina-Aegae depict Philip and Alexander hunting lions, either on horseback or on foot. Mountain lions could be found in Macedonia in that period, but lion hunts will have been less common than boar hunts. It is likely that one of the reasons for depicting lions was emulation of Persian, and before them Assyrian, kings, who decorated their own palaces with scenes of lion hunts, and close combat between the king and one or more lions. As he advanced through the territories of the Achaemenid empire Alexander visited and hunted in some of the hunting parks created by satraps and by previous kings.

As we have seen, the early history of the Macedonian monarchy was linked to the campaigns of the Persian king Darius in the north Aegean area. Even after Persian forces had left Europe at the end of Xerxes' unsuccessful invasion, the courts of the Persian satraps in Asia Minor remained powerful models for the monarchs of Thrace and Macedonia just to their west. It has been argued by some scholars that Philip II, even while he planned his campaign against the Persian empire, was prepared to emulate some of the Great King's court practices. He introduced the practice of aristocrats sending their young sons to the palace to serve as pages, and especially to accompany the king when he went hunting; the 4th-century historian Xenophon describes the Persian king as being accompanied in the same way. Alexander's upbringing will have prepared him well not only for ruling Macedonia, but for dealing with the powerful empire to its east.

Alexander becomes king

Alexander's life in the Macedonian court was interrupted when he went into exile in Illyria after quarrelling with his father, who had recently married his last wife, Cleopatra, a Macedonian woman, the daughter of one of Philip's generals, Attalus. Plutarch, who reports the incident, implies that Alexander's position as Philip's heir was under threat, although this seems unlikely. Alexander returned to Macedon not long after this, in time to be present at his sister's wedding to her uncle, Alexander of Epirus. The wedding was celebrated with a great festival at Aegae, to which ambassadors from the Greek cities were invited. It was at this wedding that Alexander's father Philip was assassinated.

The killer was arrested before he could escape. He was one of Philip's bodyguards, called Pausanias, and it is possible that his motives were entirely personal. There were, however, inevitably many suggestions that he was part of a larger conspiracy. Two men from the leading family of Lyncestis in Upper Macedonia, Heromenes and Arrhabaeus, were accused of involvement in the plot, and executed alongside Pausanias, although their brother Alexander was not implicated. Alexander the Great is said later to have accused the Persian king Darius of plotting to assassinate Philip: his death would certainly have served Darius' interests, but no ancient writer appears to have made a connection between him and Pausanias. An alternative theory that Plutarch suggests was spread at the time was that Olympias was behind the assassination, and Justin implicates Alexander himself in the plot. It is difficult to see how Philip's death at this point would have benefited Alexander, however. Nor is it plausible that Olympias would have acted for Alexander without his knowledge. There is much that remains unclear about the death of Philip, but it left Alexander as heir to all his father's positions, above all as king of Macedon, and as leader of a proposed Greek expedition to seek for revenge against the Persians for the destruction they caused in 481–479.

Chapter 3
Warrior: Alexander's army

Alexander was engaged in military campaigning throughout his reign. Before he led his army against the Persian empire he had to deal with uprisings in the areas to the northeast and west of Macedonia, and then with the Greek city of Thebes, which he besieged and sacked. After crossing into Asia he fought three major pitched battles against the Persians, at the Granicus River (334), at Issus (333), and at Gaugamela (331), as well as one against the Indian king Porus on the Hydaspes River (326), and a number of smaller engagements. He successfully besieged a series of cities on the west coast of Anatolia and in the Levant. He was also faced with a long insurgency in Afghanistan (329–326), and more trouble in Pakistan during his march down the Indus Valley. He was, in the end, always successful. We have seen that the title of 'undefeated' became attached to him: it was well-deserved.

Many books have been written about Alexander's generalship and his armed forces, illustrated with plans of his various battles. However, the evidence on which these accounts and plans are based is not easy to use, and there is much about Alexander's achievements that remains guesswork. Even though Arrian himself had experience of military command, and wrote works on tactics, the ancient accounts of Alexander's battles and sieges were less concerned with the details of military formations and command structures, and more interested in illustrating the less tangible aspects of warfare.

Forces

Some basic information about Alexander's army can be taken as reliable. He crossed into Asia to begin his campaign with around 32,000 infantry and 5,000 cavalry. There he joined up with the force of around 10,000 that Philip had sent out two years earlier. Seven thousand of the infantry and 600 of the cavalry were from the Greek cities of the League of Corinth, a further 5,000 infantrymen were Greek mercenaries, and the rest were Macedonians and their allies. The Greek cities also contributed ships to Alexander's fleet, but he was to disband this before the end of the year. As his campaign went on Alexander lost men to disease and to death and injury in battles and sieges, and through retirement, but he received a regular supply of reinforcements from Macedonia and Greece, and later on from within his newly conquered empire. Numbers provided by the ancient narratives for the size of his army remain generally consistent and believable throughout. The same cannot be said for the figures for the size of the armies he faced. At the battle of Gaugamela, for example, his second and final encounter with Darius III, figures for the Persian army range between 200,000 and 1,000,000 infantry and between 40,000 and 200,000 cavalry. Modern writers generally consider the likely number to have been below 100,000 men in total.

Alexander inherited his army from his father Philip, and its basic elements are referred to by enough ancient writers for us to understand its broad composition. The evidence from archaeology, in particular from grave goods, also helps our understanding of weapons and armour. There were cavalrymen armed with lances (but riding without stirrups, a fact which limited the impact with which they could charge); at the heart of the infantry was the so-called Macedonian phalanx, armed with

6-metre long pikes, called *sarissas*, and they are generally thought to have been flanked by men armed with thrusting spears and swords, and large round shields, like the hoplites of the Greek city states. As well as these there were light-armed troops, armed with javelins, bows, or slings. But attempts at greater specificity run into the problem that the ancient writers give a number of names for more specific units, without explaining what they are, and possibly sometimes using the same name for different units, or different names for the same units. The men of the phalanx are referred to as *pezhetairoi* ('foot-companions'), but there are also references to *asthetairoi*: it is not certain what this word means. Similarly the hoplites may be called *hypaspists* ('shield-bearers'), but towards the end of the campaign we have references to *argyraspids* ('silver-shields'), who may be an elite group of these men or something different. Such uncertainties do not cause major problems in the reconstruction of battles, but they have generated a small scholarly industry of attempts to work out what the terms referred to.

Ancient armies were made up of more than their soldiers, and the presence of camp-followers is occasionally noted by the ancient writers. Every cavalryman would have had an attendant, and although Philip is supposed to have limited infantrymen to one servant for every ten soldiers, officers would have had more. As the campaign progressed, soldiers would acquire booty, and need slaves to look after it and them. There were also, no doubt, numerous other camp-followers offering their services, of many kinds, for food or pay. Periodically attempts were made to reduce the amount of baggage and the number of hangers-on, but as war-fighting was a recognized means of acquiring possessions much of the time the camp-followers must have outnumbered the soldiers.

Sieges

Alexander's forces also included a siege train. This was an aspect of warfare that Alexander appears to have developed considerably:

catapults, battering rams, and siege towers, dismantled and loaded onto mule carts, would follow behind the army, along with the rest of the baggage train. The 7-month siege of Tyre (332) was one of his most celebrated achievements in antiquity. This is clear from the detailed accounts that we have of it, not only in the surviving historians, but also in the *Alexander Romance*, the popular version of Alexander's life that circulated widely, and was continually embellished, in the ancient and medieval worlds. And it is one case where Alexander's actions left a permanent mark on the landscape. The ancient city of Tyre was built on an island just off the Lebanese coast. During the siege Alexander built a causeway out towards the island, and although it was not completed, it led to the subsequent silting up of the channel in between, and so the ruins of ancient Tyre, such as they are, are now part of the mainland.

Battles

When it comes to reconstructing Alexander's battles, the starting point is the accounts in the surviving sources. These can be supplemented by autopsy: modern writers have visited the sites of the battles—although ancient accounts of the topography are not always precise, and in some cases it has proved difficult to identify where encounters took place. For example, the 'Persian Gates', where an Achaemenid force tried to prevent Alexander getting through the Zagros Mountains to Pasargadae and Persepolis, has not been satisfactorily located. But even when we have several descriptions of a battle, and a good idea of where it was fought, there are severe problems facing any attempt at a detailed reconstruction. Ptolemy, the historian on whose work Arrian and Plutarch draw, probably took part in all the major battles of the campaign. And yet this would not necessarily make him a good source of information. From his position somewhere in the cavalry, he would only have seen a small part of the action, and most of this would have been confused and confusing. But in any case it is likely that Ptolemy did not rely primarily on his own memory for reconstructing events. He probably based his battle descriptions on those of Callisthenes, Alexander's 'official historian', who may have witnessed the battles from a distance, and who would have been able to talk to a range of participants. But Callisthenes may not have been concerned with accuracy above all, as a consideration of the accounts of Alexander's first battle against the Persians, at the Granicus River, will show.

The Battle of the Granicus

According to Arrian and Plutarch, Alexander marched from Troy, where he had visited the tomb of Achilles, and had taken from the temple of Athena a shield supposedly used in the Trojan War, to the River Granicus where he had found a Persian force commanded by the local satraps holding the far bank, which was high and steep. Parmenion, the senior member of his staff, suggested that Alexander should postpone his attack until the morning, but Alexander is said to have responded that the Hellespont would be ashamed if, after he had crossed it, he was now held up by the trickle that was the Granicus, and with that he led his troops into the river and against the Persians. Arrian gives rather more details about what happened next, but both authors include a list of Persians whom Alexander met and killed, one after another, once he had gained dry land on the far side. It has been recognized that this is the most difficult of Alexander's battles to reconstruct, because the description is rather vague, and scholars have commented that the series of single combats fought by Alexander resembles passages from Homer's *Iliad* more than anything else. The resemblance to Homer may in fact have been deliberate, especially if it is Callisthenes' account that is being followed here. Early in the description of Achilles' one day of fighting in the *Iliad*, Homer describes how the hero leaps into the river Scamander in pursuit of the Trojans, and battles with the river itself. Alexander claimed descent from Achilles, and Callisthenes' description of the battle—first the leap into the river, and then the sequence of single-combats—will have been as much influenced by a wish to bring out the relationship between the two heroes as by any concern for accurate reportage. Diodorus gives a rather different account of the battle, in which Alexander camped overnight near the river and was then able to bring his troops over unopposed early in the morning, and fight on dry land. Whatever Diodorus' source was, in this case his version may be nearer the truth.

If Diodorus was more accurate, then one of the elements in the other version that has to be rejected is the exchange between Alexander and Parmenion about the wisdom of launching an attack across the river. There are several such exchanges described between the two men in the surviving narratives, and they have a standard pattern: Parmenion offers sensible, if cautious, advice to Alexander; he ignores it, and turns out to be right to do so. Often, the exchanges are occasions for wit: when Darius sent a letter to Alexander offering peace terms, Parmenion is said to have remarked 'I would accept, if I were you', to which Alexander responded, 'so would I, if I were you.' There is no reason to assume, as some have done, that these stories reflect a growing rift between the two men. It is true that Alexander had Parmenion killed, after his son was convicted of plotting against the king, but up until that point Parmenion remained a trusted adviser, and was given rich rewards by Alexander. It is better to recognize that these are examples of a particular kind of story, that of the 'wise adviser'. These stories depict an older man giving advice to a young ruler, so in Herodotus' *Histories* the young Cyrus the Great is given advice by Croesus, former king of Lydia, and Xerxes is given advice by his uncle Artabanus, and by the former king of Sparta, Demeratus. Normally the young man, if he is wise, accepts the advice and prospers, or, if he is foolish, rejects it and suffers. But the stories involving Alexander reverse this pattern: he rejects the advice and still prospers, revealing that he is a truly exceptional ruler. The ancient writers use their narratives to illustrate their conception of Alexander's character, sometimes at the expense of fidelity to the facts.

There were other ways of heightening the significance of Alexander's achievements in battle. The narrative of Xerxes' invasion of Greece, as told particularly by Herodotus, offered the historians of Alexander an opportunity to draw parallels between the two commanders. The clearest example of this is the description of Alexander's entry into the province of Fars, where the city and palace of Persepolis was located, through a pass in the Zagros Mountains known as the Persian Gates.

The Persian Gates

As Xerxes marched through Greece towards Athens in 480, the only place where he could be stopped was a narrow passage between the mountains and the sea in central Greece called Thermopylae, a name meaning 'Hot Gates', so-called because of a local hot spring. Herodotus describes how the pass was defended by the Spartan king Leonidas and 300 Spartan hoplites, supported by some 5,000 other troops. According to his account the Spartans, who could have held out indefinitely, were betrayed by a local man called Ephialtes, who led a party of Xerxes' troops along a little-known path that took them behind the Spartan position. On the third day of the battle, Leonidas found his troops surrounded, and he died on the battlefield. Xerxes' victory left the path to Athens open, and he was able to sack the city not long after. Although the battle ended in an avoidable defeat—Leonidas knew about the path, but did not protect it adequately—it quickly came to be considered an example of heroic self-sacrifice, and this is how Herodotus, writing around 50 years later, describes it, and how it has entered popular culture. But the narrative could also be reused.

The historians all describe Alexander's advance from Mesopotamia towards Fars through the Zagros Mountains, which involved going through a narrow pass referred to by Diodorus as the Susian Rocks, but by Arrian as the Persian Gates, held against him by a Persian commander, Ariobarzanes. Like Leonidas at the

Hot Gates, Ariobarzanes had built a wall across the pass to protect his forces, but his forces were much greater, at 25,000 infantry according to Diodorus, and 40,000 according to Arrian—although as always these figures are unreliable and implausibly high. The authors describe how, after at first failing, like Xerxes, to break through the enemy position by a frontal attack, Alexander was told by a local man about a narrow path through the mountains that would bring him out behind the Persian lines. In the fighting that followed, the Persians were defeated, but unlike Leonidas, Ariobarzanes ran away. This was Alexander's last military encounter on his way to Persepolis, which he destroyed (see Chapter 6) in revenge for Xerxes' sack of Athens after Thermopylae. The similarities between the accounts of the battles at the Hot Gates and the Persian Gates are too great to be coincidental, and it is clear that whatever may have actually happened in the Zagros Mountains, it suited those who wrote about it to present it as an appropriate inversion of Xerxes' sole victory in Greece.

Omens

Another important area where the concerns of ancient writers differ from those of their modern successors is in their attention to supernatural aspects of warfare. As a modern discipline, military history tends to focus on practical issues—the relative strength and quality of opposing forces, the nature of terrain, logistical organization, the competence of commanders and their subordinates. While the ancient accounts of Alexander's campaigns are sometimes frustratingly lacking in these details, they are generally rich in accounts of omens and the advice of seers. This emphasis does reflect important truths about ancient warfare: given the uncertainty of war in general, ancient military commanders made considerable use of divination, looking to the gods to provide information that human resources could not. As a result, good *manteis* (seers), which means men who could not only correctly advise on the outcome of future actions, but who also had a record of being on the victorious side, were highly valued, and could expect rich rewards from the individuals and communities they served.

In the surviving accounts of Alexander's campaigns, above all in Arrian, his *mantis*, Aristander of Telmessus, plays a very visible role, interpreting a great variety of things, including the entrails of sacrificed animals, the behaviour of birds, dreams, astrological events like eclipses, and unusual phenomena such as sweating statues. All these are matters on which a seer would normally be consulted, but the stories need to be treated with care. It is a feature of ancient narratives, including historical ones, that prophecies always come true, one way or another. In Arrian and Plutarch, Aristander's predictions, however unlikely, always turn out to be correct, and it is clear that once again their inclusion in the narrative serves mainly to make a point about Alexander. It is appropriate that the greatest general should be accompanied by the greatest seer, so Aristander's perfect record of prediction is a reflection of Alexander's own invincibility. Aristander is not present in accounts of Alexander's last year, presumably because he had actually died at some point in the campaign, but it is only once Aristander has left the story that Alexander starts to witness omens foretelling his own death—not all of which are understood at the time.

The campaigns

Alexander's expedition in Asia can be divided into two clear stages. In the first of these he was acting as the leader of an alliance of Greek states aiming to liberate the Greek cities of Asia from Achaemenid control, and to take revenge on the Persians for Xerxes' invasion of Greece 150 years earlier. The first of these aims, the liberation of the Greek cities, was largely achieved in 334, the first year of the campaign, as Alexander marched south through Asia Minor before turning eastwards into central Anatolia. The Persians regained control of some of the cities that he had freed in the following year, but Alexander sent a force to deal with this, and by the end of 332, Persian power in the region was permanently ended. Revenge on the Persians ultimately took the form of the destruction of the city and palace of Persepolis in Fars. Alexander's route there was by no means direct, but made sense militarily. In part it was determined by the actions of his opponent Darius in defending his territory. Alexander had disbanded much of his fleet not long after the start of the expedition, and needed to prevent Darius from using sea power. This was achieved by taking control of the major harbours along the east coast of the Mediterranean. The narratives of the Alexander historians offer additional explanations for Alexander's campaign decisions, often in terms of Alexander's personal desires: these may be accurate, but it is not clear what access they had to the workings of Alexander's mind. The march down the Mediterranean coast brought Alexander to Egypt, and although entering Egypt led him away from Darius and from Fars, detaching the wealthy kingdom of Egypt from Darius' empire would have made the detour well worthwhile. Once he left Egypt in the first part of 331, Alexander's journey took him fairly directly over the Euphrates and Tigris, then down through Mesopotamia, by way of the royal capitals at Babylon and Susa, across the Zagros Mountains, and into Fars. Alexander entered Persepolis less than a year after leaving Egypt, and destroyed the palace a few months later. That this marked the end of the allied campaign is clear from Alexander's next actions. He sent home the allied contingents, richly rewarding them, but he allowed any of the Greeks who wished it to re-enlist as mercenary soldiers. Therefore the army which set off from Persepolis in the summer of 330 was now concerned solely with fulfilling Alexander's own aims.

The second part of the expedition took Alexander first in pursuit of Darius, whom he had already twice defeated. When Darius was assassinated on the orders of one of his subordinates, Bessus, he became Alexander's new target. The pursuit led Alexander into Bactria and Sogdiana, the northeastern corner of the empire, where the local elite were slow to accept the change of regime. Hence it took three years for Alexander to settle the region.

Alexander's next move, southeast into the Punjab and the Indus Valley, is best seen as a new campaign. How many of the troops that had crossed the Hellespont with Alexander in Spring of 334 were still with him eight years later we cannot tell: injured and aging soldiers will have been sent home to be replaced with reinforcements sent from Macedonia throughout this period. Most of the older officers had also either died or been left in positions further west, but Alexander's younger companions remained with him. The Indian campaign brought Alexander downriver to the Indus Delta and his first contact with a tidal ocean. The last phase of the journey was back through southern Iran to Fars, with a fleet also being sent up the Persian Gulf towards southern Mesopotamia. Alexander then spent the last 18 months of his life in what is now western Iran and eastern Iraq.

The rest of this book will not provide a detailed narrative of the expedition. Although the following chapters are organized roughly chronologically, they are more thematic, and make use of contemporary material to show how Alexander fitted into the world through which he travelled. The simplest way to follow Alexander's campaign is by using the map and the timeline provided at the front of this book.

Chapter 4
Commander: Alexander and the Greeks

At the battle of Chaeronea in 338, Alexander's father Philip had established Macedonia as the dominant power in the Greek world west of the Aegean. The ostensible aim of the campaign against the Achaemenid empire planned by Philip and carried out by Alexander was to liberate the Greek cities to the east of the Aegean. Although Alexander's progress took him far beyond the world of the Greeks, as he took control of the kingdoms of the Near East, his relationship with them remained crucial to the security of his reign. The narrative accounts of Alexander's life have something to tell us about his treatment of the Greek cities, and ancient orators and modern scholars have debated the question of whether Alexander was a liberator or an oppressor. We can gain a bit more understanding of the issues if we look beyond the narratives and consider what inscriptions put up by the cities themselves at the time can tell us about Alexander's actions and their impact.

Autonomy and control

In order to understand Alexander's relationship with the Greek cities it is important to be conscious of two central issues. The first is the meaning of the word *autonomia* (autonomy), which was an important element in ancient Greek political vocabulary, and the other is the existence of factionalism and rivalry, which characterized the political life of almost all Greek cities.

Autonomia was not the same as independence: it meant operating under the city's own laws, and therefore was more to do with the internal administration than with involvement with other powers. But whether a city counted as autonomous might be a matter of perspective. The Greek cities of Asia Minor were from the middle of the 6th century subordinated to the Lydians, the Persians, the Athenians, the Spartans, and then the Persians again. In the 5th century, as allies of Athens (or members of the Athenian empire, to give a more negative perspective) these cities could be described as autonomous, but that autonomy was only guaranteed by Athenian naval power, and potentially the presence of Athenian garrisons, installed to protect the autonomy of the city (as defined by the pro-Athenian political leadership) from the threat of Persian-supported exiles seizing power. From the perspective of these pro-Persian citizens (or former citizens) the garrison would be a sign of lack of autonomy. There was, however, for these cities, no option of complete independence from outside interference. Only a very few Greek cities could be described as truly independent: until the battle of Chaeronea in 338, Athens, Thebes, and Sparta were the exceptions, and their relationship with the Macedonian kings remained somewhat different from those of other cities.

Competition was a central part of ancient Greek life. From the poems of Homer onwards rivalry for prestige was a driving force in the lives of the richer and more influential members of communities. The development of the institutions of the city-state, in particular citizen assemblies and law-courts, did nothing to weaken this competition, but rather provided an arena and a more defined set of rules under which it might take place. Political divisions in Greek cities were determined not so much by ideology as by the personal ambition of individuals. Even terms like 'democratic' and 'oligarchic', which were used by historians and philosophers in their discussion of civic strife, referred usually to more pragmatic distinctions (in the 5th century, supported by Athens or supported by Sparta), as Thucydides indicates in his dramatic description of the civil disorder that broke out in Corcyra in the early years of the Peloponnesian War. In smaller cities it was normal for ambitious would-be leaders to look for support—financial and occasionally military—from larger cities; and even in Athens the leading politicians were prepared to take money from external powers. Opposing demagogues would take money from Philip II and from the Persian king.

The inevitable result of this rivalry for power was the existence of political exiles. The losing faction at any one time would find themselves expelled from their city after being convicted of working against its interests, or else would leave to avoid the risk of being killed—whether as a result of judicial process or not. Deprived of their property they would either look for support from guest-friends in other cities while plotting their own return, or, if they had outstayed their welcome, they might seek service as mercenary soldiers. Exile was the experience of richer members of the community—the poorer people played a more passive role in political life, even in democracies.

The League of Corinth

When he defeated the armies of Thebes and Athens at the battle of Chaeronea, Philip II treated the two cities somewhat differently. In Thebes, an ally that had broken its agreement, he installed a garrison of Macedonian troops and, it is assumed, had the leading politicians hostile to Macedonia sent into exile. As a consequence of the advocacy of the orator Demades, no Athenian politician was expelled, and Athens was left ungarrisoned; the city became an ally of Philip, a status that made clear that the city remained an autonomous entity, even while it set limits to Athenian freedom of military action.

In the following year a more general agreement was established with the Greek cities (other than Sparta), some of the details of which are known from Athenian inscriptions. The arrangement is known as the 'League of Corinth' and involved the creation of an alliance led by Philip to campaign against the Persians. According to a speech delivered in Athens a few years later, attributed to Demosthenes but not actually written by him, the terms of the alliance began with the statement that the Greek cities were to be free and autonomous. One of the fragmentary inscriptions relating to this includes the terms of the oath sworn by the Greek cities as part of the agreement. They swear not to interfere with the constitutions of their allies, nor to seize any of their territory, or take up arms against them, or to overthrow the kingdom of Philip and his heirs, and they will fight on behalf of any ally that is attacked. It also refers to a common council of the allies—which could be called upon if any member were deemed to have broken the terms of the agreement—and to Philip as *hegemon*, that is leader of the alliance: where Philip and his successors decided to go, the allies would have to follow. An even more fragmentary inscription from the beginning of Alexander's reign provides details of what the Athenians and Alexander are expected to provide for the troops the Athenians will supply on the campaign. When Philip was assassinated Alexander acted fast to renew the terms of the alliance, but in the following year it was tested by the revolt of Thebes, which took place while Alexander was securing his northern frontier.

The sack of Thebes

We have detailed accounts of the revolt of Thebes from Diodorus and Arrian, and although there are differences between them, they make it clear that the revolt followed a pattern very similar to revolts against the Athenians described by Thucydides in the 5th century. The trigger for the revolt was the arrival of exiles, backed it would appear by Persian money, who murdered the pro-Macedonian politicians who had been in control since the defeat

at Chaeronea. This made it difficult for the citizen body to avoid
conflict with Alexander, who arrived in front of the city before the
new political leaders had a chance to rally support from other
cities. Alexander made short work of the siege, and then turned
the decision about what to do with the Thebans over to the council
of allies, as the terms of the League of Corinth indicated he
should. It was inevitable that the delegates would support the
punishment of the rebel city, and although the destruction of
Thebes that followed may appear a brutal act, it was not different
from the way Athens had treated some other Greek cities in
the 5th century.

The cities of Asia Minor and the islands of the east Aegean

When Alexander led his army into Asia the following Spring, his
first task was to take control of the Greek cities there away from
the Persian king. This was not a straightforward task, and
something of what it involved can be understood by examining the
experience of the city of Mytilene on Lesbos, which can be
reconstructed from what is said in the surviving narratives and
from the information from an inscription recording the settlement
of affairs. As it happens Thucydides gave a detailed account of the
difficulties faced by the people of Mytilene when the city revolted
from Athens in 428–427: the revolt failed when the majority of
the citizen body showed no enthusiasm for holding out against the
Athenian fleet sent to force them back into alliance. A little less
than a century later they faced a similar situation. The terms of
the treaties arranged between the Greek cities and the Persian
king in the early 4th century, which were considered by the
Persians at least still to be in force, gave control of the cities on the
mainland of Asia to the king. The islands were not covered by this,
but the Persians clearly aimed to get or keep control of these.

In 334, when Alexander led his army into Asia, he made an
agreement of some kind with those in power in the cities on

Lesbos, and sent a garrison force of mercenary soldiers to support the men friendly to him who were now controlling Mytilene. In the following Spring the Persian navy arrived off Lesbos and persuaded the other cities to come over to their side. Mytilene was besieged, and the citizens, who had little real choice, given the power of the Persian fleet, came to terms with the Persians, agreeing to send away the mercenaries supplied by Alexander and to abrogate the arrangement they had made with him by destroying the stones on which its terms had been recorded. They agreed also to let back in to the city the exiles (who had presumably left the city when Alexander's forces arrived), and to restore to them half the property that they had held when they left the city. The other half presumably stayed in the possession of the men who had supported Alexander, and had possibly themselves been in exile before his arrival. Arrian suggests that the terms of this agreement were not actually upheld by the Persians once they were back in control of the city. In the next year, 332, Alexander sent a general, Hegelochus, to regain control of the islands, and he recaptured the cities of Lesbos, including Mytilene. The terms of a new settlement are recorded on an inscription that does survive—itself an indication that they may have been honoured.

The surviving part of the inscription does not explain what the terms were on which the exiles might now return: it is quite likely that they were the same as those offered when the Persians took control the previous year. It does, however, go into great detail about the procedures for ensuring reconciliation between the two factions within the city, the returning exiles and those already in the city. It aims to prevent the use of the lawcourts to challenge the terms of the reconciliation, and it establishes a body of arbitrators drawn equally from the returned exiles and those already in the city. Modern scholars have disagreed over whether Alexander's actions were those of a liberator or of a new conqueror of these cities. The reality of his position, however, was not a choice between freeing the cities or oppressing them, but rather the need simply to prevent the divisions between the leading citizens causing instability and the opportunity for a return by the Persians. In the city of Ephesus Alexander had to step in to prevent bloodshed between the rival factions. Contemporary inscriptions from the island of Chios and the city of Priene on the mainland refer to similar attempts to settle disputes, and indicate that Alexander was engaged in a great deal of correspondence and arbitration in trying to bring lasting order to the cities of the eastern Aegean.

One indication that Alexander was successful is in the honours he received from the cities he passed through. In a number of places later inscriptions indicate the existence of festivals called Alexandreia, and priests and altars to Alexander *Basileus* (King) and *Ktistes* (Founder). By the end of the 6th century it had become a regular practice for a city to honour the man who had founded it by celebrating an athletic festival in his honour and offering sacrifices to him. If, as was usual before the 5th century, the founder had spent the remainder of his life in his new city and died there, he would be buried in the centre of the city and his tomb would be considered a sacred place. He would be treated in the same way as mythical heroes, like Orestes in Sparta and Theseus in Athens, whose supposed bones were found and brought to those cities for formal burial. But there was no very clear distinction between the kind of honours paid to a hero and those paid to a god. On a number of occasions in the 5th century those in control of a city might decide that a new person deserved to be recognized as their founder. Most significantly at the end of the Peloponnesian War the Spartans installed a new regime on the island of Samos after taking it from Athenian control. The new rulers decided to honour the Spartan commander Lysander as their new founder, and created a festival in his honour, and honoured him as a god, according to a 3rd century Samian historian. It was in line with this that cities set up cults of Alexander and maintained them in the following centuries. Of course it was those individuals who benefited from Alexander's settlement of Asia Minor who would have had most cause to introduce such honours. They served to bolster the position of Alexander's supporters for example by attributing to him, as founder, responsibility for the very existence of their city; but this is not to deny the sincerity of the actions.

At Priene an inscription records that Alexander dedicated the newly built temple of Athena (Figure 4). In other cities, too, new temples started to be built in the wake of Alexander's passage. At Miletus the oracular temple of Apollo at Didyma, destroyed by the Persians in 494, was restored, and the oracle could once again be consulted. Such developments were not necessarily immediate, but they are witness to a significant transformation of the fortunes of those Greek cities.

Sparta

One Greek city stood aloof from the rest and from the Macedonians. Sparta had, until its defeat by the Theban general Epaminondas in 371, been one of the most powerful cities in Greece, directly controlling 40 per cent of the Peloponnese, and leading an alliance that covered most of the rest. Since then Sparta had lost much of its territory and all of its dominance. The Spartans refused to join the League of Corinth, or to serve with Alexander, and instead negotiated with Darius for financial support to lead an uprising in Greece. After an abortive attempt in Crete in 333–332, the Spartan king Agis launched his revolt in the Peloponnese in 331. Anti-Macedonian politicians were able to mount support for Agis in many Peloponnesian cities, but the Athenians did not join him, and the crucial city of Megalopolis in Arcadia in the southern Peloponnese also stayed loyal to Alexander. Agis was killed when the Macedonian regent Antipater led an army against him as he was besieging Megalopolis, and that marked the end of significant opposition to Alexander anywhere in Greece.

Athens

Athens appears to have received more honours from Alexander than other cities did. After his first victory, at the Granicus,

4. Inscribed blocks from the temple of Athena at Priene. The first inscription records the dedication of the temple by Alexander the Great

Alexander chose to send his share of the battlefield spoils to Athens to be dedicated on the acropolis: three hundred suits of armour, displayed with a pointed message: 'Alexander the son of Philip and the Greeks, except the Spartans, [set up these spoils, taken] from the barbarian living in Asia.' When Alexander took over the royal palace in Susa he found there a pair of statues that the Athenians had erected in honour of the Tyrannicides, Harmodius and Aristogeiton, two men who had assassinated the brother of the last tyrant of Athens, and were held to be heroes of liberation. Xerxes had taken the statues home with him to Persia after the sack of Athens in 480 BCE, and, according to Arrian, Alexander now sent them back. When Alexander had the palace at Persepolis destroyed as the final act of the campaign of the League of Corinth, it was Xerxes' sack of Athens that was most obviously being avenged.

As in all Greek cities, as we have seen, the politicians of Athens were divided between those who supported Alexander and those who did not. After Alexander's first victory over Darius himself, at Issus, when Darius was no longer in a position to offer financial support to them, the anti-Macedonian politicians remained quiet until the year after Alexander's death. Under the leadership of the orator Lycurgus, the Athenians increased their state revenues and used the money to restore and improve civic buildings including the Theatre of Dionysus and the Stadium (restored again for the first modern Olympic Games in 1896); the practice was established of performing the plays of the great tragedians of the 5th century, Aeschylus, Sophocles, and Euripides, at the festival of the City Dionysia, and considerable attention was paid to the *ephebeia*, the training of young men. After the tension and danger of the period from before the battle of Chaeronea until the destruction of Thebes, Athens flourished while Alexander was on campaign in the east, benefiting from the wealth that came back from the Persian empire in the hands of discharged veterans returning home. Modern scholars sometimes suggest that the Athenians were continually looking for ways to oppose Alexander, but the evidence to support this view is difficult to identify.

In 324 Alexander returned victorious from his campaign in Pakistan, emerging from the desert of Gedrosia at the head of his army. While this caused concern for some officials in his empire who had used his absence to enrich themselves from public funds, it was treated as an occasion for celebration by those in power in the Greek cities, who sent embassies to Susa and Babylon to congratulate him. In Athens a decision was taken to honour Alexander with a statue bearing the inscription 'King Alexander, Invincible God'. There is no reason to believe that this did not reflect the popular view of Alexander at that point as more than a conquering hero, and there was no significant objection to the proposal, which is known from a fragment of a contemporary speech. Although Alexander is referred to as a god, the statue was not accompanied by the setting up of an altar or the appointment of a priest, so it is not the same as the cult offered by the cities of Asia Minor. Its rather extravagant description of Alexander could be justified by the claims made, amongst others, that in Pakistan Alexander had travelled further than the god Dionysus, and captured places that even Heracles had failed to capture. Similar decisions may have been taken by other Greek cities, but such evidence as we have is of questionable value.

Exiles

One of Alexander's most controversial acts on his return from the east, at least in the eye of modern scholars, was to require Greek cities to take back their exiles. As we have seen, exiles were a problematic phenomenon for nearly all Greek cities. It was not normally possible for individuals to possess land in cities other than their own, so those in exile for any length of time had to find some way of supporting themselves. Among the higher social groups who made up the majority of political exiles, fighting as a hoplite soldier or a cavalryman was one of the few forms of employment available, and many of the mercenaries who had served with Alexander would have been exiled from their cities at some point. As part of his reorganization of his empire on his return from the east, Alexander required many of his satraps to disband their mercenary forces, and some solution had to be found to make sure that these men had somewhere to go. The best solution was for them to return to their cities and settle on land there.

Alexander followed an established practice of using a major panhellenic festival, in this case the Olympic Games of 324, as the occasion for announcing his decision. Every Greek city would send sacred ambassadors to the festival, and it was therefore the ideal place for communicating important information. Requiring cities to take back exiles was to interfere in their affairs, reversing decisions taken by their courts. As such it challenged their autonomy, but the surviving histories disagree over how far the Greek cities did object. For Athens it presented particular problems, because many Athenians owned plots of land on the island of Samos, from which the Samian owners had been expelled. Those Athenians potentially faced a substantial loss of income if the previous owners were able to return.

An inscription survives relating to implementation of the decree in the city of Tegea in the Peloponnese. This makes clear that there was an opportunity for the cities to negotiate on how the restoration would take place, and it also shows that the concern to ensure reconciliation between the exiles and those who had stayed behind, which we saw in the settlement of Asia Minor, was a major issue here too. The surviving part of the inscription describes the procedure for allocating houses and garden plots to returning exiles, who would have to recompense the existing owners for them. It also mentions a special court made up of jurors from outside the city who are to deal with disputes. This was not a crude or heavy-handed action by Alexander. Had the years after 324 been as peaceful for the Greek cities as the years before (at least since the defeat of Agis in 331), it might have been possible to judge the impact of the exiles decree. However, Alexander's death the following year and the subsequent wars, not only in Greece but across the whole of Alexander's former empire, created disorder on an even larger scale than had hitherto occurred.

Modern scholars, following the lead of the ancient narratives, have tended to see the imposition of the 'Exiles Decree' as an authoritarian act, forcing cities to take in their former enemies against their will. This view is part of a wider interpretation of Alexander as an oppressor whose promise of 'freedom for the Greeks' was never anything more than an empty slogan. There were no doubt people who lost out from Alexander's actions—not least those who had been comfortable working with their previous Achaemenid overlords—but the evidence of the inscriptions above all suggests that Alexander wanted a good relationship with the Greek cities, and the wealth that he released from the treasuries of the Achaemenid royal capitals was to enrich the cities of Asia Minor and the mainland hugely over the following decades and centuries.

Chapter 5
Pharaoh: Alexander and Egypt

Alexander entered Egypt late in 332, facing no opposition from the inhabitants or from the Persian satrap Mazaces, who had too few soldiers to attempt any resistance. This was the first of the major Near Eastern kingdoms to come under his control, with a system of government that had its roots in over two-and-a-half millennia of Pharaonic rule. The popular image of Egypt as an unchanging civilization should not, however, be exaggerated: the centuries before Alexander's arrival had seen many changes of rule since the end of the imperial period of the Late Bronze Age New Kingdom. The end of the New Kingdom had been followed by four centuries of the 'Third Intermediate Period' (1069–664), when the kingdom had been disunited and ultimately conquered by the Assyrians. Following that, Dynasty XXVI (664–525) had ruled Egypt until the Persian invasion under Cambyses, which had led to 120 years of Achaemenid rule. Egypt broke away from the Persian empire in 404, but was reconquered sixty years later, only twelve years before Alexander's arrival. The conflicts which led to these transfers of power left their mark on Egyptian society. Nonetheless rulers would adopt the practices and forms of representation used by their successful predecessors, as they attempted to confirm their authority, and so maintain the appearance of continuity.

For the surviving Alexander historians two events are of crucial importance in Alexander's time in Egypt: the foundation of the city of Alexandria and the visit to the oracle of Amun at Siwa. Arrian introduces his accounts of both these episodes saying that Alexander was seized by *pothos*, that is, overwhelming desire: these are actions driven by his own personal emotions rather than from any practical considerations. This interpretation has been largely followed in recent scholarship. The ancient writers disagree about the relative chronology of the two events, and this may add to a suspicion that one of them, the story of the foundation of Alexandria, is not all that it seems.

Alexandria

In the period of the Roman empire Alexandria, on the Egyptian coast at the western edge of the Nile Delta, was one of the most important cities in the world. Already by the end of the 3rd century BCE it had grown through trade to become the largest city in the world, and in antiquity only Rome ever grew larger. It was a great centre of trade and a crucial point of contact between the Mediterranean world and the East. The Library at Alexandria gathered together all of Greek literature, and became a centre of science and scholarship. It was at Alexandria, about a century after the death of Alexander, that the first calculations of the circumference of the earth were made; the Jewish Bible was also translated into Greek there in the 3rd century, and it was mainly through this translation, known as the Septuagint, that the Hebrew biblical texts were known to early Christian writers.

All the ancient Alexander historians emphasize Alexander's personal involvement in the construction of Alexandria, suggesting that he determined where it would be built (after receiving advice in a dream, according to Plutarch) and how the walls and the major public buildings would be laid out. They also all provide versions of a prophetic story about the foundation. They say that the outline of the city was marked out using barley grains (either because this was the normal Macedonian practice, or because no chalk was available); and then, according to some versions, birds flocked down and ate the barley. The use of barley was interpreted to mean that the city was destined to grow rich from the fruits of the earth, but in the versions involving the birds, their arrival was taken to predict the fact that people would come to Alexandria from far and wide to settle. How much, if anything, of these accounts can be trusted? The answer is that possibly none of it can be.

After Alexander's death his body was sent west from Babylon for burial in Macedonia. En route it was captured by Ptolemy and brought to Egypt, where it was entombed in Memphis, not Alexandria. Memphis remained the administrative centre of Egypt under Ptolemy, who had taken control of Egypt as satrap on Alexander's death, until at least 311. In a document he composed in that year, known as the 'Satrap Stele' written in Egyptian, Ptolemy states that he moved to 'the Fortress of King Alexander, formerly known as Rakotis, on the shore of the Greek sea'. This event, 12 years after Alexander's death, and 20 years after he left Egypt, may mark the real beginning of Alexandria. Ptolemy proclaimed himself king in 304, and it is probably only after that point that the city began to become a major cultural centre. Its most famous buildings, the library and museum, are usually associated with Ptolemy's son and successor Ptolemy II Philadelphus (283–246). It is not clear from the text of the Satrap Stele whether the site was named 'the Fortress of King Alexander' before Ptolemy I moved there or whether it still had the Egyptian name Rakotis. Archaeology has provided little information about the earliest history of the site, since the ancient city is buried beneath the modern city and the sea, although excavation is ongoing, and something may emerge in the future. At the moment there is little contemporary evidence to support the idea that Alexander himself was responsible for much of what was to become the most important city to bear his name.

As his campaign took him into eastern Iran, Afghanistan, and beyond, Alexander did start to create settlements, usually named

Alexandria, including what is now Kandahar in Afghanistan. Plutarch, in his essay 'On the Virtue and Fortune of Alexander the Great', suggests that Alexander founded more than 70 cities, and claimed that his purpose in doing so was to spread Greek culture and learning among the 'barbarians'. The number is probably an exaggeration, but at least 20 settlements named Alexandria are known from inscriptions and written accounts. Not all of these have been securely located, and some, like Alexandria Troas near Troy, previously named Antigonia Troas after its founder Antigonus the One-Eyed, were given their name by later rulers. Some were refoundations of previously existing settlements, and others were new creations. Excavations at Ai-Khanoum in northeastern Afghanistan, which is thought to be the site of Alexandria-on-the-Oxus, have revealed a Greek theatre and temples, built some decades after Alexander's time, but Plutarch's idea that his foundations were intended as cultural centres is unrealistic. These settlements were mostly little more than fortresses, occupied by veteran Macedonian soldiers prepared to start a new life in Asia, supported perhaps by local inhabitants brought in from surrounding villages. These were not intended to be major commercial centres but points of control in regions where there was a danger of insurrection. When compared with all the other Alexandrias, the idea of Alexander deliberately created a new commercial city in Egypt seems out of place. It is possible that he might have wanted to leave a garrison fort there, and that this is what Ptolemy is referring to in the Satrap Stele, but the site of Alexandria is not an obvious one for a military settlement.

The stories of the omens surrounding the foundation of the city are above all reflections of its future success: the greater the fortune of the city, the more incentive there was to associate it with Alexander himself. Three of the early histories of Alexander had their origins in the city: Ptolemy, whose history is the main source for Arrian, Cleitarchus, whose work lies behind Diodorus and Curtius, and the so-called *Alexander Romance*, the fanciful popularizing account of Alexander's career that is known from versions from the 3rd century CE and afterwards, but which had its origins in the 3rd century BCE. Ptolemy in particular associated himself with Alexander, as we have seen, putting Alexander's head on his coins, and to credit Alexander with the founding of his royal city would assist him in this. Other authors would have no reason not to promulgate a version of the facts that raised the status of their own city. Older Greek cities claimed mythical heroes as their founders, and Alexander the Great was a hero worth claiming as founder by the Alexandrians, but the stories that Alexander did personally found the city belong more to legend than to history.

The oracle of Amun

The Egyptian episode that receives the most attention in the surviving histories is Alexander's visit to the temple of Amun in the Siwa oasis in the Libyan desert. In addition to the accounts in Diodorus, Curtius, Plutarch, Arrian, and Justin, we have much of what Alexander's court historian Callisthenes wrote, as reported by the geographer Strabo, who wrote under the emperor Augustus, that is, a little later than Diodorus. Modern scholars have followed the ancient sources in seeing Alexander's encounter with the oracle as a turning point in his understanding of himself. As with other cases of Alexander's involvement with religion, however, the evidence is complex and confused.

The principal temple at Siwa was built in the reign of the pharaoh Amasis (570–526) for the god Amun, whose main centre of cult was at Thebes. At Thebes the oracle of Amun functioned in the traditional way of Egyptian oracles. At major festivals the image of the god would be carried in procession in his sacred boat, on the shoulders of eight priests. Those who wished to consult the god could ask their question as the god approached. If the god 'nodded' to them, that is if the cult image swayed towards them as it was being carried along, this would be taken as a positive answer, but if it swayed away from the enquirer it would indicate a negative response. Another method of questioning would be to place two alternative written statements along the path the god was travelling, and whichever of the two the god swayed towards would be taken to represent his decision. At Siwa the oracle operated in the same way. When Alexander visited the sanctuary the processional way led from the principal temple to a second smaller temple, built by Nectanebo II, and it was along this route that the cult image would have been carried. Since the oracle was in existence before the time of Nectanebo, his temple must have been constructed to increase the monumentality of the existing processional route.

From the time of the creation of the temple under Amasis, Siwa was visited by sacred ambassadors (*theoroi*) from the Greek city of Cyrene (near modern Benghazi), and Amun received cult in Cyrene under the name of Ammon or Zeus Ammon. He was depicted as a man with ram's horns, reflecting the Egyptian practice of representing Amun with a ram's head. Herodotus reports a consultation of the oracle by the Lydian king Croesus, which, if the report is accurate, would have taken place early in its history. Ammon was recognized in the Aegean in the 5th century, and in the early 4th century inscriptions indicate that the Athenians sent *theoroi* to the temple. But while the temple had some prestige in the Greek world, it was very much on the edge of Egyptian territory, and had far less prestige than Amun's much older temples in upper Egypt. It is unlikely therefore that Alexander visited it to impress the Egyptians, and the ancient writers do not describe the visit in those terms. It would make more sense to link Alexander's visit with his interest in establishing his authority over the Greek cities of Cyrenaica, which had come under Persian control in the time of Darius I, but had been left free from external control after the revolt of Egypt in 404.

Callisthenes claims that Alexander wanted to visit the oracle in emulation of his ancestors Perseus and Heracles, although there is no suggestion in earlier writers that these heroes did go to Siwa. Herodotus, who visited the oracle himself, and who tells stories of

Heracles' adventures in Egypt, tells how the hero went to visit the temple of his father Zeus at Thebes, and how Zeus, in order to prevent Heracles from seeing him as he was, wore a ram's head as disguise. But he says nothing about Heracles going to Siwa. Arrian, whose whole account appears based on Callisthenes (possibly by way of Ptolemy's history), gives the same explanation, but adds that Alexander wanted to find out about his *genesis*, that is his birth or his origins. Neither Callisthenes nor Arrian says what it was that Alexander asked the god. Of the other narratives only Justin offers an explanation of why he wanted to consult the oracle, elaborating the story that he wanted to know about his birth, but all four other authors do give a fuller account of Alexander's conversation with the priest—even if not a reliable one.

Ancient historians are often vague about the role of translators in encounters between foreigners. When Alexander visited Siwa it is unclear in what languages the various parties spoke. Plutarch, who several times in his *Life of Alexander* identifies linguistic jokes and puns, presents the Egyptian officials as speaking Greek, but doing so poorly: he suggests that the priest of Amun may accidentally have addressed Alexander as *Pai Dios* (Son of Zeus), because he was trying to say *paidion* (child). It would be, for Plutarch, a clever accidental omen, but none of the other writers describes the events in this way. They give the impression that all communication was direct, and could be interpreted in straightforward Greek terms. It is unlikely that Alexander understood Egyptian. It is possible that the priest of Amun understood Greek, since there was an established pattern of Greeks visiting the oracle. However, it is certain that Alexander will have been accompanied by interpreters, so that he will have known precisely what was being said. It is also likely that he will have been recognized as Pharaoh, or at least as the man soon to be crowned as Pharaoh, and therefore addressed with the formality that his office required.

This is significant because the ancient writers claim that when he first arrived at Siwa the priest of Amun addressed Alexander as son of the god (Diodorus), or specifically of Zeus (Callisthenes and Plutarch), Jupiter (Curtius), or Hammon (Justin). According to Diodorus, Curtius, and Justin, Alexander responded to this by saying that he would from this point on call himself by this title—suggesting that this was the beginning of a process that would end up by alienating Alexander from his men, because he was denying that Philip was his father. As we will see, however, Alexander's titles in Egypt, following Egyptian tradition, included the name 'Son of Re'; for him to be addressed as such by an Egyptian (or Libyan) priest will have been protocol, not revelation.

The more elaborate descriptions of Alexander's visit are generally thought to derive from the work of Cleitarchus, who was not an eyewitness to the visit, but, writing in Egypt, did understand how Egyptian oracles functioned: we are given slightly confused, but essentially authentic, descriptions of the statue being carried in its boat on the shoulders of the priests. But stories about the consultation of oracles in ancient historical narratives tend to conform to certain patterns, and the readers of the Alexander historians will have expected a spoken exchange between enquirer and priest, as was the pattern at the most famous Greek oracle, Delphi (although Delphi was notorious for the obscurity of its responses). The consultation of an oracle that responded solely by the movements of a statue would have been less easy to dramatize. As a result we are given a story that is not compatible with what we know about how Egyptian oracles functioned. Some scholars, including the excavators at Siwa, have attempted to reconcile the accounts by postulating a separate 'Royal Oracle' that was closer to the Greek model, but this is not compelling, and it makes more sense to allow the historians some dramatic licence in their retelling. These writers claim that Alexander asked two questions: whether his father's murderers had been punished and whether he would rule the world. The first of these seems designed in these accounts to reinforce the notion that Alexander had accepted divine paternity, as the oracle is said to have responded that his father could not be harmed by mortals (but that Philip's killers had been avenged). The second question received a positive response, and we will consider the implications of this later.

Stories about the consultation of oracles are common in Greek literature. The oracle of Delphi plays a major role in Herodotus' *History*, the first work of history to be written and one of the most influential. Oracular consultations feature prominently in many of Plutarch's *Lives*, and he wrote a series of essays about Greek oracles. It is therefore not surprising that the expedition to the oracle at Siwa is given a lot of attention in the narratives of the Greek and Roman Alexander historians. It demonstrated the involvement of the gods in Alexander's achievements, and revealed his greatness through the responses that the oracle gave. These confirmations of the nature of Alexander were important for the readers of those narratives, but the Egyptians themselves had other ways of making clear Alexander's significance and his relationship with the gods, above all by recognizing him as Pharaoh.

Pharaoh Alexander

If we read the Greek and Roman histories with an understanding of what the Egyptians would have wanted from a new ruler, we can see that Alexander was able to live up to their expectations. Memphis, at the apex of the Nile Delta, the royal centre of Lower Egypt, was the administrative centre of Egypt in this period, and that is where Alexander went first. The normal rituals associated with the accession of a new pharaoh would start with the ceremonial proclamation of his royal names, and this would be followed by the pharaoh-to-be travelling to the major temples of the kingdom on a royal barge, a journey known as 'The Creation of Order in all Provinces'. All the kingdom's officials would be expected to renew their oaths of office, and foreign allies to renew their alliances at this time. The process ended with the coronation itself in Memphis, which would ideally take place at the time of the Egyptian New Year festival in June. None of the surviving authors actually describes Alexander's coronation, but they do refer to the occasions when the various rituals would have taken place. Arrian mentions two festivals at Memphis, one on Alexander's arrival and one shortly before his departure. Curtius says that from Memphis Alexander travelled up-river, presumably by boat, and he also reports a tragic incident when a young Macedonian noble drowned after the boat he was in capsized while it was attempting to catch up with Alexander. Arrian also describes Alexander receiving embassies and distributing offices while he was at Memphis before his departure.

The reluctance of the Greek and Roman authors to mention an actual coronation is significant. The same reluctance occurs in their accounts of Alexander's time in Babylon, where it is certain that he was enthroned as king, and at Susa, where it is highly likely. In part this may be a result of the authors' chosen narrative structure. They all, to a greater or lesser extent, present Alexander as being gradually corrupted by contact with the 'East': he is depicted as becoming increasingly interested in 'barbarian' practices and losing control over himself. This is a theme that we will consider elsewhere, but it is a storyline that would be weakened if Alexander were seen to be adopting the practices of the peoples he conquered too early in the journey.

Egypt had many temples, and work on restoring or extending them was one of the activities expected of a pharaoh. Two of the last native Egyptian rulers, Nectanebo I (380–362) and Nectanebo II (360–343), had been energetic in their building works, and it is likely that a number of works had been started by Nectanebo II but left unfinished when the Persians regained control of Egypt after its period of independence from them (404–343). Egyptian evidence indicates that Alexander was ready to follow in the tradition of temple-restoration.

At the great temple of Amun-Re at Luxor, near the ancient royal city of Upper Egypt, Thebes, Alexander is depicted on the walls of

5. Alexander the Great (on the right) depicted as pharaoh in the temple of Amenhotep III at Luxor

the 'chapel of the barque', which he is credited with restoring. In a sequence of reliefs in the traditional Egyptian style, Alexander is depicted dressed as pharaoh, facing the god Amun-Re. The accompanying texts identify him as 'King of Upper and Lower Egypt, Lord of the Two Lands, *Setepenre Meryamun* (Beloved of Amun, Chosen of Re), son of Re, possessor of the crowns, Alexander' (Figure 5). This is the standard form of address for a pharaoh, and the inscribed texts note that he has carried out the work for his father Amun-Re. The 'chapel of the barque' would have contained the cult image of the god, standing in a ceremonial boat. At major festivals the image would have been carried by the temple priests in procession in the boat. In the other great temple of Amun, nearby at Karnak, an inscription announces that Alexander had renovated the chapel of Tuthmosis III (Pharaoh 1475–1429) and once again Alexander is given his full pharaonic titles. Further downriver, at Hermopolis, inscriptions record further restoration work by Alexander. The picture we get from Egyptian monuments is of Alexander following in the footsteps of his predecessors, a picture significantly different, as we have seen, from that presented by the Greek and Roman accounts of his time in Egypt.

Chapter 6
King of the world: Alexander and Persia

The historian Appian, a contemporary of Arrian, reports a conversation between the Roman general, Scipio Africanus, and his tutor, the Greek historian Polybius, which took place outside Carthage in 146 BCE as that city was being sacked by the Roman army. Appian says that Polybius recorded the conversation as he heard it. Scipio, watching the destruction of the ancient city, was drawn to reflect on

> the inevitability that cities, nations and empires would be overthrown: such a fate had befallen Troy, a once fortunate city, and had befallen the Assyrians, the Medes and the Persians, whose empire had been greatest of all, and most recently the glittering empire of the Macedonians.

He went on to quote lines from the *Iliad*, where the Trojan prince Hector predicts the fall of Troy, and he explained to Polybius that he was thinking of the future time when Rome itself would fall.

The idea that different nations followed each other in ruling over large parts of the world, and in particular over Asia, was a well established theme in historiography by the time the surviving Alexander historians were writing. At the start of the last book of his *Anabasis* of Alexander, Arrian reports the unlikely suggestion that Alexander was planning to circumnavigate Africa and attack

Carthage from the west, and adds that in Alexander's view the Medes and Persians had no right to the title 'Great King' as they had only controlled the smallest part of Asia. This is probably a reflection of Arrian's own view rather than Alexander's, but Herodotus' account of the rise of the Persian empire, written a century before the reign of Alexander, presented the Persians as successor to the power of the Medes. Although 'rule over Asia' was not a precisely defined idea, it was what Alexander could expect to gain by defeating Darius, which he duly did for the second and final time at Gaugamela, near the modern city of Mosul in northern Iraq, on 1 October 331.

'King of the World'

We know the precise date of the battle of Gaugamela, and about some of the surrounding events, from a Babylonian astronomical diary like the example we met earlier in this book, noting Alexander's death. The Gaugamela diary, which covers the sixth and seventh months of the Babylonian year, equivalent to 8 September to 6 November 331, as all such diaries do, records each night's observations, and, if anything significant occurred, what rituals were carried out in response: on 25 September a dog was burned, possibly in response to a bolt of lightning (the tablet is broken at this point). At the end of the sixth month, *Ulūlu*, the tablet indicates how much barley, dates, mustard, cress, sesame, and wool could be bought in the market for a silver shekel; then which planets were in which constellations; and the height of the Euphrates. These data are followed by reports of other events, including an outbreak of panic in the camp of Darius on 18 September; the arrival of the Macedonian army at the battlefield; and the battle itself, during which Darius' troops, having been defeated, abandoned the king in their flight. This detail is of interest because it helps to resolve a disagreement amongst the Alexander historians: while Diodorus and Curtius claim that Darius held firm until after his troops began to flee, Plutarch and Arrian present Darius as the first to run. It is a case where the normally more reliable Arrian turns out probably to be incorrect.

The scribe who wrote out the tablet refers to Darius as 'the King', but to Alexander as 'King of the World'. There is some uncertainty about this translation, but similar titles are used to refer to Alexander in the surviving historians. Since the division of the world into continents was a creation of Greek geographers, Babylonians had no distinct concept of 'Asia', and 'King of the World' may have been a Babylonian way of rendering the term 'King of Asia'. Plutarch takes Alexander's victory at Gaugamela as the climax of his campaign, stating 'With the battle turning out this way, the rule of the Persians was considered to be completely overthrown, and Alexander, proclaimed as King of Asia, sacrificed to the gods on a grand scale and rewarded his friends with wealth, estates, and provinces.' This would be the situation the Babylonian scribe was responding to in his choice of title.

The title 'King of the World' first appears in the narrative of Alexander's campaigns in the story of the Gordian knot. At Gordium, the ancient capital of Phrygia, Alexander was shown a cart connected to a yoke by a complex knot, and was told that whoever could undo the knot would become either 'Ruler of Asia' (according to Arrian and Curtius) or 'King of the World' (according to Plutarch). Two versions of Alexander's response to this are reported—the more popular was that he simply cut the knot with his sword, but the alternative was that he pulled out a peg that held the knot together. In either case he was recognized as having fulfilled the prophecy. The versions of Alexander's consultation of the oracle at Siwa found in Plutarch, Diodorus, and Curtius (but not Arrian) also have Alexander being told that he will rule the world. There is no suggestion in these accounts that Alexander misunderstood the meaning of the oracle, or that it was unreliable. The responses can be understood as foretelling the outcome of Alexander's meeting with Darius, at Gaugamela, which followed his departure from Egypt.

Susa

Defeated at Gaugamela, Darius III fled eastwards, and Alexander was able to lead his army south through Mesopotamia towards Persia. The first major city he came to was Babylon, and we will consider his relationship with that city later. From there he moved on to Susa, like Babylon an Achaemenid royal capital. Two of the Alexander historians report an odd story about Alexander's visit to the palace at Susa, which might be concealing an important event in Alexander's career. According to Diodorus and Curtius, Alexander went on a tour of the palace, and when he reached the throne room he sat on the royal throne. As he was not tall, Alexander's feet would not reach the floor in front of the throne, and so a page brought over a low table to serve as a footstool. At this one of the palace eunuchs began to wail, and eventually explained that this was the table at which Darius had formerly eaten his meals: the eunuch could not keep silent seeing this transformation of Darius' fortune. Alexander at first wanted the table removed, but his friend Philotas told him to treat the situation as an omen acknowledging Alexander's triumph.

What does the story tell us? It is unlikely to be true. Depictions of Achaemenid kings on their thrones generally show them with a footstool, and everything we know about 'the King's table' suggests that any table at which Darius dined would be unsuitable to act as a footstool. It is also unlikely that Alexander would have shown the kind of insensitivity the story implies. One possible interpretation of the episode is that it is a confused description of Alexander being enthroned and crowned as Great King. Plutarch, in his essay on *The Fortune of Alexander*, mentions an aged Greek called Demeratus weeping with happiness at the sight of Alexander sitting on the throne of Darius at Susa, and Susa was the usual place where Achaemenid kings were crowned. Plutarch, in his *Life of Artaxerxes*, describes his subject, Artaxerxes II, undergoing a different succession ritual, which took place at Pasargadae, but it is clear that Achaemenid kings performed different rituals in different places. The Alexander historians may have been uncomfortable describing Alexander willingly taking part in an Achaemenid ceremony, and thus retold the events as an omen-story, but we should not assume that Alexander shared their scruples.

This raises the question of what Alexander's ultimate aims were. Some historians have described Alexander as 'the last of the Achaemenids', suggesting that he saw himself as the successor to Darius III. On this view Alexander was planning to move the centre of his kingdom from Macedonia to the Achaemenid centres at Susa and Babylon. Associated with the move are his adoption of Persian dress and Persian court protocol, which are described as disturbing to his Macedonian companions. The alternative view would see these practices as necessary for the administration of the eastern parts of Alexander's empire, and would suggest that, had he lived longer, Alexander would have turned his attention westwards, and probably returned to Macedon.

To find our way through this uncertainty we have to start by thinking about the intended readers of the surviving narratives of Alexander's campaign. For the Roman readers of the histories of Alexander, the Persians were still the enemy. In place of the Achaemenid kings, the Romans faced the Parthian empire just across the Euphrates. Several Roman commanders had led expeditions across that river to take on the Parthians, with mixed results. Arrian had the emperor Hadrian in mind as a reader of his history, and Hadrian had campaigned with his predecessor Trajan in Armenia and Mesopotamia, and then, once he had become emperor, had withdrawn from the territories east of the Euphrates. Arrian tries to set Alexander up as a figure worthy of emulation by his Roman readers: he therefore plays down as far as possible any suggestions that Alexander might willingly have set himself up as Great King. But as we have seen, there is good reason to suppose that Macedonian court practices had always owed something to Persian models. Persian kingship will have appeared far less outlandish to Alexander and his Macedonians than it would have done to the Romans who read about him in the surviving accounts.

The burning of Persepolis

Alexander understood the importance of gestures. He adopted Achaemenid protocols where it helped him maintain his authority, but his Achaemenid predecessors were prepared on occasions to demonstrate their power by destructive acts. One of the most notorious of Alexander's actions on his campaign was the burning of the palace of Persepolis. The palace had been built by Darius and Xerxes, the kings who had led armies into Greece, and the more popular story recorded in the surviving sources is that it was burnt down after a drunken party at which an Athenian courtesan, Thais, encouraged Alexander to take revenge for the destruction of Athens by Xerxes by destroying the palace that he had built. Versions of this story are told in all of the surviving accounts except that of Arrian, who reports that Alexander had the palace deliberately destroyed—an action Arrian himself appears not to have approved of. The material evidence tends to support Arrian's more sober view, and indicates that it was the contents of the palace as much as the building that were targeted (although the gold and silver were carried away first). The evidence of burning on the surviving stonework suggests that the furnishings had been piled up and set on fire.

Why Alexander should want to destroy Persepolis when he had done no damage to the other royal centres, Susa and Babylon, has puzzled scholars. It was not an act that would endear him to his new subjects, the Persians. The most likely explanation is that this was indeed a symbolic revenge for Xerxes' destruction of Athens. This was part of the justification for the participation of the Greek cities in the campaign, and it would have been difficult for Alexander to ignore it. He could rule his empire from the other royal centres, and did not need Persepolis. Later Persian tradition magnified the impact of the burning, claiming that along with the palace Alexander had destroyed the texts of ancient Zoroastrian religious works, but this is not plausible.

Dressing as a Persian

For the Alexander historians, his campaign in Iran led to a relentless decline in Alexander's character, as he became increasingly drawn into 'eastern' forms of behaviour. They describe how he began to adopt Persian (or Median) forms of dress and court practices, including the mutilation of his opponents, and requiring his friends to prostrate themselves before him. At the same time they picture him becoming increasingly tyrannical: former friends were executed on trumped-up charges or murdered in violent rages. Modern scholars, while modifying elements of this narrative of corruption and decline, have tended to accept it as largely true. This is a mistake. Alexander's decline and fall was held up by moralists as the clearest example of seduction and corruption by the east. This reading of his life became the pattern for biographers and historians to use, but it obscures some important facts. Macedonian kings were part of a network that included the western Persian satraps, and many of the practices of satrapal courts, themselves influenced by the court of the Persian king, were adopted or adapted by the Macedonians and the other kings of the Aegean world: Alexander came to 'the east' familiar with its practices. We have also seen how in Egypt and Susa Alexander had no difficulty taking on the required role of pharaoh or king. The surviving narratives present Alexander gradually beginning to adopt Persian clothing, and later to 'experiment' with formal court protocol, facing the suspicion and even hostility of his fellow Macedonians in the process. But other stories, more favourable to Alexander, found particularly in Plutarch, depict his Macedonian friends sinking into luxurious living while Alexander set them an example of frugality and self-control. Neither version is convincing: both are more concerned with providing moral examples for the reader to emulate or resist than with accurately reporting what actually happened. It was the Roman writers and readers who might pretend to be shocked by Alexander's adoption of Persian dress in an Iranian climate, not his fellow Macedonians. So we may take it for granted that, from his time in Babylon and Susa onwards, if not earlier, Alexander's travelling court adopted protocols appropriate to the circumstances, and the king himself fully retained his intellectual capacity.

Court ceremonial

The issue that most concerned the ancient writers, and many modern scholars, is the question of whether Alexander wanted his companions to prostrate themselves in his presence. The Alexander historians all appear to have believed that it was normal practice for Persians to prostrate themselves before the Great King, although this was not the case: only defeated enemies would have been required to do this. To make matters more complicated, the historians also suggested that prostration was a way of acknowledging the divinity of the Persian king. They report stories of how Alexander tried to introduce this practice into the protocol of his court, using social occasions as experiments and claiming that his achievements merited his being worshipped. In the stories, however, opposition to these changes is successfully led by Alexander's court historian, Callisthenes, and the practice is dropped.

Callisthenes, however, is an implausible leader of the resistance. His history of Alexander's campaign was notorious for its flattery. It was probably the source for the stories about Alexander's emulation of his heroic ancestors, Achilles, Heracles, and Perseus, and for depicting Alexander's expedition as a divinely ordained sequence of triumphs. In his description of Alexander's march along the south coast of Asia Minor he described the waves of the sea prostrating themselves before Alexander. Nor was Callisthenes himself popular: some stories told about him in the memoirs of Alexander's companions suggest that he was irritable and boorish at social occasions. But in 327 he was implicated in a plot against Alexander, was arrested, and died while under arrest. In the decades after his death he was reinvented as a principled opponent of Alexander's adoption of Persian practices and claims to divine descent. It is likely that the stories about the introduction of prostration, and Callisthenes' objection to it, were invented to make Callisthenes' death fit an established pattern of stories of philosophers standing up against tyrants. Encounters between philosophers and monarchs were a common subject for Greek writers, starting with Herodotus' account of the meeting of the Athenian philosopher-statesman Solon and Croesus, king of Lydia in the 6th century. Later history also had an influence: in the period shortly before Curtius, Plutarch, and Arrian were writing, the philosopher Seneca was ordered to commit suicide by the emperor Nero, whose tutor Seneca had been. So by the time the Alexander historians were writing, Callisthenes had become a philosophical martyr, killed for speaking truth to tyrannical power, and the stories about his opposition to prostration were too well known to be ignored. However, they are not compatible with what we know about Persian practices in Alexander's time and earlier, so they are not the best way of approaching the question of Alexander's interest in court ceremonial.

What we can say with more confidence is that Alexander appointed men to ceremonial positions that were a normal part of Achaemenid court life. He had a chamberlain or usher, a post known from Herodotus' description of palace organization under Darius I, where the usher controlled access to the king; his friend Hephaestion was given the title of *chiliarch*, another position that had been usual in the Persian court. He kept high ranking Persians in his entourage, including the son of his opponent Darius III, and when he distributed estates to his friends after the victory at Gaugamela, Alexander was acting like a Persian king, and effectively establishing these friends as the nobility of his new empire. Later in his reign, the descriptions of banquets that he organised for large numbers of leading Persians and Macedonians appear very similar to those known from earlier documents from Achaemenid Persepolis. The Alexander historians mention these facts in passing, and they do not suggest that they led to difficulties between Alexander and other Macedonians.

Alexander's queens

Alexander's marriages demonstrate how he integrated himself into his new kingdom. As we have seen, his father Philip had several wives, and used marriage as a means of maintaining relationships with Macedon's neighbours. Persian kings bound powerful nobles to themselves in the same way, and especially in cases where the succession was not direct, they would marry former wives or daughters of their predecessors. As part of Alexander's settlement of the northeastern part of his empire, as we will see, he married Rhoxane, the daughter of a leading Iranian nobleman. On his return from the East in 324 he married two more women: Parysatis, the daughter of Artaxerxes III and sister of Artaxerxes IV, and Stateira, the daughter of Darius III. These marriages connected him to the families of the last two Persian kings, and, had Alexander lived longer, might have produced heirs to Alexander's throne who were direct descendants of his Achaemenid predecessors. Stateira and Parysatis had been captured by the Macedonians, along with the rest of Darius' household, in Damascus after the battle of Issus. The Alexander historians report that Alexander treated these captured women, who included Darius' wife and mother, with great respect. He might have married Stateira rather earlier than he did. All the Alexander historians mention letters sent by Darius to Alexander at times before the battle of Gaugamela, in which Darius offered him marriage to Stateira along with control of the territories west of the Euphrates. Such an agreement would effectively have made Alexander co-ruler with Darius, and presumably would have made it likely that a son of Alexander would inherit the whole empire eventually. Alexander's military triumph rendered this offer redundant, but a child of Stateira would have been a potential successor to Alexander. It is perhaps for this reason that Rhoxane, anxious to protect the status of her (as yet unborn) child, probably had Stateira and Parysatis killed not long after Alexander's death.

Discussion of Alexander's marriages inevitably leads to consideration of his attitude to sex more generally. This was a topic that ancient writers did not ignore, and which has interested modern scholars and influenced modern representations of Alexander. But the questions raised by the ancient writers were rather different from those which have been debated more recently. The Alexander historians do not give a great deal of detail about Alexander's sexual relationships, although Plutarch mentions briefly that he took as a mistress Barsine, the daughter of one of the leading Persians, Artabazus, and the widow of Darius' naval commander, Memnon of Rhodes, who was captured along with the rest of Darius' household after Issus. They are more interested in the issue of Alexander's self-control and sexual continence, as illustrated by his treatment of Darius' captured wife and daughters. Such continence was considered to be a particularly masculine virtue by ancient writers, who did not discuss sexuality in terms of sexual orientation. It is modern writers, including the novelists Klaus Mann and Mary Renault, and the film director Oliver Stone, who have drawn attention to the question of whether Alexander had sexual relations with men as well as women, drawing particular attention to Alexander's friendship with Hephaestion, and to stories about a Persian eunuch called Bagoas. While there is no explicit reference in the surviving texts to such relationships, they would not be inconceivable. There is, however, a danger that suggestions of Alexander's homosexuality romanticize him as much as references to his sexual continence, if they focus exclusively on consensual sexual relationships. Alexander spent most of his adult life on military campaigns and in a royal court where displays of power were a means of preserving order. Perhaps there should be debate, not on whether

Alexander ever had sex with another man, but on whether, or how often, he had sex by force with an unwilling partner, male or female. That kind of behaviour would have been beneath the notice of those who wrote about Alexander in his lifetime, but it has been a feature of all courts and all armies, so it would be truly remarkable if it was not part of Alexander's experience.

Chapter 7
Traveller: Alexander in Afghanistan and Pakistan

In the late Spring of 330 Alexander left Persepolis on a new campaign in the eastern parts of the empire he had won. It would be over five years before he returned. From the very start this journey to the east attracted more strange stories, and more moralizing commentary, than any other part of his career, and it has been a continuing source of fascination for historians in recent centuries. For ancient writers this was when Alexander was seduced by the luxuriousness of the east, and lost control of his passions. It was also when his unquenchable desire to go ever forward was eventually brought to a halt by his soldiers' refusal to go on. For modern writers Alexander's difficulty in dealing with insurgency in Afghanistan and the surrounding areas is the earliest evidence of the impossibility of governing that country; his killing of members of his court is presented as a sign that he was becoming a paranoid tyrant; and his treatment of the people of the Indus Valley is considered little short of genocide. Until recently there was little firm evidence to show what Alexander's eastern campaign involved, but the work of archaeologists, and the appearance and publication of documents from the Persian satrapy of Bactria, in what is now Afghanistan, offer some important correctives to the views of the ancient writers.

Alexander and the queen of the Amazons

One episode in particular shows how early some fantastic stories were spread about Alexander's activities in the east. Curtius describes in some detail the visit of Thalestris, the Amazon queen, to Alexander's camp near the Caspian Sea. She was accompanied by 300 women warriors, and came with the intention of being impregnated by Alexander. To that end she spent 13 nights with the king before returning to her people. Plutarch provides details about where this story came from, saying that most of the authors he had read reported it, and naming five of them, but listing nine other authors who did not mention it. Both lists included men who had accompanied Alexander, but Plutarch tells a further story which casts doubt on the episode. Some years later, one historian, Onesicritus, was reading to Lysimachus, who had been one of Alexander's companions on the campaign: when he came to the story of the Amazon queen, Lysimachus is said to have smiled and asked, 'And where was I at the time?'

Curtius associated this story with Alexander's adoption of Persian dress and court practices, which he saw as a sign that Alexander had lost all self-control. Other historians also chose to wait until this point in the narrative to describe Alexander's adoption of Persian clothing, although, as we have seen, it is likely that the Macedonian court had been influenced by Persian protocol before Alexander's reign, and Alexander had already been acting in accordance with local expectations in Egypt, Babylon, and Susa.

Into Afghanistan

Alexander's initial aim was to prevent Darius III from raising new forces in the eastern parts of his empire. However, by the summer of 330, Darius was dead, having been betrayed by his general Bessus, who declared himself king and took the throne-name Artaxerxes V. Alexander was then able to claim that, as the legitimate king, he was avenging Darius' death. His march took him through what is now northern Iran to Afghanistan, where he turned south to skirt the mountainous interior and then followed the route of the modern road from Kandahar to Kabul before turning northwest to Bactra (modern Balkh), and then across the Oxus River, which is now the border between Afghanistan and Uzbekistan, and in Alexander's time between the satrapies of Bactria and Sogdiana. By now Bessus had lost the trust of his fellow Persians, who turned on him and handed him over to Alexander. That was the Spring of 329, but there were another two years of fighting before Alexander was able to leave Sogdiana and Bactria: he faced insurgency in his rear and hostile neighbours on the other side of the River Tanais or Jaxartes.

The Greek and Roman narratives present the story of these years from the perspective of the Macedonian army and court. There are skirmishes fought and cities sacked, and from time to time troubles within Alexander's entourage. Little is said about those they were fighting against. As a result it is easy to imagine that Alexander was facing the same difficulties that the British had to deal with in the 19th century, the Russians in the 20th century, and NATO forces in the 21st. The historian George Grote, writing in the middle of the 19th century, referred to 'the rude, but spirited tribes of Baktria and Sogdiana', and the novelist Steven Pressfield depicted Alexander's infantrymen using the language, and sharing the attitudes, of contemporary US soldiers. But the region was no isolated wilderness in Alexander's time. Recently a number of documents dating from the reigns of Artaxerxes III and Alexander himself have revealed that it was very much integrated into the rest of the Persian empire.

These documents include letters written on leather, several of which were sent by Akhvamazda, who was probably the satrap of Bactria, to another official, Bagavant, in the period from 353 to 348. Akhvamazda has to deal with complaints about Bagavant's behaviour, and to make Bagavant get on with tasks set him. The

6. A document from Bactria, written in Aramaic in 324, listing supplies being distributed in the satrapy

responsibilities of both men extended to Sogdiana as well as Bactria. There are other letters and records of the distribution of supplies. Some of these records are very similar in form to documents recovered from Persepolis dating to the 5th century. All the Bactrian documents are written in Aramaic, which, by the 4th century, had become the language of administration throughout the empire (Figure 6). It is clear that Bactria, when Alexander arrived there, was a well organized region, integrated into the rest of the empire. The difficulties he faced in bringing the area under control were not that it was in the hands of quarrelling warlords, but that its administration could be effectively used by his opponents, in particular the rebel Spitamenes, who had turned Bessus over to Alexander, and then turned against him.

The edge of empire

The northern boundary of Sogdiana, and of the Achaemenid empire, was the Jaxartes River, which was also known to the Greeks as the Tanais, and was recognized as dividing Asia from Europe.

Beyond lay Scythia, and Arrian and Curtius each have accounts of how Alexander crossed the river to take on the Scythians beyond. The two accounts are significantly different from each other, although each starts with Alexander sacrificing, with the intention of crossing the river, and receiving unfavourable omens. In Arrian's version, when a subsequent sacrifice also turns out unfavourably, Alexander decides to ignore the omens. He crosses the river and is initially successful, but then drinks some tainted water, falls seriously ill, and has to return across the river. In Curtius' story the second sacrifice is very positive; the bad omens turn out to have foretold an ambush of Alexander's men that had not yet been reported to Alexander, but the campaign across the Jaxartes is a complete success. Which of the two stories is correct is impossible to decide, but both suggest that the symbolic importance of Alexander crossing the Jaxartes was considerable.

Darius I had campaigned in the area in around 518, and in a later addition to the account of his reign he had inscribed at Behistun, he described how he crossed the 'sea' to fight the Scythians. Darius and his successors considered their empire to stretch from sea to sea, and in this conception the Jaxartes counted as a northern sea. In crossing the Jaxartes, but not attempting to hold on to the territory to its north, Alexander was following the practice of his Achaemenid predecessors in asserting the extent of his authority from sea to sea. And his later actions at the Hyphasis River in Pakistan were probably intended to achieve the same end.

Alexander was eventually able to settle affairs in Sogdiana and Bactria. As part of this process he followed an established Achaemenid practice of linking himself to the local Persian nobility by a marriage. His new wife was Rhoxane, daughter of Oxyartes, a leading Sogdian, whom Alexander later appointed as satrap of the area south of Bactria. The Greek and Roman historians appear unwilling to recognize Rhoxane's significance, suggesting that the marriage was a love-match, and in Curtius' case claiming that Rhoxane was socially far inferior to Alexander.

It is clear, however, that it was the marriage that consolidated Alexander's control of the region. One of the Bactrian documents discussed earlier is a long list of supplies which covers three months in year seven of Alexander's reign, that is 324: the satrapal administration was working smoothly then. In the following centuries Bactria was to become one of the most prosperous parts of what had been Alexander's empire.

Court intrigues

Quite apart from the dangers of military activity, Alexander was at risk from attacks from within his court. The threats, such as they were, did not come from his close advisors, but on two occasions they had repercussions that led to the deaths of senior courtiers. For Alexander and his contemporaries, plots were an inevitable part of court life. His father had been assassinated by a former bodyguard, and it remained unclear whether that was part of a wider conspiracy. But for later writers, especially for those living under Roman emperors, these events were opportunities to consider how courtiers ought to behave in an autocracy. The dictatorships of the 20th century in turn provided models for modern scholars writing about Alexander's court, sometimes adding a further layer of anachronism to their accounts.

In the Autumn of 330 a conspiracy to assassinate Alexander involving a number of minor figures in his entourage was revealed. One of Alexander's companions, Philotas, son of Parmenion, was said either to have been implicated, or to have known about the plot, and done nothing to prevent it. Philotas was put on trial and condemned to death, and Alexander also ordered the death of Parmenion, who had been left in command in Ecbatana in Media. It is impossible at this distance to determine whether Philotas and Parmenion were guilty of anything, and it is likely that their deaths resulted from the inevitable rivalry between individuals of a royal court whose members were competing for the favour of the king. Arrian gives a brief account taking Philotas' guilt for granted. Curtius on the other hand provides a very elaborate description of Philotas' trial, complete with speeches of accusation on both sides. His version of events has some resemblance to accounts of trials of Roman senators under the emperor Tiberius, for which we have descriptions in the *Annals* of Tacitus. This was a way of bringing to life for his Roman readers the events of an earlier period when a ruler was becoming increasingly despotic and suspicious.

A second conspiracy led to another courtier's death. In Spring 327, around the time that Alexander married Rhoxane, a group of royal pages conspired to assassinate him. This followed the humiliation of one of the pages, named Hermolaus, during a hunt. The pages had easy access to the king, so were in a good position to carry out a plot against him, and this is what Hermolaus planned. It was only Alexander's staying up all night that saved him, and the next day the plot was discovered. In the investigation that followed, Callisthenes, Alexander's court historian, was implicated in the plot and arrested. As with other plots, we cannot know whether or not he was guilty, and in this particular case we do not even know what happened to him. Arrian says that the historians who were there at the time give conflicting accounts of his fate: Ptolemy said that he was executed, while Aristobulus stated that he died of disease while in custody. In the surviving narratives the real reason for the death of Callisthenes is taken to be his opposition to Alexander claiming divine status, and requiring his companions to prostrate themselves before him; the pages' plot merely provided the pretext for his arrest. Most modern scholars have accepted this version of events, but, as we have seen, it has its problems.

One other significant death of a courtier occurred between the arrests of Philotas and Callisthenes: Alexander ran his companion Cleitus through with a spear after a drunken dinner. Cleitus was a cavalry commander under Alexander's father Philip, and had kept that role under Alexander. He was said to have saved Alexander's life at the Battle of the Granicus in 334. In the autumn of 328 Alexander appointed him satrap of Bactria. At a dinner soon after this, according to all the surviving narratives, an argument broke out between the two men. Accounts of the substance of the argument, and of what the protagonists actually did, are inconsistent and probably unreliable, but the evening ended with Alexander killing Cleitus. Both men were probably drunk. Roman moralists drew parallels between the deaths of Cleitus and Callisthenes, as two examples of the king killing his friends, and the authors of the surviving narratives put similar accusations into the mouths of both men—in particular that Alexander was dishonouring the memory of his father Philip by claiming to be son of Zeus. This was a standard accusation made against Alexander in later periods, and gave greater significance to Cleitus' death as being one more example of a death resulting from Alexander's increasing loss of awareness of his own mortality. But in all likelihood it was the proximity of men, alcohol, and weapons in the atmosphere of rivalry and ambition that would characterize any royal court that best explains what happened.

To the Indus Valley

From Afghanistan Alexander marched southeast through the Hindu Kush and into the northern part of the Indus River basin in what is now Pakistan. According to Herodotus' *Histories*, Darius I had campaigned in this region, and the parts of what he calls India west of the Indus paid tribute to the Persian king. Not a lot is known about the region between the time of Darius I and Alexander, so it is not clear how far to the east the authority of the later Achaemenid kings reached, although Arrian says that a contingent of the Indians who bordered Bactria fought alongside the Bactrians at the battle of Gaugamela. For the Greek and Roman historians, this was not a significant issue in any case. Their narratives focus more on the idea of Alexander travelling further east than his heroic predecessors had gone. Alexander captured a supposedly impregnable fortress, the Rock of Aornus, which even Heracles was said to have been unable to storm, and he and his companions spent time in the city of Nysa, once visited by Dionysus, as was proved by the presence there of ivy, a plant particularly associated with the god, which was apparently found nowhere else in the region.

Four major tributaries flow into the Indus from the east, coming down from the Himalayas: from west to east, the Hydaspes (modern Jhelum), Acesines (Chenab), Hydraotes (Ravi), and Hyphasis (Beas). The territory between these rivers was controlled by a number of rival Indian princes. Alexander adopted a different pattern of control here from other parts of the empire. He did not appoint satraps and local military commanders, but rather he confirmed in their positions those princes who agreed to accept his authority. The first significant ruler to do this was Taxiles, whose territory lay between the Indus and the Hydaspes. Consequently Alexander was faced with opposition from Taxiles' neighbour Porus, on the east side of the Hydaspes.

Alexander's defeat of Porus, which followed his rapid crossing of the river, was the fourth and last major pitched battle of the campaign in Asia. A series of large silver coins, or medallions, were struck to commemorate the victory. Known as Porus decadrachms or Elephant medallions, these depict on one side a lone horseman attacking an elephant with two tall riders, one of whom is throwing a spear at the horseman—generally assumed to be a depiction of Alexander and Porus—and on the other side Alexander himself in full armour, holding a thunderbolt and being crowned with a wreath by a winged victory (Figure 7). These attributes should probably be associated with the title of 'unconquered god' that the Athenians were to bestow on Alexander some two years later on his return from this campaign. The coins or medallions were probably issued to Alexander's soldiers as a reward for their service. They show Alexander as his troops would want to imagine him, all-powerful

7. A coin or medallion issued by Alexander to celebrate victory in his Indian campaign. The obverse shows a horseman attacking an elephant with a warrior on its back, probably representing Alexander and Porus. The reverse shows Alexander, in armour, holding a thunderbolt and being crowned by Victory

and victorious, and the Greek cities would have recognized his success in similar terms. But the coins should not be seen as Alexander making claims himself for any 'divine status'.

Alexander's treatment of Porus after the battle became a popular subject, not least in a series of operas using a libretto by the 18th-century Italian poet Metastasio, and in the first full-length movie about Alexander, Sorab Modi's *Sikandar* of 1941. Porus pledged allegiance to Alexander, who restored him to his position, and even increased the size of his territories.

Turning back?

After this Alexander continued eastwards over the Acesines and Hydraotes as far as the Hyphasis, which became the scene of one of the most frequently told stories about Alexander. It was on the banks of the Hyphasis, according to tradition, that Alexander's soldiers finally refused to accompany him any further. In response Alexander supposedly shut himself up in his tent and refused to see anyone, and then said that he would go on alone. But when even this would not make his soldiers change their minds, he submitted to their will and turned back. This is one of the stories found in all the surviving narratives, and as a result its veracity has seldom been doubted, but all that this unanimity really proves is that the story had come into circulation before the earliest of the surviving narratives had been composed: it was so memorable a story that no subsequent narrator could ignore it. There is good reason to suppose that the story is an invention. Before he marched east from the Hydaspes, Alexander had commissioned the building of a fleet of transport ships to take his army down-river. It is likely that the Hyphasis was considered the boundary of the Persian empire towards India, just as the Jaxartes was north of Sogdiana. It may have been the case that Alexander had intended to cross the Hyphasis to assert his authority, and then return to its west bank, just as he had done both at the Jaxartes and also at the Danube at the start of his reign. If so, then according to Ptolemy, as reported by Arrian, it was unfavourable omens rather than Alexander's soldiers that prevented him. Alexander's activities in the eastern part of the empire make more sense as the consolidation of his rule over the territory he had won from Darius III, rather than an endless quest for new conquests. The authors of the Alexander histories had no interest in where the existing boundaries of the Achaemenid empire lay, so they present Alexander's every move as winning new territory, but Alexander himself will have known better. Having reached the eastern edge of the territories he had already laid claim to, he was ready to turn south and march towards the ocean. He was not turning back homewards yet.

To the ocean

For the story of Alexander's journey through the Indus Valley to the Indian Ocean we are entirely reliant on the Alexander historians. No inscriptions from Greeks or Indians have survived, and the constantly changing courses of the major rivers have erased any archaeological remains that there might have been.

Alexander sailed down the Hydaspes while contingents of his army marched alongside on either bank. His aim appears to have been to assert his authority by confirming those local leaders who acknowledged his sovereignty in their positions, and campaigning vigorously against those who resisted him. This was no different from his policy elsewhere, but modern scholars have tended to present this phase of the campaign as particularly violent and destructive. Certainly Alexander did face resistance in some places, and he received his most severe wound during the siege of a city somewhere in the southern Punjab. South of Punjab, although his army marched, and where necessary fought, through the territory on the eastern side of the Indus, Alexander was not concerned to establish direct rule over that territory, and he probably followed Darius I in treating the river as the eastern boundary of his empire. As it turned out, this was one of the first parts of Alexander's empire to be taken over by others. Plutarch reports a visit by a young Indian prince (whom he calls Androcottus) to the court of Alexander when he was in the Punjab. That prince was Chandragupta Maurya, who came to power in around 322, and rapidly gained control of most of northern India from the Ganges Delta to the Indus. By the time he abdicated in 298, the Mauryan empire included most of South Asia, including the satrapies along the west bank of the Indus.

For Alexander it is clear that his arrival at the Indian Ocean marked the successful end of his campaign, and this was celebrated by sacrifices to the gods made out at sea. But the final stage of his campaign was to become the most notorious of all his travels, and possibly the most misunderstood.

The Gedrosian Desert

Alexander had brought a fleet down from the Punjab to the Indian Ocean, and his intention was to send it on up the Persian Gulf to the mouths of the Tigris and Euphrates, and from there upriver to Babylon. To have a naval route that reached from Mesopotamia almost to Afghanistan would have been of great value, but it relied on the fleet being supplied as it sailed along the largely inhospitable south coast of Iran. It was for this reason that Alexander led a land force through the region of Gedrosia in southern Iran on his way from the Indus Delta back to Pasargadae. His purpose, as Arrian describes it, was to make sure that there was fresh water and supplies of grain available to the fleet as it sailed up the gulf. There is no doubt that this was a difficult task, as the territory was mostly desert and there were few good anchorages at the coast. The land expedition took two months, but it should be judged a success, as the fleet, under the Cretan commander Nearchus, was able to complete its journey without difficulty.

Ancient authors writing after Alexander's time transformed the march through Gedrosia into a disaster resulting from Alexander's arrogance and folly. After a sober account of how, with some difficulties, Alexander was able to achieve his aim, Arrian reports a series of stories about the hardship of the desert journey that he did not find in his main sources, but must have considered 'worth telling and not entirely implausible'. Plutarch claims that he lost three-quarters of the army he took to India in the Gedrosian desert, even though he took far fewer than half of his troops into Gedrosia. Modern scholars have perhaps been too ready to believe the horror stories, even suggesting that the march through the desert was Alexander's way of taking revenge on his soldiers for forcing him to turn back at the Hyphasis. This was not what the ancient writers thought. Arrian reports the view that Alexander was seeking to outdo his famous predecessors, Cyrus the Great and Semiramis, the legendary queen of Babylon, each of whom had gone through the desert and lost almost their entire army. We should recognize in the stories of the desert journey an interest not in Alexander's folly, but in his superhuman endurance.

Once he had led his army out of the desert, the road was open first to Pasargadae and Persepolis, and then to Susa and Ecbatana, before the final chapter in Alexander's life opened on the road to Babylon.

Chapter 8
Doomed to die: Alexander in Babylon

The final chapter of Alexander's life was set in Babylon. He had spent a short time there earlier in his campaign, and it had been the first Achaemenid royal centre that he had visited. We have already come across the fragment of a Babylonian astronomical diary that reports Alexander's victory at the battle of Gaugamela, and refers to him as 'King of the World'. That diary goes on to report his negotiations with the governor of Babylon, his promise to restore Esagila, the sanctuary of the god Marduk, and his entry into the city of Babylon itself on 20 October 331. Alexander was to return to Babylon nearly eight years later, in Spring 323, and it was there that he died. Babylonian documents can illuminate important aspects of Alexander's actions in the city and his relationship with its scholar-priests. They can also help us make sense of some puzzling stories in the Greek and Roman accounts.

Babylonian scholarship

The scholars who produced the astronomical diaries were also responsible for composing the Babylonian royal chronicles. Like the diaries these record significant historical events, without commenting upon them, and they therefore differ from the royal inscriptions, which were designed for public consumption and which emphasize the virtues and power of the king. The sequence of chronicles starts at the accession of king Nabonassar (747–734), and is known to carry on at least into the later 2nd century BCE. The eight years during which Alexander was king, though they were important in Babylonian history, are only a brief moment in this context.

As well as making records of the present, the Babylonian scholars also created works of guidance based on past events. These included the *Enūma Anu Enlil*, which listed celestial events, in particular eclipses, with guidance as to what they portended. The aim of all this was to support the king, so that his reign would be long and the city of Babylon would benefit from it. So as well as recording celestial events and identifying potential threats to the king, the scholar-priests would advise him on what actions to take to avoid the predicted dangers.

Alexander's entry into Babylon, 331

When Alexander entered Babylon after his victory at Gaugamela, he was following in a line of previous victorious new rulers that included Sargon II of Assyria (722–705) and Cyrus the Great of Persia. The account of Alexander's entry into Babylon recorded by Curtius follows a pattern known from official documents produced by these earlier kings. The people of the city are described as rejoicing, and the new king in turn sacrifices to the gods and promises to restore their temples. The promise to restore the temples did not necessarily indicate that they had been damaged earlier: large brick-built buildings were in need of constant attention, and kings could improve them as well as keep them standing: the king's concern for the fabric of the city was a sign of his virtue. Arrian claims that Xerxes had destroyed the temples of Babylon, but there is no mention of this in any Babylonian documents.

None of the surviving narratives mentions a coronation of Alexander in Babylon, but he was certainly recognized as king from the time of his arrival, and described as such in Babylonian documents from this time and afterwards. For Plutarch, the fact that Alexander was prepared to surround himself with Babylonian soothsayers was a sign that he was becoming enmeshed in superstitious practices, but it was an inevitable consequence of his position as king that the religious-administrative organization of the city would be deployed to advise and support him. He did not stay long in Babylon on this occasion, moving on to the other Persian royal centres at Susa and Persepolis. But Alexander was to return to Babylon at the end of his life, and once again he would follow the guidance of its priests.

On 20 September 331, the 13th day of the month *Ulūlu* in the Babylonian calendar, 11 days before the battle of Gaugamela, there had been a lunar eclipse. Saturn was in the sky, and Jupiter had set. This is recorded in the astronomical diary already discussed, and the eclipse is mentioned by the surviving Alexander historians. In the *Enūma Anu Enlil* there is an explanation of the meaning of an eclipse on that day. Not only does it foretell the death of the current king, but also that his son will not inherit his throne, and a new ruler will come from the west and rule for eight years. The battle that followed the eclipse in September 331 did indeed ensure the end of Darius' reign, and sometime after that of his life. He was indeed succeeded by a ruler from the west, Alexander. But October 323 would mark the end of eight years of Alexander's reign. Unless fate could be avoided, Alexander's future was looking bleak.

Alexander's entry into Babylon, 323

Alexander had returned from his Indian campaign at the end of 325. After spending the summer of the following year in Ecbatana in Media, and campaigning against the Cossaeans in the northern Zagros Mountains in the autumn and winter, Alexander made his way to Babylon in the spring of 323. There, according to Arrian and Diodorus, he was discouraged from entering the city by the

Babylonian priests, on the grounds that it would be dangerous for him. Possibly they were influenced by two eclipses, one lunar, one solar, that had occurred the previous May. The meaning of the lunar eclipse on that particular day was that 'the King of the World would die and his dynasty would come to an end'. Such predictions were supposed to come true within 100 days, but occasionally came into effect later. It is also likely that the priests were expecting solar eclipses in April and May 323, although these turned out not to be visible. Arrian says Alexander was advised not to enter the city from the west, and he adds that according to Aristobulus, who was with Alexander at the time, the king attempted to follow this advice, but was prevented from getting round the city because the ground was waterlogged and marshy. It is common in narratives involving prophecies of misfortune that the central character tries to avoid ill luck, but is prevented by circumstances beyond his control, and Arrian is clearly conscious that this is the message of this story, but that does not mean that it is not a basically accurate account.

It seems likely that, either after Alexander had entered Babylon against advice, or while he was waiting to enter the city, another ritual was performed to protect him from ill fate. This was the 'substitute king ritual', which is known from Assyrian texts. The ritual involved the temporary abdication of the king, usually for 100 days, with a criminal or madman being made king in his place. The idea was that any misfortune would fall on the substitute instead of the real king. Once the predicted risk period was over, the substitute would be executed, and the real king would resume his reign. There are no Babylonian documents that refer to this ritual, but the Greek writer Dio Chrysostom, a contemporary of Plutarch, makes a confused reference to it as a Persian custom. It was probably taken over by the Babylonians from the Assyrians, and used by them into the Persian period and beyond. In the narratives of Diodorus, Plutarch, and Arrian, stories are told about a madman or lunatic being found sitting on the throne, wearing Alexander's royal gown and diadem. In the stories this is presented as an omen of Alexander's impending death, and it is suggested that the man went to the throne of his own accord. However, the similarities to the elements of the substitute king ritual are too close to be coincidental, so they may be taken as evidence for Alexander undergoing such a ritual in 323. However, he was clearly back on the throne by June.

Death

Plutarch and Arrian both give quite detailed accounts of the last days of Alexander's life. They based these on what they believed to be genuine reports of his daily activities recorded in the so-called 'Royal Journals'. While it is not unlikely that such records might have existed, most scholars doubt that what was available to writers of the 2nd century CE bore much of a relationship to them. Following the account in these journals, Plutarch and Arrian describe how Alexander caught a fever and spent the last few days of his life mainly lying on his couch, conducting the religious rituals required of him as king and giving instructions to his officers about a planned invasion of Arabia. He gradually weakened, and sometime before he died he lost the ability to speak. None of this is implausible. Although Alexander was only 32 years old, he had suffered a number of injuries, including a severe chest wound in the Punjab. He also drank alcohol heavily. His companion Hephaestion had died under similar circumstances in Ecbatana the previous year, with no foul play suspected.

Inevitably, however, within a few years of his death, stories began to circulate that claimed that Alexander had been poisoned. The version we find in most of the Alexander historians claims that Alexander's regent in Greece, Antipater, organized the assassination, sending his sons Cassander and Iollas to Babylon with poison provided by Aristotle. It is most likely that this story was invented to damage the reputation of Antipater and Cassander in the conflicts between Alexander's successors that broke out immediately after his death. Alexander's mother, Olympias, working in the interest of her grandson, Rhoxane's infant son Alexander IV, found herself in opposition to Antipater and Cassander and may have been the source of the story.

The most widespread story about Alexander's death, however, concerns his supposed last words. Arrian reports, on the basis of the supposed 'Royal Journals', that Alexander lost the power of speech a few days before he died, but, because the story was too well known to be ignored, he also notes that some writers said that Alexander's companions asked him to whom he left his kingdom, and that Alexander's reply was 'to the strongest'. The events of the years following Alexander's death made such a response seem prophetic. Alexander's generals fought among themselves over the next decades, attempting either to take control of his whole empire or, eventually, to carve out kingdoms for themselves. Even when he was dead, Alexander was still a part of this conflict. As we have seen, his body, which was being sent back to Macedonia to be buried in the royal tombs at Vergina, was diverted to Egypt, where Ptolemy, who made himself first satrap and later pharaoh in Egypt, used it to legitimize his rule.

The empire which Alexander had created began to fall apart even before his body had been properly buried. There is no space in a book of this size to tell the story of the following years, which has in any case been told often before. What remains is to look at how the historical Alexander, whom we have glimpsed through the fragmentary contemporary evidence, and through the distorting lens of later historical tradition, reached the position he occupies in the imagination of the modern world.

Chapter 9
After Alexander

This book has tried to show what we can say with confidence about Alexander and his world, on the basis of evidence from his own time. Often this has meant challenging commonly held ideas about how he acted, why he did what he did, and even questioning whether he did do some of things attributed to him. But if long-held ideas about Alexander are unreliable or wrong, where did they come from in the first place? In this last chapter we will look at Alexander's afterlife, and how some of the images of Alexander that are prominent in popular imagination came into existence.

Roman Alexanders: Julius Caesar and others

In 45 BCE the Roman Senate voted to put up in the Temple of Quirinus in Rome a statue of Julius Caesar, with the title *Deus Invictus* ('The invincible god'). Caesar, who was to be assassinated the following year, at this point held the position of dictator, with what amounted to absolute political power in Rome. The title *Deus Invictus* (Greek *Theos Aniketos*) was identical to that the Athenians had given to the statue of Alexander they voted in 324, ironically also the year before his death. It is unlikely that the choice of title was coincidence. At the time that the statue was voted on, the leading politician (and part-time philosopher) Cicero was attempting to compose a letter of advice to Caesar on how to rule, in deliberate imitation of a letter supposedly written to Alexander by his former tutor, Aristotle. In the end Cicero abandoned the idea, noting in a letter to his friend Atticus that 'even Aristotle's pupil, whose temperament and self-control were of the best, became proud, cruel and intemperate once he was addressed as king'. It suited the moralists of the Roman republic, which had an ideology of opposition to monarchy, to see Alexander's taking of Darius' throne as the beginning of a decline into tyranny.

Parallels between Julius Caesar and Alexander, the two greatest military figures of their ages, were readily drawn. Plutarch's *Life of Alexander* is paired with his *Life of Julius Caesar*, and several writers tell a story of how Caesar, in Spain, before his career had taken off, saw a statue of Alexander and wept at how little he had achieved by the age at which Alexander had died. He was not the only Roman to see Alexander as a potential model. His older contemporary and rival Pompey, who had annexed the territories of the eastern Mediterranean, which had formerly been part of Alexander's empire, for Rome, adopted the cognomen Magnus, 'the Great', and modelled the hairstyle of his portrait statues on that of Alexander. So Alexander could provide a model for ambitious individuals. The man who commissioned the Alexander Mosaic in Pompeii (see Figure 1 in the Introduction) around the time of Pompey's birth presumably also saw Alexander as a figure worthy of being depicted in the more public area of his home. The implication might be that visitors would associate Alexander's virtues with his own.

On 15 February 44, at the festival of the Lupercalia, Caesar's lieutenant Mark Antony offered a diadem to him, which Caesar declined. It was suspected by some contemporaries that Caesar had arranged the event as a way of claiming the title of king, as if by popular demand; others interpreted his action, placing the diadem on a throne next to him, as making a claim for worship as a god, since gods were regularly represented in Roman

processions by attributes carried on thrones. It is probable that
these two interpretations could have been held together. Kingship,
in this period, was considered a characteristic of the Persian and
Hellenistic east, and Romans were under the impression that in
that part of the world, kings were worshipped as gods. Whatever
precisely happened, this diadem incident has been seen as a
trigger for Caesar's assassination exactly a month later by men
claiming to be defending the republic. It was in the years after this
assassination that the earliest of our surviving narratives of
Alexander's life, Book 17 of Diodorus' *Library of History*,
was written, and memories of Caesar's life and death must have
influenced the way he and his readers will have interpreted the life
of Alexander. It will also have influenced Diodorus' contemporary,
Pompeius Trogus, whose history survives now in an epitome, an
abbreviated version made around 300 years later by Justin.

Julius Caesar had come to power during the period of political
chaos and civil war which led to the collapse of the Roman
republic. His adopted son, who took the name Augustus, brought
an end to the wars and, while claiming to be restoring rule to the
senate and people of Rome, established himself as the first Roman
emperor. For Augustus and his successors, the question of how
to reconcile the need for a single leader with the Roman tradition
of republican rule was an on-going concern, and this is an
underlying theme in the stories we find in the narratives of Tacitus
and Suetonius, who were writing at about the same time as
Plutarch and Arrian, and of Cassius Dio, writing in the early 3rd
century CE. Some emperors are portrayed as less successful than
others, in particular Caligula, who became emperor in 37 CE.
Caligula is said to have taken Alexander the Great's breastplate to
wear when, like Julius Caesar and Augustus before him, he visited
Alexander's tomb in Alexandria. He is also said to have required
Roman senators to prostrate themselves in front of him, offering
them his toe to kiss instead of his hand. Curtius' generally negative
depiction of Alexander may have been influenced in part by
memories and representations of Caligula: Curtius was writing

either in the reign of Caligula's successor Claudius, or under Vespasian a few decades later.

By the time Plutarch and Arrian were writing, under the successful emperors Trajan (98–117) and Hadrian (117–38), it was accepted that the Roman Empire was an autocracy. Alexander came to be presented as a model of correct kingship: these writers emphasized his wisdom and self-control while warning of the potential dangers of adopting the habits of eastern rulers. Both emperors led armies across the Euphrates into Mesopotamia, following in the footsteps of Alexander, so it was appropriate for contemporary writers to present him as both a symbol of military success and a warning about the dangers of luxury and excess.

The Alexander that has come down to us in the ancient historical narratives grew under particular circumstances. He is the creation of Roman authors (even if several of them wrote in Greek), writing for a Roman audience. Roman concerns, about how to be a ruler, and how to live as a subject under an autocracy, which are central themes in Roman histories of Rome, are equally present in histories of Alexander the Great, as is a suspicion and hostility of their eastern neighbours. In more recent times these concerns have sometimes arisen again: the period of dictatorship in Europe in the second quarter of the 20th century, and the rebirth of the idea of the 'clash of civilizations' in the wake of 9/11 have both had their impact on Alexander studies, as the prejudices of the Romans have seemed to pre-echo the politics of the 20th and 21st centuries.

Medieval Alexander

If we want to know about Alexander today, it is to the Alexander historians of the Roman period that we turn for our information. However, for most of the period between Alexander's death and the present there was another tradition of stories that was much more prominent. In his *Monk's Tale* Chaucer gives a brief account of Alexander's career and comments that:

> The storie of Alisaundre is so commune
> That every wight that hath discrecioun
> Hath herd somwhat or al of his fortune.

The story that the Monk is referring to is known as the *Alexander Romance*, an account of Alexander's life that had its origins in Egypt in the 3rd century BCE, and was developed over the following centuries, translated into numerous languages, until versions of it were known from Iceland to India.

The earliest version of the *Alexander Romance* that we can read comes from the 3rd century CE. It tells the story of Alexander's life, with fanciful elements that became even more exaggerated in later versions. Alexander is said to be the son of the last Egyptian pharaoh, Nectanebo, who is also a magician, and who comes to Philip's court and seduces Olympias by disguising himself as the god Ammon in the form of a serpent. Nectanebo acts as Alexander's first tutor, but Alexander kills him when he reveals himself to be his father. In later Persian tradition, as recorded in the *Shahnameh*, or *Book of Kings*, written around 1000 CE, Alexander has become Sekandar, supposedly son of Philip, but actually the son of Darab, king of Persia, and therefore half-brother of his opponent Dara (Darius III). These alternative filiations tie Alexander more firmly to the kingdoms he comes to rule. Other elements of his early life are made more fantastical: for example in the *Romance* his favourite horse, Bucephalas, is depicted as not just untameable by anyone but Alexander, but also as a man-eater. Another story tells of the young Alexander going in disguise to spy out the court of the Persian king before he begins his campaign. In versions of the story told after the Arab conquests of the 7th century CE, Alexander is said to have gone in disguise to the royal court of Islamic Andalusia, where the queen immediately sees through his disguise.

Many of the events recorded in the more sober accounts of Alexander's career are also described in the *Romance*, although not in the same order. In particular Alexander's siege of Tyre is described with considerable detail. Later versions of the *Romance* include more miraculous tales: Alexander is taken up into the sky in a chariot drawn by griffons, and goes down to the depths of the sea in a glass diving bell; he visits paradise and has his own death foretold. Over time the story told in the *Romance* tells more and more about Alexander's search for wisdom, and in the versions written down in medieval western Europe Alexander becomes a symbol of chivalry and goodness.

It is through this *Romance* tradition that Alexander, under the name *o Megalexandros*, continued to be known in Greece through centuries when knowledge of classical history and mythology was lost. An early modern Greek version of the *Romance*, the *Phyllada*, or *Book of Alexander the Great*, was published in Venice in 1670, and remained in circulation continuously from then onwards. Alexander also became, uniquely among figures from classical antiquity, a character in a number of Karagiozis shadow-puppet plays. This form of popular entertainment grew out of an Ottoman Turkish tradition, developing its Greek character through the 19th century, and reaching the peak of its popularity in the first half of the 20th. *O Megalexandros* appeared in several plays, most notably in 'Alexander the Great and the Cursed Snake', in which, in keeping with the development of his character into that of a brave warrior righting wrongs, he kills a dragon which is terrorizing a kingdom: he has become a version of St George.

The presence of Alexander in Greek popular culture in the role of a largely Christianized warrior hero may be part of the explanation for the strength of the reaction in modern Greece to the deployment of the image of Alexander. This has been a particular issue in the relationship between Greece and the (former Yugoslav) Republic of Macedonia, where the decision in 2006 to name the airport at Skopje after Alexander the Great, and to erect a huge equestrian statue of him on the site, led to protests from the Greek government.

Alexander, the Enlightenment, and empire

The chivalrous Alexander of the *Romance* suited the medieval world, and the courts of the absolutist monarchs like Louis XIV and Catherine the Great. New Alexanders emerged in the Age of the Enlightenment, the period from the late 17th until the early 19th century. Initially in France, but then in Scotland and England, and eventually Germany and elsewhere, *philosophes* and historians brought a more critical approach to the study of ancient history and of Alexander the Great in particular. New editions and translations were made of the Greek and Latin Alexander historians, and their reliability was held up to scrutiny. At the same time Alexander was reconsidered as model ruler. Some writers chose to stress his negative characteristics, his cruelty, and, not least, his persecution of scholars like the court historian Callisthenes. But this was a period of European expansion overseas, and for others Alexander's campaigns were seen as bringing the benefits of a lively and progressive European civilization to the slothful and unchanging east. For such writers there was effectively no difference between the empire of Darius III and the Ottoman Empire of their own time. The most positive assessments of Alexander can be found in a number of essays by Voltaire and in the treatise on *The Spirit of the Laws* by the Baron de Montesquieu: they suggest that Alexander's greatest achievement was to open up the east to trade and commerce, through his city-foundations, and the naval voyages he organized.

For writers in England and Scotland, the loss of Britain's American colonies in the War of Independence was the impetus for renewed study of ancient Greek history. In 1786 the Scottish historian John Gillies published a two-volume *History of Ancient Greece, its Colonies and Conquests*. Dedicated to the king, George III, it was written in reaction to the events in America with the explicit intent of demonstrating the dangers of democracy or republicanism and the superiority of constitutional monarchy. Two years earlier the English Conservative MP William Mitford had published the first volume of his eight-volume *History of Greece*. By the time he published his last volume, the French Revolution had taken place, offering an even clearer lesson about the dangers of the unrestrained rule of the people. For Gillies and Mitford democratic Athens, defeated in the 5th century by monarchic Sparta and in the 4th by the Macedonians under king Philip, represented all that was wrong with democracy, and in contrast the career of Alexander was the best example of what monarchy could achieve. For Gillies, Alexander was 'this extraordinary man, whose genius might have changed and improved the state of the ancient world'.

Alexander's 'civilizing mission' was a theme that was used to justify British involvement in India, which after the loss of the American territories became the main focus for colonial expansion. Following the example of earlier French writers, advocates of imperialism depicted the British as Alexander's heirs, bringing European energy and civilization to Asia, sunk in lethargy. But Alexander's legacy could be claimed by others too. Sir Alexander Burnes, who was British political agent in Kabul before he was assassinated in 1841, shortly before the British forces were driven out of Kabul and destroyed at the end of the First Anglo-Afghan War (1839–42), travelled widely in central Asia in the 1830s. He took with him texts of the Alexander historians, and went in search of the sites they mentioned. But he also noted that in parts of the region Alexander was considered an Islamic prophet, and mentions in his memoirs the (unprompted) claim of a local ruler to be a direct descendant of Alexander. These ideas of Alexander would probably have come through the *Romance* tradition as transmitted in Persian texts.

Hero or villain

Perhaps the most influential study of Alexander to emerge from this period was that of the German historian Johann Gustav Droysen, whose *Geschichte Alexanders des Grossen* (*History of*

Alexander the Great—a work never translated into English) was published in 1833. Droysen studied in Berlin, and was influenced by the philosopher Hegel and the geographer Alexander von Humboldt. Enlightenment scholars in Germany identified their country closely with ancient Greece, not least because both were made up of a large number of small states surrounded by larger kingdoms. Droysen supported the cause of German unification, and his Alexander was also a unifier, not only of the warring Greek city-states, but of the whole of western Asia. For him the period that followed Alexander's death, until then seen as a time of decline in the Greek world, was actually one of triumph, as Greek culture sprang up in the territories through which his army had passed. What is more, Droysen suggested, Alexander's welcoming of men from many cultures into his court encouraged them to think about what they shared, including the idea of a single god: and therefore, perhaps, he paved the way for Christianity.

Alexander's contribution to civilization was depicted less positively by George Grote, a friend of the political philosopher John Stuart Mill and a radical MP, in his very popular 12-volume *History of Greece*. For Grote, Alexander represented all that was worst about autocracy and imperialism:

> As far as we can venture to anticipate what would have been Alexander's future, we can see nothing in prospect except years of ever-repeated aggression and conquest, not to be concluded until he had traversed and subjugated all the inhabited globe...Now, how such an empire thus boundless and heterogeneous, such as no prince has ever realized, could be administered with any advantage to subjects—it would be difficult to show.

The terms of the modern debate about Alexander were set in the Enlightenment. Historians still try to decide whether he was a romantic hero or a bloodthirsty tyrant, and whether or not his campaigns brought more good than harm. This is because, to a great extent, the arguments are based on the same limited collection of texts—the Alexander historians we considered at the start of this chapter. It is not my intention, at the end of this *Very Short Introduction*, to offer my own judgement on Alexander or his legacy. The surviving narratives can be interpreted to support a variety of assessments. It has been my aim, however, to show that these narratives are not necessarily reliable enough for us to use them to draw any clear conclusion at all. Material from Alexander's own time, in the form of the Greek and Egyptian inscriptions, the speeches of Athenian politicians, and the diaries of Babylonian scholar-priests, as we have seen, can offer some limited alternative perspective. Before asking, 'What should we think of Alexander the Great?', we should perhaps ask, 'What did his contemporaries think of Alexander the Great?'. That question has not yet been convincingly answered, but this book has been a start in that direction.

References

Introduction

Ada Cohen, *The Alexander Mosaic: Stories of Victory and Defeat* (Cambridge University Press, 1997)

Andrew Stewart, *Faces of Power: Alexander's Image and Hellenistic Politics* (University of California Press, 1993)

Chapter 1: Before Alexander

Pierre Briant, *From Cyrus to Alexander: A History of the Persian Empire* (Eisenbrauns, 2002)

Lindsay Allen, *The Persian Empire* (British Museum Press, 2005)

Amélie Kuhrt, *The Persian Empire: A Corpus of Sources from the Achaemenid Period* (Routledge, 2007)

Robin Lane Fox (ed.), *Brill's Companion to Ancient Macedon: Studies in the Archaeology and History of Macedon, 650 BC–300 AD* (E.J. Brill, 2011)

Chapter 2: Prince: Alexander in the Macedonian court

Elizabeth Carney, *Women and Monarchy in Macedonia* (University of Oklahoma Press, 2000)

Robin Lane Fox (ed.), *Brill's Companion to Ancient Macedon: Studies in the Archaeology and History of Macedon, 650 BC–300 AD* (E.J. Brill, 2011)

Chapter 3: Warrior: Alexander's army

Donald W. Engels, *Alexander the Great and the Logistics of the Macedonian Army* (University of California Press, 1978)

Waldemar Heckel, *The Marshals of Alexander's Empire* (Routledge, 1992)

Chapter 4: Commander: Alexander and the Greeks
A.J. Heisserer, *Alexander the Great and the Greeks: The Epigraphic Evidence* (University of Oklahoma Press, 1980)

P.J. Rhodes and R.G. Osborne, *Greek Historical Inscriptions, 404–323 BC* (Oxford University Press, 2004)

Chapter 5: Pharaoh: Alexander and Egypt
Philip Bosman (ed.), *Alexander in Africa* (University of South Africa Press, 2014)

Chapter 6: King of the world: Alexander and Persia
Ernst Fredricksmeyer, 'Alexander the Great and the Kingship of Asia' in A.B. Bosworth and Elizabeth Baynham (eds), *Alexander the Great in Fact and Fiction* (Oxford University Press, 2000): 136–66

Hugh Bowden, 'On Kissing and Making Up: Court Protocol and Historiography in Alexander the Great's "Experiment with *Proskynesis*"', *Bulletin of the Institute of Classical Studies* 56/2 (2013): 55–77

Klaus Mann, *Alexander: A Novel of Utopia* (Brewer and Warren, 1930)

Mary Renault, *The Persian Boy* (Longman, 1972)

Chapter 7: Traveller: Alexander in Afghanistan and Pakistan
Joseph Naveh and Shaul Shaked, *Aramaic Documents from Ancient Bactria from the Khalili Collections* (Khalili Collections, 2012)

Frank Holt, *Into the Land of Bones: Alexander the Great in Afghanistan* (Second edn, University of California Press, 2012)

Steven Pressfield, *The Afghan Campaign* (Doubleday, 2006)

A.B. Bosworth, *Alexander and the East: The Tragedy of Triumph* (Oxford University Press, 1998)

Chapter 8: Doomed to die: Alexander in Babylon
Amélie Kuhrt, 'Alexander and Babylon', *Achaemenid History* 5 (1990): 121–30

R.J. van der Speck, 'Darius III, Alexander the Great and Babylonian Scholarship', *Achaemenid History* 13 (2003): 289–346

Chapter 9: After Alexander
Diana Spencer, *The Roman Alexander: Reading a Cultural Myth* (University of Exeter Press, 2002)

Richard Stoneman, *Alexander: A Life in Legend* (Yale University Press, 2008)

Claude Mossé, *Alexander: Destiny and Myth* (Johns Hopkins University Press, 2004)

C.A. Hagerman, *Britain's Imperial Muse: The Classics, Imperialism, and the Indian Empire, 1784–1914* (Palgrave Macmillan, 2013)

Further reading

Ancient narrative sources
All modern reconstructions of the narrative of Alexander's life have to start with the ancient accounts, which are available in translation.

Arrian, *The Campaigns of Alexander*, translated by Aubrey de Sélincourt (Penguin Classics, 1958; revised edn 1971)

Arrian, *Alexander the Great: The Anabasis and the Indica*, translated by Martin Hammond (Oxford World's Classics, 2013)

Arrian, *The Landmark Arrian: The Campaigns of Alexander*, translated by Pamela Mensch (Anchor Books, 2012)

Plutarch, *The Age of Alexander*, translated by Ian Scott-Kilvert, revised by Timothy Duff (Penguin Classics, 1973; revised edn 2012)

Plutarch, *Greek Lives*, translated by Robin Waterfield (Oxford World's Classics, 2008)

Quintus Curtius Rufus, *The History of Alexander*, translated by John Yardley (Penguin Classics, 1984)

Diodorus Siculus, *Books 16.66–17*, translated by C. Bradford Welles (Loeb Classical Library, 1963)

Justin, *Epitome of the Philippic History of Pompeius Trogus. Volume I Books 11–12: Alexander the Great*, translated by John Yardley (Oxford University Press, 1994)

Waldemar Heckel and John Yardley, *Alexander the Great: Historical Sources in Translation* (Wiley-Blackwell, 2004) contains a wide selection of texts from more fragmentary sources.

Modern biographies of Alexander
Biographies of Alexander the Great continue to be published at a rapid rate. Two that have stood the test of time are:

> Robin Lane Fox, *Alexander the Great* (Allen Lane, 1973)
> A.B. Bosworth, *Conquest and Empire* (Cambridge University Press, 1988)

A useful reference work is:

> Waldemar Heckel. *Who's Who in the Age of Alexander the Great* (Wiley, 2006)

Something of the landscape through which Alexander travelled can be seen in:

> Michael Wood, *In the Footsteps of Alexander the Great* (BBC DVD, 1998)

"牛津通识读本"已出书目

古典哲学的趣味	福柯	地球
人生的意义	缤纷的语言学	记忆
文学理论入门	达达和超现实主义	法律
大众经济学	佛学概论	中国文学
历史之源	维特根斯坦与哲学	托克维尔
设计,无处不在	科学哲学	休谟
生活中的心理学	印度哲学祛魅	分子
政治的历史与边界	克尔凯郭尔	法国大革命
哲学的思与惑	科学革命	民族主义
资本主义	广告	科幻作品
美国总统制	数学	罗素
海德格尔	叔本华	美国政党与选举
我们时代的伦理学	笛卡尔	美国最高法院
卡夫卡是谁	基督教神学	纪录片
考古学的过去与未来	犹太人与犹太教	大萧条与罗斯福新政
天文学简史	现代日本	领导力
社会学的意识	罗兰·巴特	无神论
康德	马基雅维里	罗马共和国
尼采	全球经济史	美国国会
亚里士多德的世界	进化	民主
西方艺术新论	性存在	英格兰文学
全球化面面观	量子理论	现代主义
简明逻辑学	牛顿新传	网络
法哲学:价值与事实	国际移民	自闭症
政治哲学与幸福根基	哈贝马斯	德里达
选择理论	医学伦理	浪漫主义
后殖民主义与世界格局	黑格尔	批判理论

德国文学	儿童心理学	电影
戏剧	时装	俄罗斯文学
腐败	现代拉丁美洲文学	古典文学
医事法	卢梭	大数据
癌症	隐私	洛克
植物	电影音乐	幸福
法语文学	抑郁症	免疫系统
微观经济学	传染病	银行学
湖泊	希腊化时代	景观设计学
拜占庭	知识	神圣罗马帝国
司法心理学	环境伦理学	大流行病
发展	美国革命	亚历山大大帝